T0026292

SCAVENGER TIDES

A MYSTERY

Susan Hanafee

This book is a work of fiction created by Susan Hanafee, who has also written under the pen name of E. C. Thomas. All names, characters and events are products of the author's imagination and are used fictitiously. Any resemblance to current events or living or dead persons is entirely coincidental and unintentional.

Cover photograph by the author.

Copyright © 2020 by the author. All rights reserved. No part of this book may be reproduced, stored in a retrieval system or transmitted by any means without the written permission of the author.

ISBN 978-1-09836-473-1 ebook 978-1-09836-474-8

The cruelest lies are often told in silence.

– Robert Louis Stevenson

CHAPTER 1

The sign in front of the little island church promised eternal life. The man inside had death on his mind.

It consumed his thoughts as he and Pastor Billy Cordray walked to the altar at the front of the sanctuary. It stayed with him as he lit two candles to open the service.

He took a seat near the organ and tried to focus on the pastor's words. "Gracious and loving God…." But his eyes wandered to his watch. *Ten minutes. The son of a bitch better be on time. No excuses either.*

When Pastor Billy lifted his Bible into the air and walked into the congregation to read the scripture, all eyes turned toward him. *It was time.* The man slipped out the exit door near his chair and through the sacristy. Outside, he surveyed the alley across from the church.

Where the hell is he? Maybe he wants to weasel out of the deal.

As if responding to a summons, a tall figure in jeans and a long-sleeved shirt stepped out from behind a row of bushes. A cap and sunglasses obscured his face, but he walked like a man with nothing to hide. He carried a paint can.

"What's that?" the man asked as he handed the figure a thick envelope.

"A souvenir." The tall figure removed the lid and thrust the can forward. Inside was a dog's head: Yellow fur matted with blood, tongue hanging to one side of its mouth and eyes glazed.

The man shuddered. "You sick bastard. What am I gonna do with this? You were supposed to take care of…."

"I did. You wanted a message sent. This is your receipt." The figure stuffed the envelope into his pocket and disappeared into the hedge.

The man grunted, then chucked the open can into the trash bin. He re-entered the sacristy, and when he heard the organ and the shuffle of people standing, slipped back inside the church sanctuary and stood in front of his seat by the organ.

His alto voice joined with the others. "So, I'll cherish the old rugged cross, till my trophies at last I lay down…."

A prideful smile crossed his face, then faded when he saw a gray-haired woman in the front row staring at him and scowling.

⁓⊃C⁓

Pastor Billy, in his first year of ministering to a flock of wealthy Southwest Florida retirees and assorted other island residents, left the church with his Bible in one hand and a bag of trash in the other. His words from the pulpit had been inspiring, he was sure of it. It appeared that no one nodded off, and he thought he'd even heard a whispered "amen" now and then.

He considered putting out the trash a demeaning job for a man of the cloth, but the church sexton, whose job it was to clean up after the service, had phoned in sick. Someone had to dispose of the pew programs and Styrofoam coffee cups from the Fellowship Hall. Yes, he thought, he could humble himself to do this part of the Lord's work.

When he lifted the top of the trashcan near the church office he gasped. Staring back at him were the lifeless eyes of a bloody devil dog.

The words were out of his mouth before he could stop them: "Jesus Christ!"

CHAPTER 2

I t was early October in southwest Florida: The air was oppressive and pungent with the aroma of dead fish. But it wasn't the smell that put me off my stride, it was the black buzzards that I saw landing on the second-story porch of a house under construction and filing through what looked like an opening for a double door.

When I returned to my condo after my morning walk, I attempted to capture the scene in my writer's journal before the horror of it faded.

"The smell of death called them to this place. It wafted through the opening and into the morning air. It was irresistible. First one, then another landed. They walked through the doorway and into the area where breakfast was being served. They stuck their beaks into the rotting hulk and began ripping off pieces of flesh."

Kind of gory. Grotesque. Who knows? Going with it for now. I closed the journal and tossed it onto a nearby Adirondack.

"Another day in paradise." There was no one around to hear the sarcasm in my voice or see me yawn. It couldn't be boredom. Not in this beautiful place. Maybe it was the slow pace of life.

It was only five months ago that I walked away from a lucrative and frenzied public relations job at a Midwestern utility and, at the same time, ended a marriage and a subsequent relationship that made me want to swear off men. Forever. Again.

My destination was an island where I hoped to live a simpler life as a writer and mother to my 21-year-old daughter, Meredith. She was in her junior year at college and would be joining my mother and me for Christmas.

One of the first things I did after I moved in was set up a writing table with a view of the Gulf of Mexico. On the wall to the left of my desk, I hung a small plaque. It was a picture of an old-fashioned typewriter with the words: "You must not come lightly to the blank page." Stephen King.

I hadn't even opened my first ream of printer paper when I realized that a mental haze had descended onto my creativity. I had a journal full of ideas but nothing else. No plot, no characters, no storyline. I wasn't going "lightly." I was going nowhere.

It wasn't the same for my mother, Ruth Harvey. She was a widow of 20 years, who moved south with me into her own condo close by. Mother played bridge, took mah-jongg lessons and had a calendar full of luncheon and dinner dates. She was on such a social fast track that some days it felt like I needed an appointment to say hello.

Although Mother's new friends did not know me well, I suspected they had bonded with her over my writer's block and then exaggerated my frustration level. *Poor Leslie's not writing. She's not fitting in. She's not happy. What can we do about it?* I could see the pity in their eyes when, on the rare occasion, I was invited to join them for lunch.

I checked my watch. More than an hour had passed since I spotted the buzzards. I picked up my cell phone.

"Sheriff." The raspy voice that answered and listened to my story was perfunctory. "Prob'ly a dead animal. We'll check it out."

I thanked him, wondering if someone would show up anytime soon. And if it would be okay for me to be there when that person did arrive?

My next call was to the realtor who sold me the two condos; one for me and one for Mother.

"This is Gordon Fike. Let's make it happen."

It was his usual greeting. Every time I heard the sales pitch, the more annoying I found it to be.

I turned on my upbeat persona: "Gordon, it's Leslie Elliott."

"Leslie! How's the novel coming?"

He sounded genuinely happy to hear from me. With Gordon you couldn't be sure.

"Like fishing for tarpon in September. Nothing much on the line."

He laughed a little too long. "That's a good one. What can I do for you? In the market for a house for you and your mother? Um, such a charming lady."

Mother had sized up Gordon the day of her condo closing and decided she didn't like him. She gave no reason why; she said it was one of her "feelings." While his attempts to charm her proved useless, I was sure he never complained publicly. Unpleasant or not, we would always be potential buyers and sellers in his mind.

"Mom's still unpacking, if you can believe that. I did call about a property, but not one I'm interested in buying. It's the yellow house on Oceanview Drive. The one that looks like someone stopped work halfway through the project. I see it on my walk every day."

The lingering silence on Fike's end was way out of character.

"Sorry. Don't know anything about that house," he finally said in a tone that reflected none of his earlier enthusiasm.

"What's happened? Did the owner run out of money? Did he die?"

"Don't know."

"Com'n Gordon. You know everything that goes on around here." I laughed. "Especially when it comes to real estate."

More silence. I decided to push on.

"This morning there were buzzards walking in an open door on the second floor. I called the sheriff."

That statement seemed to loosen his frozen tongue.

"The sheriff? Listen, Leslie, people around here like their privacy. It's best to mind your own business." His manner was now uncharacteristically brusque, almost angry.

A realtor should care about those things — vultures in a house — even if he doesn't know anything about the property.

"I see." I paused for what seemed like an eternity to give him time to respond further. Hearing nothing more, I ended the conversation. "Sorry to have bothered you, Gordon. Have a nice day." I clicked *end*, wondering what his problem was.

Besides irritating me, Gordon Fike's warning made me want to know more. There was no ignoring the fact that buzzards entering an open, vacant house was odd. And the house itself? When a place meant for life is empty, they say it has no soul. I had to see what it was in this lifeless house that the convention of vultures found so compelling.

CHAPTER 3

Tattered black plastic on the construction fencing around the yellow structure danced in the Gulf breezes. Volunteer palmettos that had staked their territory in the front yard bobbed and twisted, and a little dust devil stirred up and made its way toward me from a pile of stones, drywall and timber that formed a monument to days when this had been a more productive worksite.

There was no sign of the sheriff. I looked around, saw no one watching me and squeezed through an opening in the fence. A few skittish buzzards, gobbling up remains of something near the house, darted their beady eyes in my direction but kept on eating.

I worked my way through the construction debris to a door on the lowest level and reached for the knob. It turned, opening a crack to an area that looked like it would be used for storage when finished.

When I was little, my mother was full of warnings. *Don't touch the stove, it's hot. Don't cross the street without looking both ways.* As I prepared to enter, I could hear her saying, *"Don't go in that door."*

When I did open it fully, bits of foam insulation, cigarette butts and Mountain Dew cans skittered across the cement floor with the incoming breeze. Men at work. *You worried for nothing, Mother.*

I was surprised to see the newest edition of *The Island Sun*, the weekly newspaper on the ground, its front page rustling in the wind as I shut the door behind me. It was an indication that the birds weren't the only recent visitors. I picked it up, stuck it under my arm and headed for a makeshift stairway.

The steps to the next level were on the east side of the house. The scavengers had landed and entered from the west. If they were still there, I didn't want to disturb them. They are large birds, and they outnumbered me.

Several days ago, Yahoo carried a story about black buzzards killing calves in Tennessee. A sidebar told of vultures attacking feral pigs on the island of Cayo Costa, Florida.

Buzzards are normally nature's clean-up crew, not the aggressors. Still, I didn't want to chance ending up like one of the eyeless victims in Alfred Hitchcock's movie *The Birds*.

The door at the top of the stairs opened to my left, blocking my view of the kitchen where I suspected the buzzards might be having breakfast. Across a hallway were more stairs leading to the third level. I chose to explore what seemed a safer path.

On the top step, I happened to glance down and noticed reddish-brown dots in the construction dust. I pulled out a Kleenex from my shorts pocket, moistened it with my tongue and rubbed it over the area. I felt compelled to do that. Maybe it was because Mother had read too many Nancy Drew mysteries to me when I was a kid.

The first door I came to on the third floor had a lock and a brass handle that wouldn't budge. The door across from it led to an unfinished bathroom. A dirty green towel was draped over the edge of a sink. Behind a half wall was a toilet, lid up. The area was in need of sanitizing but offered no clues.

In the larger room at the end of the hallway, a row of windows overlooked the island's North Pass – the gateway to the Gulf. I stood for a minute just for the wonder of where I now lived. *I will never tire of it,* I said to myself. The view included a shell path that wandered through a mangrove swamp and ended up at a long dock.

The room was empty except for some paint cans stacked in a pyramid along one wall. A few of them had drips of the same reddish-brown color I'd seen on the stairway. I grabbed the thin metal handle of the can at the end to get a better look. It came off the ground so easily, I almost lost my balance. I decided to take it with me.

Satisfied there was nothing else to discover on the third level, I retraced my steps down the back stairway, yelling and stamping my feet in hopes of scaring off any remaining buzzards. For good measure, I reached around the wall and heaved the paint can into the room toward the west side of the house. It bounced, banged and rolled, then fell silent. As I rounded the door, I saw that it had come to rest against a mass on the floor.

The buzzards had vanished, but the stench that attracted them hadn't; it came from the clumps of yellowish-white fur and bits of red meat clinging to exposed bones.

The mass on the floor looked to be the partially decomposed body of an animal, likely a dog. There were pads on the end of paws, the remnants of a tail, but no head. It appeared sliced off on the spot, hopefully after the poor creature was dead. Everywhere were large patches of the familiar reddish-brown color. There was no question that it wasn't paint.

In a corner was a blue denim dog collar with two silver tags. I walked over and picked it up. The name *Whalen* and a phone number were embroidered in white. There was little wear and no sign of blood. As I slipped the collar into my pocket, a sense of fury overtook me.

My God. What sadist did this?

"Whatcha doin' here, lady?" The voice was raspy, as if the speaker needed to clear his throat. Whoever it was had entered quietly, surprising me. My hand went to my heart.

"Oh, Sheriff," I gasped as I turned around to see a slight man in matching tan shirt and pants. "You startled me. I-I'm Leslie Elliott. I called about the buzzards. I-I think I spoke with you."

During my short time as an island resident, I'd never seen the sheriff or any of his deputies. This man had an emblem on his sleeve, a badge attached to his breast pocket and a holstered firearm. He wore no hat, and his slicked-back brown hair was long enough to brush against his shirt collar. His rugged face, lined by excessive sun and years of smoking – I guessed – didn't look happy to see me.

"Ya shouldn't be here." He retrieved a small tin from his pants pocket, opened it and smeared a greasy substance under his nose. Then he thrust the container my direction. "Since ya are, want some? Helps with the god-awful smell."

I reached my forefinger into the box and smeared some of the substance under my nose. It smelled like Vick's VapoRub, the substance you see coroners using on TV shows to lessen the stink of death.

"Yer trespassing. Jus' because you called, don't give ya the right to be here. I won't do anything but don't come back," he said as he reached for a thin notepad in his back pocket and started writing.

"I wasn't trying to create problems," I said.

"Folks here tend to keep to themselves. You'll learn." He kept his eyes on his writing as he issued my second warning of the day on island etiquette and minding my own business.

"Since yer here, I'll ask ya some questions. When did ya see the birds and was there anyone else around?"

"About 8:30. I usually walk by here at that time. There was no one else. So, when did the work stop?"

He looked up and, to my surprise, provided an answer. "Ten months. A year. Nobody paid much attention 'til the weeds started growin.' Then we got complaints. How many buzzards did ya see?"

"It's hard to say. 10, 15. I'm not sure how many were already inside. The owner. Did he die or run out of money or what?"

He shrugged. "Haven't seen him around lately."

"Didn't you say the house was abandoned?"

"Said the owner stopped work. Didn't say he was gone. I'll ask the questions." He narrowed his eyes and shook his head.

"Oh, sorry, Sheriff. Being new to the area, I'm interested in learning about my neighbors."

His lips spread into an exaggerated grin that exposed a gap in his smile, a couple of teeth back from the two in front. "He's not yer neighbor yet, is he?"

I wanted to keep the conversation going to see if I glean any more information from the recalcitrant law enforcement official. I also didn't want to alienate him completely.

"Do you think it's a dog? I mean, it seems obvious that it was at one time. Unless it was a coyote or something. Did the owner have a dog?"

He paused and flipped through his notebook. "Yeah. I thought so. Got a call from the pastor about a dog's head in the church's trash. Might be the same animal. Like I said, no need to go nosin' around. I'll figure out what happened."

"I'm sure you will, Sheriff," I said. *Body one place, head in a trash can by the church. I'm not sure that's a mystery you can solve, but maybe I'm wrong.*

"It's Deputy. Deputy Bruce Webster. If ya see anythin' else when yer walkin' by, call me. But don't come in the house again. It's not safe." He handed me a card with his name and phone number and a fingerprint that appeared to be part of the design.

"Sure, Deputy." I took a piece of paper and golf pencil from my pocket and scratched my name and cell number on it. "Call me if you find out anything."

I reached for the paint can I'd pitched in the buzzard's direction. "This can was upstairs. Empty. I'll put it in the recycling bin at my condo," I said, trying to sound as though it was no big deal.

To my surprise, Deputy Bruce Webster did not object.

ꙮ

Back in my condo, I pulled the dog collar out of my pocket and ran my fingers over the embroidered letters. How did poor Whalen meet his brutal end? How long had he been there? And where was his owner?

I picked up my cell phone and punched in the number on the collar. After a dozen rings, it switched to a man's voice.

"Leave a message. I'll get back to you."

It was hard to say the words. I pictured Whalen whole again, running in and out of the Gulf waves, his yellowish-white fur ruffled by the wind. He was digging for sand crabs and scattering flocks of terns and seagulls. His throaty bark was cutting through the sound of the surf. He'd done all those things. Now he was a pile of rotting flesh and picked-over bones.

"I, uh, I have some information, uh, about your dog." My voice broke, and I realized I should have given myself more time to think about my message. "His remains were, uh, found in a house on Oceanview Drive. I'm not sure if it's your house, but you can reach me by returning this call."

What the hell would I say if and when the owner contacted me? *I saw buzzards going into a house and decided to investigate. That's where I found your dog dead and missing its head."*

My thoughts turned to the paint can I'd left on the small table by the front door. I took it over to the kitchen counter and popped off the lid, using the screwdriver from the utility drawer.

Except for traces of white powder – drywall dust, I guessed – it was empty. It was obvious the can's shiny interior had never been used for paint.

CHAPTER 4

After 20 years of bitterness because of the untimely and disturbing death of my father – her beloved husband – Mother was finally transitioning to a good place. Today, the local beautician, Dianna, had completed another step in this welcome transformation.

"Wow, Mom, look at your hair! The gray is gone and it's, um, auburn like mine!" I enthused when mother strolled through the door of my condo looking ten years younger.

"It takes me back to the days when I was the spitting image of Maureen O'Hara, before you and your escapades stripped me of my youth," she said, as she primped her newly-colored locks.

I grabbed Mother's hand, laughing while I positioned the two of us in front of the floor-to-ceiling mirror in the condo's tiny dining area.

At one time we were both 5'8", 115 pounds. We still weighed about the same but gravity had taken an inch from Mother's height and settled it on her waist. Her thin nose turned up at the end. My slightly wider nose was complements of my dad's genes. We both had pale eyes; Mother's blue, mine green. Other than those few details and 26 years difference in our age, we looked a lot alike.

Though Mother had lived all those years with melancholy, there were a few occasions when the old Ruth would surface. The mother that was spunky, fun and slightly irreverent when I was growing up. The one that was a wiz at card games. I once caught her stuffing the Queen of Spades in her bra during a heated game of Hearts; she was only sorry she'd been caught. The one that delighted in reading and then talking about the sexy novels of Jacqueline Susann.

Now I was seeing a lot more of the happy Ruth. The one that was always grousing and complaining and ready to pick a fight with me was becoming a distant memory, thank God.

"No one would guess we are mother and daughter," I said, giving Mom a squeeze around the waist and the chance to embellish on my observation, as I knew she would.

"More like sisters," Mother quipped.

Our two condos were on the northernmost part of the island, which was ten miles long and one mile wide. Public beaches flanked the west and south sides, and mangrove swamps adorned the north and east fringes of our strip of sand. The Gulf waters surrounding us transformed daily from blues to greens, their changing colors more intense than any artist could capture. Photos of the island's dramatic sunsets often posted on Facebook were never as vibrant as the real thing.

A 15-minute drive in a golf cart took us to a village with touristy shops, a small grocery, a couple of churches, an art gallery and a community center that showed free movies several times a week.

A historic hotel that had survived hurricanes, many remodeling projects and the occasional termite infestation stood like a proud matriarch in the heart of the village. Tourists, attracted to the hotel's five-star accommodations and 1950's ambiance, brought with them a hustle and bustle that kept the community's seasonal merchants in business.

Warm sunny days, tropical breezes and an abundance of game fish were the elements of the siren song that lured 4,000 souls from the north to this paradise from October to April. The other five months of the year folks like us – "rounders" we were called – numbered about 800.

Some claimed that only the hardy could tolerate the summer, with its soaring temperatures, oppressive humidity, mosquito infestations and threats of violent storms. But it didn't take long for me to discover that the island was at its best when most everyone else was gone.

It was with summer ending – and paradise lost for a while again – that Mother, with her new hairdo, her friend Mary Sanders and I were attending the seasonal opening of the Gallery Centre and going out to dinner afterward.

At 79, Mary was five years older than Mother, petite and dark-haired, with a wispy southern voice that motivated listeners to move closer when she spoke. She was also a widow. She and Mother had lunch and shopped at least once a week. On those few times I was invited to join them, I felt like the odd woman out. It was that whole pity thing. But that was okay. I was glad Mother had made a close friend.

What interested me most about Mary on this particular day was that she lived around the corner from the mysterious yellow house. I was looking forward to quizzing her about the goings-on, or lack thereof, at the property. I was also wondering if she had seen the buzzards.

"You want a glass of wine before we go? We have time," I said as Mother entered my condo once again after changing into a pale-yellow shift dress with a wrap decorated in colorful butterflies. Another sign she was emerging from her cocoon of sadness.

"Oh yes, *dear*, something light. My God, it's been a day. The beauty parlor was packed. And there was so much good gossip, I wanted to take notes."

"Notes. Um, yes. It must have been something." I filled the glass half-full and handed it to her. "You wanna tell me about it?"

"Not now, dear. Mary might find it interesting and I don't want to repeat myself." She paused, then slipped back into a character I knew all too well.

"Is that what you're wearing?" she said, raising one eyebrow.

My long-sleeved black knit top and ruffled skirt with black-and-white polka dots seemed a good choice for an art event. I thought the black complimented my hair and eyes, but for some reason Mother deemed it unworthy, and was giving it the evil eye.

"You'll roast. At least put on something sleeveless that shows some cleavage."

"Cleavage? You know I don't have much, and I'm not on the prowl if that's what you have in mind. There have been too many men in my life. All unsuitable."

"Do as your mother says, dear. You never know who'll be there."

CHAPTER 5

When the historic preservation bureaucrats were finished with it, the island's Gallery Centre cost $1 million to renovate, and it still didn't have a bathroom.

The tiny structure was once home to a fisherman and his wife who survived into their 80s with outdoor plumbing and a cistern for rain water. Now, the remodeled 1920's residence provided a lovely but limited space for local artists to exhibit and sell their works.

"Limited" was the key word. Decades of pent-up creativity oozed from the septuagenarians who had once busied themselves raising families or running multi-billion-dollar corporations, and were now living in Florida during the winter months.

With time at their disposal, they took up painting or writing or acting in little theater groups – searching for latent talents. As the artist in many emerged, gallery walls filled to overflowing.

The resulting disputes over space and painting placement led to the occasional outburst of temperament and more than a few headaches for the gallery manager Deb Rankin.

I knew all of this because Deb, a painter of landscapes and my new friend, often bent my ear about the challenge of keeping her artists happy; a task she likened to corralling fire ants.

Tonight, however, the atmosphere was festive and all disputes on the back burner, as the historic house stood ready to show off its contributors' latest works.

The gallery's entryway deck served as a makeshift bar, with two volunteer bartenders who were husbands of exhibiting artists. Leon was well-groomed, with his meticulous handlebar mustache and Tommy Bahama shirt. Jerry, in a pink polo that didn't quite cover his expanding waistline, was mopping his brow with a handkerchief when Mother, Mary and I approached.

"You ladies working tonight?" Leon inquired, flashing a grin our direction. "You want a glass of wine?"

"You'll need something," Jerry chimed in. "It's hotter than Hades."

"It's not so bad, Jerry. You're having old man hot flashes," Leon said, laughing.

Before we could respond, Deb emerged from the entrance, clutching four bottles of champagne against her sequined blouse. Droplets of perspiration dotted her forehead. She wore no make-up except for a splash of pink lipstick that looked like it was applied without benefit of a mirror. Her long, brown hair fell down to her waist and brushed against the top of her buttocks as she walked.

"I'm so disorganized. Will you help with this, honey?"

"Sure, Deb. Anything for you," I said.

Deb pointed to a table with a hand-lettered *Welcome* sign, a white lace tablecloth and several rows of plastic champagne glasses. "Figured we might as well go all out tonight."

On my first visit to the gallery, I was admiring one of Deb's oil paintings – a summer scene with billowing clouds that forecasted rain – and reaching for my credit card when the artist cornered me.

"That piece would look wonderful in your living room, honey. I'll give you a deal." Her manner was sincere. I liked her, even though I knew this woman had no idea what my tiny living room looked like.

"Sold!" was an easy response since I'd been planning to buy it at the original price. When Deb handed over the artwork, she signed me up for a season of volunteer activity and what I was confident would become an enduring friendship. I liked her.

"I want your pretty face to be the first thing people see when they come up that ramp," Deb said as she put the champagne bottles on the table. "I'm puttin' your mother and Mary Sanders in charge of passin' appetizers."

She turned to Leon and Jerry. "Pour the expensive stuff first. If we run out, the cheap stuff will be okay. After a couple of glasses, they won't know the difference," she said. They snapped a pair of salutes her way.

As I eased the bubbly into the plastic glasses, I wondered if Mother would be happy with an assignment that involved serving others. Being waited on was more her style. But, in a few minutes, Mother breezed past me with a tray of canapés and a cheesy smile on her face.

"Mary says my new hair color will attract men in droves."

"No doubt about it." I responded with only a hint of playful teasing in my voice.

She fluffed her hair with her right hand and swung the tray in her left hand in front of me. "Try these. They've got shrimp AND bacon. Quite tasty."

I popped one into my mouth. "Ummm. You want some champagne?"

"Not until my job is done, dear. You don't want me spilling appetizers all over these art patrons." To my amazement, Mother giggled.

"I'll take some, please." The stranger's words came at me like a request for something more than a glass of the bubbly stuff.

When I turned, I found myself looking up at a square jaw and dimpled chin. His sandy hair was tousled as though he'd sailed in on the breezes from the Gulf. His lips remained closed, the corners of his mouth turning up slightly. I sized him up and determined he must be in his late 40s.

I hurried to swallow my appetizer and found my throat had gone dry. That's how it always started.

"Help yourself," I mumbled.

He reached for the glass and took a drink, never taking his eyes off me. They were bluish-gray like gunmetal and cold.

I was scrambling for something else to say – the sudden heat came to mind – when the sound of a woman's voice drew the stranger's attention from me to an old Lincoln town car parked at the curb.

"Frank! Come talk to your son. He can't sit in the car listening to that music all night. We're here to see the show."

"Excuse me," he said, once again offering me that closed smile.

My eyes followed him as he strolled down the ramp to where a woman with teased black hair stood, hands on her hips. She lowered her voice. I couldn't hear her words, but her body language said she thought she was in charge. The man named Frank nodded, saying something that must have satisfied her. She turned from him and marched up the ramp, stopping at my table.

"Is this free?" She reached out and swooped up a drink before I could answer. Her multi-colored diaphanous blouse with flowing sleeves traveled over the top of several glasses, causing the liquid inside to shudder. I grabbed the last one to stop its precarious teetering.

"Yes, help yourself. Or there's red or white wine," I said, nodding in the direction of the two bartenders.

The woman eyed Jerry and Leon. "This'll do. My daughter-in-law. She's in there. Makes scarves. Maybe you've seen them. Pretty but they don't pay the bills." She put down the empty glass now marked with bright red lipstick and headed to the entrance without further comment.

My glance wandered back to the man named Frank and lingered there. He was leaning through the car's open window, directing his conversation to the passenger side. The thin white shirt he was wearing, with sleeves rolled to his elbows, clung to his muscular arms and back.

After a few minutes, a boy emerged from the car. He was maybe 13 and was dressed like his father in jeans and cowboy boots. He kept his eyes down as he walked up the ramp, but I recognized the facial expression. I'd seen it many times on my daughter's face when she was younger – acquiescence to authority masking teen-age rebellion. The boy clearly didn't want to be at an art show, and the man named Frank didn't seem to be keen on it either.

"Just a few minutes, Stevie, and you can go back to the car," Frank said as the two of them passed my table. He gave me a sideways glance and disappeared into the building.

When the champagne was gone, Deb Rankin pronounced me free to do whatever I wanted. There was no doubt what that was. I was looking for another encounter with the sandy-haired man and hating myself for it.

⁓◯⁓

Mother was in the high-traffic foyer that connected the center's two exhibition areas. She looked like one of those whimsical butler statues you order from a catalogue, holding the tray of appetizers to one side so people could help themselves while she engaged in an animated conversation with two men.

When she spotted me, she moved her head to the left, rolled her eyes and raised her eyebrows. I shrugged as though I didn't understand, but I knew what she was up to.

After purchasing a pair of pearl earrings with tiny gold leaves from a jewelry table and exchanging small talk with Candace, the artist, I strolled into the larger exhibition area.

The artwork in the second gallery looked interesting, but it was the scene unfolding in front of a display of colorful scarves that captured my attention.

The woman of the diaphanous blouse and red lipstick was wagging her finger at a female in her early forties who was remarkable not just for her good looks but her edgy hair. It was shaved on the sides, moussed into a pompadour on top and fashioned into a comma-like curl in the back. The hairdo was part of a look-at-me package that included tattoos on her arms and defiance on her face.

Frank and the boy stood to one side, seeming like they wanted to be somewhere else.

Deb Rankin joined me. "Opening night and she's determined to cause trouble," she said, shaking her head.

"They don't act happy with each other. Do you know them?"

"Oh, yes, honey. Everyone knows them. The man kind of takes your breath away, doesn't he? He's Frank Johnson. Fisherman. He's been around here 18 years or so. The artist is his wife, Janis, soon to be his ex. She does scarves and the occasional painting. The bossy woman is Frank's mother, Georgia."

She paused to check her watch and then went on. "You don't mess with Georgia. She rules with an iron fist. I'm surprised Frank lets her get by with it. He's quiet, but he's as strong-willed as his mother. Maybe it's because she takes good care of him and the boy now that Janis lives on her own off-island."

"Janis? That's her name? She's a beautiful woman. I could do without the hair and the tattoos. Guess I'm too conventional."

"In high school, I'm told, the boys followed her around like a dog in heat. Didn't seem she'd settle down with one guy. Then Frank showed up. He's got that bad boy look women dream about."

Hearing the beginning sounds of a skirmish, she paused.

"Uh-oh. I'd better go break this up," she said.

Deb approached the two women, putting her arm around the artist named Janis, while cajoling Georgia whose flowing sleeve was being tugged at by Frank. *Let's go. Let's go,* I could hear him saying. When she finally relented, he led her out the door at the end of the main gallery.

"What was the problem?" I asked when Deb returned.

"Who knows. Georgia and Janis are oil and water," she said, wiping the perspiration off her forehead as she surveyed the room, which had returned to normal.

"So, go on with your story," I urged.

"Where was I? Oh yeah. Janis and Frank separated a year ago, and Mama moved in to help out. Now Frank hangs out with Scooter and me at our place once or twice a week. To get away from Georgia."

I pictured the three of them sitting in Deb's messy backyard, drinking beer, trading gossip and enjoying doing nothing. "Um, why did you say Frank was bad?"

"Just a figure of speech. Isn't that the kind of man all us women are attracted to? I know I am, though my Scooter's neutered after all these years," she chuckled. "Frank's not really a bad boy. More the mysterious type."

"It must be tough on the teenager, not being with his mother and having so much drama in his life," I said, pursuing still more details.

"Drama? Their family troubles aren't so unusual around here, honey."

"Really? I was told people on this island don't talk much about their private lives. In fact, I was told to mind my own business."

"Who said that?" Deb looked surprised at my remark.

"Gordon Fike and Deputy Bruce Webster. Earlier today." My mind replayed the unfriendly conversations.

"That Gordie's the biggest gossip on the island. The truth is that no one around here minds their own business unless they're up to no good," Deb said, smirking.

"And there's plenty of no good in this place. That's for sure. You be as nosy as you want. Adds to the fun of livin' here."

She glanced at the watch again and patted me on the shoulder. "See you later, honey. Gotta check on those appetizers. Hope we aren't running out."

She left me standing alone, hungry for even more information about Frank Johnson. Two mysteries in one day: the yellow house and the handsome bad boy. Maybe my creative juices would soon be flowing again. *I had to smile at that. My "whatever" juices.*

CHAPTER 6

"Did you see him?" Mother inquired after she, Mary and I placed our dinner orders at Mullet's, a beachfront eatery on the island's south end.

I acted like I didn't hear her question, pretending to gaze around the dining area looking for familiar faces. Did I really want to have this conversation with my mother? If anything, I wanted to know more about the house with the buzzards.

With its varnished wooden tables, 1940's linoleum floor and imbedded smell of fried foods, the restaurant had the kind of ambiance tourists love.

Snook and tarpon were mounted on the walls, along with pictures of fishermen and their boats. An 80's-style band – musicians with more hair on their faces than their heads – played on Friday and Saturday nights with no cover charge. An outdoor eating area, with ceiling fans clicking overheard, offered a view of the Gulf waters and access to a public beach.

Mother and I had eaten at Mullet's two, maybe three, times since moving south. Prices were a little stiff for us. A hamburger was $13. Add another $5 for onion rings. And they stubbornly refused to split the bill, no matter what size the party. If we wanted to pay for our own food, we had to put our math skills to the test.

"What'd you say?" I finally responded.

"Did you see him?" Mother said, emphasizing the word "him."

"See who?" I took a sip of Michelob Light, relishing the idea of having a little fun at Mother's expense.

Mother's sigh was so loud that Mary Sanders giggled and the people at the next table stopped eating and looked over at us.

"The man with the sandy hair and the dimple in his chin. He came into the beauty shop this morning to talk to one of the customers who was getting her hair dyed. The ladies told her it would be too dark, but she wouldn't listen…."

"What about him?" I interrupted before Mother could go too far off-track. I hoped I didn't appear too eager, even though I was.

"After the woman left, the girls told me that he's one of the local fishermen and the customer was his mother. He and his wife are getting a divorce. She's seeing another man. I can't imagine why. You should have seen the old ladies' heads snap when he strolled into the shop. Made me wish I was a couple of years younger."

I continued toying with her "That's why you had me change clothes? You think I should hook up with a fisherman who's still married? Really, Mother?"

"You want me to think you aren't interested in men right now, but I'm not buying it." Mother gave me a pat on the arm and flashed a knowing smile. "You're a Harvey woman. We can't help ourselves. We like men, and we like them strong and good looking. Like that fisherman."

She waved her empty wine glass at the waitress. "I'll have more wine. How about you, Mary?"

"No thanks. Why don't you find a handsome man for me, Ruth?" she asked. She often talked about her late husband, Chester. Behind her sweet smile was a yearning for male companionship that she didn't try to hide.

"Come to think of it," Mary said with a devilish smile, "I'll take someone who's breathing. He doesn't have to look that good. Sometimes a man's touch can make you feel whole again."

Mother seemed oblivious to Mary's comments, clucking instead about her second glass of wine being slow to arrive.

"Speaking of men, Mary," I said, "what do you know about the one that's building the house around the corner from you; the yellow one? I'm guessin' it's a man."

She looked at me for a second, questioning, and then her eyes brightened. "Oh, that house. Such a shame. The owner's name is Peter something. Thompson, I think. Don't know much about him. He's got dark curly hair and a goatee. Appears to be good looking from a distance, but I've never seen him up close. When he's around, which isn't much lately, I wave. But he's always in a hurry. Too busy to talk."

"So where is he, and has he abandoned the house?"

"That's what all of us want to know," she said, sighing.

Was there more to learn from Mary? "Where's he from?" I pressed.

"Canada, I think. There are a lot of them down here. Canadians. Nice people. I can't say for sure about him, whether he's nice or not. Like I said, he keeps to himself."

I thought of poor Whalen once more. "Does he have a dog?"

"Why, yes, uh, I think he does. I've never seen him with anyone else, like a woman, but I did see a dog, a yellow Lab. The two of them go for walks when he's here."

I could feel my eyes beginning to sting as I pictured the mass of bones, blood and fur that had attracted the vultures to Mary's neighbor's house.

"Did you notice a large group of buzzards entering the house this morning?" I continued.

"Buzzards? Oh my! Can't say that I did. Oh, dear. We're plenty concerned about the situation, but what can we do? We're just waiting. Waiting to see what happens next," Mary said.

I was right there with Mary and her neighbors, wondering what was going on. But my curiosity – maddening as it sometimes was – had no intention of waiting around for the answers.

CHAPTER 7

The water in the island's South Pass was churning like a washing machine. I tried to focus on the horizon, but all I could think about was keeping the contents of my stomach in place as we rolled, up and down, back and forth, up and down in the fishing boat named *Dreamcatcher*.

When the urge overwhelmed me, I rushed for the side and deposited my fruit-and-yogurt breakfast into the aquamarine water. The wide-brimmed straw hat I was wearing went with it, ripped off my head by a sudden gust.

Damn. I liked that hat. I wiped my mouth on a towel tossed my direction. I might have been embarrassed if I didn't feel so bad.

"Honey, next time someone asks if you get seasick, be sure and say yes," my friend Deb Rankin said, showing no empathy for my discomfort.

I nodded weakly. It was she who had arranged the fishing charter to take place a couple of days after the Gallery Centre's opening. When I arrived at the marina, Deb was there with her husband Scooter. Setting up the tackle was Frank Johnson, the *bad boy* from the art show and our captain for the morning.

I wasn't surprised to see him. Deb had a habit of meddling in other people's lives. She thought I'd taken a liking to him at the art show. She was right but wrong. Even though he was separated, he was still married. I'd been in those situations before with no happy ending for me. No, not this time.

There was also a deck hand who looked to be about 16. Frank called him Gator. He was lean, with thick dark hair and tawny skin. I watched him apply sunscreen on his face, arms and torso and then slip into a lightweight long-sleeved shirt. When I was his age, I never gave skin cancer a second thought. I hoped I didn't come to regret my cavalier attitude.

Frank helped me onboard, his hand grasping mine and holding on longer than necessary I thought. "Ever been fishing? You need something for seasickness?"

"No thanks. I'm fine."

We all soon realized I wasn't fine, and since Deb had arranged for the trip, and I assumed paid for it in some fashion, I felt like I was stuck on the boat until the four-hour session ended. *Just let me fall overboard and wash ashore,* I prayed as the waves grew in intensity.

After my third trip to the edge of the boat, I guess Frank took pity on me. He steered to calmer waters even though the new location still had plenty of swell. I didn't feel like fishing, and my protective hat was gone, so I sat under the cockpit Bimini to watch the others as I tried to keep my stomach in line.

By the time we motored alongside the dock and departed the boat, I was feeling humiliated and rung out. I stood by, watching as Frank sliced through the grouper Deb caught, tossed the unwanted remains in the water to waiting pelicans and slipped eight perfect fillets into a plastic bag.

"Here you go," he said, handing the fish to Deb and avoiding eye contact with me.

"Sorry. Guess I'm not a boat person," I said, looking for absolution from any of my fellow passengers.

Frank mumbled something I couldn't quite hear.

"You'll be prepared next time, honey," Deb said.

"If there is a next time," I said, wondering how another fishing trip could ever be in my future.

When we turned to leave, I recognized Frank's teenage son, Stevie, ambling toward us. His head was down as though watching something important in each step he took on the wide planks of the pier. His thick brown hair was unruly. His oversized t-shirt, imprinted with a jumping fish and the year 2019, flapped around in the stiff breeze like an unsecured sail.

The boy was about 30 feet from me when a large dog bounded around him, almost knocking him over. It was a yellow Lab.

"Whalen?" The name rolled off my tongue in an unconscious response. The dog hesitated. His brown eyes focused on me. His mouth opened, exposing white teeth and a pink tongue. He looked like he was smiling.

Frank's sharp whistle projected over me. He slapped his leg several times. "Here Buddy. Good dog, good dog."

The Lab trotted to Frank, who bent down and scratched his ears. When the fisherman gazed up at me, his gunmetal eyes had gone cold again.

ꝏꝏ

The morning light found its way through my eyelids and popped them open at 8:12. I stretched, got up and reached for the shorts, t-shirt and sandals I'd laid out the night before.

I opened the sliding door that led to the lanai. Below me, a long-legged blue heron the neighbors called Wilt was patrolling the seawall. The sentry with the fearsome orange bill was on the prowl, looking for something to slide down his S-shaped neck.

The concrete wall on which he strutted was designed to protect our condos from the vagaries of the North Pass. Having noticed water under our structures after a particularly heavy storm, I was skeptical the barrier could do the job in desparate times.

But there were no worries about that today. The skies were blue and the water was like glass, with no bad weather in sight. I took a deep breath, sucking the salt air into my lungs and descended the steps to the strip of sand that served as our beach.

"Good morning, Wilt." The large bird eyed me as if looking for a handout. Observing that I had nothing to offer, he began moving in the opposite direction.

"Guess you don't want to be seen with me – a landlubber," I said as I sat down on the seawall and dangled my feet in the blue-green water. *Not so warm as in the summer months but soothing.*

My mind flashed back to a long, hot car trip with my family.

Me and my older brother in the back seat reading comic books. Mom and Dad in the front. I was 6 and fighting a sense of nausea that grew with each passing mile. Maybe it was the greasy hot dog I ate for lunch. Perhaps it was the excitement of the trip. When I could no longer contain the contents of my stomach, I opened my mouth to announce impending disaster.

"I think I'm gonna...."

The warning came too late. The back seat floorboard of the family's 1974 Buick was the recipient of a pinkish mass of stomach bile and partially digested meat. Although

Mother defended me, my father complained that the car would never smell right again, and it didn't.

Why didn't I remember that awful incident when Frank asked me about motion sickness? I did manage to make it to the side of his boat, at least twice. It's not like I wanted to be seasick. Still, I should have known better.

The roar of an engine from a fishing vessel distracted my self-recrimination. The white vessel with a platform on top cut through the calm water. A second and third followed in a parade through the Pass to the Gulf. Wilt squawked as the boats' wakes splashed against the seawall, spraying the two of us with fine droplets of salty water. He spread his massive wings and took off.

As I stood up and started for the condo steps, I noticed one of the boats make a sharp turn and head my direction. I shielded my eyes. By the time the vessel came to rest about 10 feet from me, I'd identified the captain.

"Hey," Frank said as he throttled back on the engine and let the boat drift closer to the seawall. "How're you feeling?"

He was wearing long sleeves and a baseball cap; the uniform for men and boys like Gator who spend their days in the sun. The disgust he displayed yesterday had been replaced by a broad smile. Friendly or mocking? I couldn't tell.

"Still embarrassed. I should have, um, listened to you."

Frank nodded, as if agreeing with my comment, but then adopted a look of sympathy. "You could say that. But I've been in this business a long time and stuff like that happens. I was out of line. Sorry."

"Please don't apologize. You didn't do anything wrong."

"I was upset that you didn't warn Gator. But that's history. I'd like to make it up to you."

"After what happened you want to take me fishing again? No thanks." I laughed to avoid appearing rude.

Frank took off his cap, ran his fingers through his sandy hair and then re-positioned the hat to shield his eyes from the morning sun. "I was hoping we could have dinner."

Uh-oh. Hello, resolve. I'm gonna need you. Where are you?

"Dinner? You want to have dinner with me?"

"I can bring the fish. You got a grill?"

"There's a community one by the parking lot," I heard myself say.

"Good. How about tonight? About 6?" He nudged the boat so that it pointed toward the Gulf, giving me time to ponder his invitation. What did Deb say? He wasn't a bad guy? He was married. But he was separated.

"Uh. Okay. Sure. I'll fix a salad. The gate code is 1972. Easy for me to remember. That was the year I was born."

"A good one," he said and grinned.

"See you tonight" was all I could think to respond.

As I watched him head out, I wondered if our meeting was a chance encounter. It didn't feel like it. I thought back to the look he gave me when I called the dog on the pier Whalen – and shuddered. Why was I being so suspicious? About everything.

CHAPTER 8

The man at the paint store off-island joined the growing ranks of people that looked at me like I'd lost my mind.

"You want what?" he said, stroking the wattle under his chin.

"I want you to tell me what's on the side of this can, Willy," I said, checking out the nametag on his short-sleeved red shirt in the hopes of more personalized service. "And on this tissue. Is it the same thing?"

"Looks the same, but I ain't no scientist, ma'am. I jus' mix paint," he said, looking like he expected me to say okay and leave.

I wasn't about to walk out the door empty-handed. "Well, can you match the color and tell me what it is?"

Willy sighed and took the can from my hand. He reached for an opener.

"It's empty," I said.

He popped the top off. "Empty." A puzzled look crossed his face.

Like I said, I whispered to myself.

He turned the can over. A few whitish specks fell onto the counter. He pursed his lips and blew, dispersing the fine material into the air.

I let out a shriek. "Oh no. What if that was….?

"What? Looked like drywall dust to me."

"It could have been a clue," I said.

A second man, standing off to one side, began chuckling. "You a detective or somethin'?"

"A writer," I said, although the jury was still out on that one.

"That figures. You got some 'magination. Or maybe you been watchin' too many TV shows." The two laughed.

My face contorted into a Ruth-like scowl, which appeared to have some impact on Willy. The look of humor on his face vanished as he attempted to cast himself as a serious technician.

"All right then. I'll run these and see if we could match the colors." He took a small knife and scraped some of the drip material off the can, putting it under a scanner. In a few minutes, a piece of paper emerged with some numbers on it.

"Looks like the closest color is Sierra Redwood, SW 7598," Willy said. "You wanna can?"

I shook my head. There were no paint jobs in my future, and even if there were, I wasn't inclined to have walls that looked like they were covered with blood. "No thanks. What's this one?"

He took the tissue from my hand, scratched his head and put it under the scanner. "Um. Flower Pot. That color's close but no cigar."

My dad used to say that for no particular reason. Guess some men from another generation liked the sound of the corny phrase.

"So, they're not the same color?" I asked.

"Nope. But this could be throwin' it off," he said, returning the flimsy Kleenex to me.

I persisted. "I don't suppose you could tell me if anyone bought either of those colors in, say, the last year?"

He looked at the other man who seemed to want no part of a conversation with an obvious nut case. Especially one that was asking them to research a year's worth of receipts.

"Not sure the colors came from our store. We jus' matched what you give us. There's plenty of paint places around here."

"But this is your can," I protested.

"That don't mean nuthin'."

There was a fractional pause on my part, long enough to make itself felt.

"You're telling me that someone could have gotten hold of one or more of your empty cans and dribbled another brand of paint down the sides?"

"Couldn't say," Willy said, eyeing the other man again. "Uh, why would some-one do that? Sounds like a pretty stupid idea – even for a, um, writer."

I sighed in frustration. Bringing the can and the Kleenex remnants to the paint store for some sort of identification had seemed like a good idea. Now I wasn't sure. Maybe these good ol' boys were right. Maybe the whole thing was a figment of my imagination – a hairbrained search for something to grab onto.

Once again, Willy assumed the demeanor of helpful sales assistant. Maybe he remembered there was one of those email surveys waiting for me on my iPhone at the end of my visit.

"Tell you what. Bud here and I'll check to see if anyone bought one or both of these colors or some cans recently. Maybe one of the local painters or contractors. If we find somethin', we'll let you know."

"Great! How long will that take?"

"Can't be sure."

I handed my card to Willy, snatched up the empty paint can and the Kleenex. "Thanks. I'll look forward to hearing from you."

When I left the building, I was pretty sure that was another call I'd never receive – like the one I hadn't gotten from Deputy Bruce Webster about the headless dog the two of us encountered in the mystery house.

I grabbed the cell phone from my purse and hit the number for Royal Palm Cleaners.

When I moved into my condo, the business owner, Jackie Gates, and her helper removed about 10 years of grime from the expensive bamboo furniture the former owners had left behind. Jackie also cleaned up the red wine my mother spilled on her new couch two days after she moved in.

"How you doing, Leslie? Your mother have another accident?" Jackie was always cheerful, even when faced with the worst of messes.

"Not that I know of. She started drinking white wine after that near disaster." I switched the cell to speaker so I could hear better. "Jackie. Need a favor. Are you on-island?"

"I'm just wrapping up on Ficus Road. 252."

"This sounds silly, but I'd like you to take a look at something and tell me what you think it is. You've cleaned so many things off furniture and out of carpeting…."

"I don't want to brag, but if anyone can identify a stain, it's me. Come on over."

Jackie was packing her van when I pulled up. She was a tiny woman but was handling the heavy fans and cleaning equipment like a professional weight-lifter. I got out of the car and offered to help. When she turned me down, I waited until she finished then gave her the paint can and tissue.

"I found these in that half-built house on Oceanview Drive."

She took them and looked at me quizzically. "What were you doing there, girlie?"

"Getting inspiration for my book."

"Hah. Snooping around. Your favorite pastime. You know what they say about minding your own business." She giggled, sticking the tissue in her pocket, then turning the paint can upside down to examine it further.

"Yeah, yeah. Everybody says that but no one around here does it, I'm told."

"You got that right," she said. "You know, seems obvious this is paint." She moistened one of the drips on the can, ran her finger over it and then put a dab on her tongue.

"Jackie! Be careful!"

"Don't worry. I've had worse in my mouth. If you know what I mean. It's paint. Latex."

"Wow. You can get a taste from old paint? What about the tissue?"

The cleaner removed the Kleenex from her pocket. When the material made it to Jackie's tongue, she smacked her lips and crinkled her nose.

"It's pretty faint. But there's no mistaking that metallic taste. Even though it looks like your paint color here, it's blood."

ꝏ

I had one more call to make before Frank arrived for dinner.

"Seaside Veterinary Clinic," the woman said. "How may I help you?"

I steeled myself for the conversation that was to follow. I needed to give the clinic some information but not too much. I wanted a lot in return.

"Oh, hi. I found this dog. A Lab, a yellow Lab. I wonder if he might be a, uh, patient at your clinic."

"Is there a number on his collar?"

"Yes. I called and no one answered."

"Why don't you bring the dog in, and we'll see if he has a chip."

"Uh, it's kind of a long drive and the dog is in no condition to travel."

"All the more reason to bring him in," the woman responded.

There was no more skirting the truth. "To be honest, the dog is dead," I said.

There was a pause on the other end of the line. "Did you say dead?"

"I found him on my walk and brought his collar home with me. I called the sheriff and, well, I thought I should alert the owner."

"My suggestion is that you turn the collar over to the sheriff and let him try to contact the owner. Or he can bring the remains to us. We dispose of dead dogs for the county. We can examine the body for a chip at that time."

I was thankful I hadn't identified myself. I was sure the woman had already pegged me as a whacko. "It was about, uh, a couple of days ago that I found the carcass. I'm guessing the sheriff has gotten rid of it. And it was more a pile of bones and meat picked over by the buzzards than an actual, uh, animal."

A sigh, fueled by what must have been a very deep breath, hissed from the other end of the phone. "What exactly would you like me to do?" the woman finally said.

"I'm wondering if anyone remembers treating a dog named Whalen or if you have a record of him."

"We treat hundreds of animals at this clinic. Many are pets of transient residents, northerners. Unless you have a last name for the dog...."

"Hold on." I searched for the little scrap of paper on which I'd written the name that Mary Sanders gave me.

"Thompson. The dog's name is Whalen Thompson."

"Just a minute," the woman said as the phone went silent.

I checked my watch. It was 3:47. I hadn't made the salad or cleaned up for dinner. Maybe I should have called the vet earlier.

The line clicked after about five minutes and the woman was back on. "Found him. He was in earlier this year for his shots. Owner is Peter Thompson, Toronto Canada." She reeled off his phone number.

"Oh gosh, thanks, but that's the same number that was on the collar," I said, trying to hide my disappointment. "Do you have any other contact information?"

"No, he pays in cash. We've only seen the dog twice. No current mailing address either. Guess we tried to send him something and it came back. Maybe we didn't have enough postage. Canada costs more, the post lady told me."

I was about to move on when she spoke again. "Oh wait. That's interesting. There's a handwritten note. Says someone brought Whalen in recently and wanted to make sure his shots were current. Um, not the owner. Said the dog was a stray. We checked the chip, told him the dog was current on his shots and gave him the owner's name and number."

"Do you have that person's name?" I asked.

"It's not in the file. I can check with the girl who was here that day and get back to you."

"Thanks. I'd appreciate that."

While I was eager to hear from the deputy and the man at the paint store, this was one call I didn't need. I already knew who had brought the dog to the vet's.

CHAPTER 9

He pressed his lips against hers, running his fingers through her short hair and down the sides of her face. She felt the urge within her growing stronger as his kisses drew her in. Now his hands were moving down to her neck, caressing, then encircling it. His thumbs reached into the hollow of her throat and began pressing. Their lips broke apart. Wait. Stop. She couldn't breathe. She tried to focus on him, questioning why it had come to this. His cold eyes held no answers. They were the last thing she saw.

How stupid, I thought as I wiped my damp forehead with the back of my hand. I was letting my thoughts wander as I stood in the kitchen slicing carrots and tearing lettuce leaves. My mind had taken me down a very dark path. A ridiculous one at that.

What did the man at the paint store say? *Too many TV shows. Some imagination.*

The abandoned house, the buzzards and the headless carcass, a dog's collar and an empty paint can: I'd linked those relatively innocuous items to a web of criminal activity of my own fantasy. And tonight, I was having dinner with a man I suspected was involved, simply because he had the dog whose collar I'd found in the mystery house.

There must be a logical explanation. Frank Johnson was a fisherman. Nothing else. He appeared to be a quiet man. A peacemaker. He didn't get involved in the clash between his wife and his mother at the art show. He urged his mother to leave.

If I was worried about him, why had I spent so much time getting ready for his arrival? It must have taken me 10 minutes to select a dress from my closet. Was it too short? Was it age appropriate? Whatever that was. Would he think it looked good on me?

In case you've forgotten, he's still married, a little voice inside my head admonished.

Yeah, but he's separated. That makes it okay, my libido responded. I opened a pinot noir and poured a glass, carrying it through the second bedroom to my small deck at the front of the condo. My mind needed numbing.

There was just enough room among the pots of geraniums, hibiscus and desert rose plants for the two plastic chairs I'd purchased several months ago. The deck was my refuge for reading in the late afternoon. From this vantage point, I also could see visitors arriving.

As I sat there waiting for Frank, my eyes traveled from the gated parking lot entrance to the buzzards circling overhead. It was easy to see their skeletal structure; each feather fused to a bone extending from the curved neck. The feathers: black to gray then back to black, beautiful and ominous at the same time.

Their numbers were growing daily, lured here by the scavenger tides; waves that carried in hundreds of fish and other sea life killed by toxic algae blooms offshore.

The rotting fish disgusted beach walkers but gave life to the vultures above. *Life to death. Death to life. It's nature,* my thoughts whispered to me.

The distinctive rumble of a Harley drew my attention from the skies to the condo entrance. I watched my guest punch in the number and rev the engine while he waited for the wrought-iron gate to rumble open. He pulled the Harley between two white lines, got off and unstrapped a brown paper bag from behind his seat.

"Hello," I shouted from my perch.

"This the grill?" he said, stopping by the Webber that was chained to a post on the edge of the asphalt parking lot.

"Nothing fancy, but that's it," I said.

He opened the top, looked up at me and sent his understated grin my way. "It'll do."

When he came through the screen door, he set the brown paper bag on the kitchen counter and gave me a peck on the cheek. Everyone on the island seemed compelled to offer a kiss as part of their greeting. The custom worried me during cold and flu season, but I participated anyway.

"Four fillets. Beer," he said.

He smelled of Dial soap and a spice I couldn't identify. There was a pinkish glow on his cheeks and the bridge of his nose – signs of a long day on the water. His mood was cordial but restrained.

In the corporate world I was used to the quick talkers who were comfortable working the room; men who had a sharp wit, a glib comeback and all the answers. At first blush, Frank appeared to be – there's no other way to put it – the strong silent type.

I gave him the tour, moving him through my living area, the two bedrooms and onto the lanai where we settled into my Adirondacks. In front of us was a sky of blue and shades of pink, a palette created by the setting sun and reflected in the water below. The view was so spectacular it felt as though no words were needed. *And where to start anyway?* I wondered.

"How was your day?" I finally asked.

His face hardened. "One of the worst of my life. Had a couple of bad actors onboard. Real jerks. I'd rather not talk about it."

"Oh. Sorry to hear things didn't go well."

We continued sipping our drinks as I searched for another conversation starter. When I realized he was okay with the silence, I decided to keep still for a change.

The quiet was interrupted by the voices of small children strolling on the beach below. When their silhouettes appeared, I could see they were carrying miniature poles and buckets.

"I caught lots more fish 'n you," the girl said as she pushed wisps of hair from her face.

"You say that and I'm gonna push you in the water and you'll be eaten by a shark," the boy countered. His baseball cap was turned backward. His tummy protruded over a bathing suit that reached below his knees.

"Mommy, Mommy. Kurt's gonna kill me."

The little girl's screams startled a group of seagulls nearby waiting for a hand-out. They took off, emitting cries louder than hers.

"You'll be okay," we heard a distant voice say. "He doesn't mean it. Now hurry up. It's getting dark."

Frank's face relaxed into a smile, opening the door to small talk at least.

"Did you have a little sister to torture?" I asked.

"Just brothers. They beat up on me. That's how I learned to be tough."

"Don't mess with you?"

"Right. Don't mess with me, Leslie." He grinned that half-smile of his and ran his fingers through his sandy-colored hair. I tried not to stare. I never felt at ease around good-looking men. My former boss, Brad Stewart, had been one of those beautiful on the outside, wretched on the inside kind of guys. I hoped Frank wasn't like that. But as Deb had said, he definitely could take your breath away.

"So, is the fishing business good? Seems like it would be around here," I said. I was getting warmed up for the big question that I absolutely had to ask.

"Some years, yes. Others, not so much. There was a big fish kill several years ago from the cold. Red tide's a problem. It's out there now. Lots of us did odd jobs, tried to sell boats, did home maintenance during the last downturn. I've painted houses on the island, but I'm a fisherman. That's all I want to do."

I wondered how anyone could make a decent living catching fish. "And your family?" I asked.

"I've got Stevie. He's 13 and does okay in school, but I worry about him. He doesn't have many friends his age. Keeps to himself."

"Kids are always a concern. My daughter Meredith's a junior in college. She's talking about going to South Africa next summer. Scares me, but I try not to think about it."

He stood up, clutching his empty beer can. To my surprise, he leaned over, cupped my chin and brushed my lips with his. With this tender connection, my pulse picked up its pace. It was still tripping along when he returned with another beer for himself and my bottle of pinot noir.

"Were you born around here?" I asked.

"Kentucky."

"What brought you here? Did your family fish?"

"They were carpenters. Most of them."

"But you became a fisherman instead. You've been a fisherman all your life?"

"Something like that," he said, shifting in his chair.

"Do you have any hobbies?"

44

"Staying out of trouble and not answering too many questions." He smiled. I was surprised he had tolerated the interrogation for so long.

I studied him for a minute and decided to take a chance. "Well, sorry, but I have at least one more question. Why do you have Whalen?"

"Who?" His face was blank. Totally unreadable, as though he'd never heard that name before. And, yet, he must have remembered when I called to the dog on the dock. It was just yesterday.

"The yellow Lab, the dog with your son. Whalen's his name. I've seen him a couple of times in the neighborhood. You know how you remember a dog's name and not its owner? After I saw him with you yesterday, I checked with the vet, thinking I was crazy or something and that it wasn't Whalen. How could it be?" I paused, watching his eyes. They were steady in their focus on me. "They said you brought him in recently to see if his shots were current."

He looked out to sea, took a gulp of beer and then zeroed in on me again.

"Someone found the dog. Gave him to me. I thought he'd be good for Stevie, so I agreed to keep him. The owner didn't seem to care much about him," Frank said. "I guess the lady at the vet did tell me his name is Whalen. We call him Buddy."

Sometimes it's expedient to bend the truth. Was it just me or was he also hedging his answer?

"All I know is that I saw Whalen's collar and what I thought were his remains in that yellow house on Oceanview Drive. The one that's under construction. Why would someone want the owner or anyone to think Whalen was dead?"

"I know the house you're talking about. You went in there? Why?"

"There were buzzards walking through an open door on the second floor. I was, um, being nosy. The house gives me the feeling that there's something not right there." I stood up and pointed to the south. "You can see it from here."

The unfinished yellow house in the middle of a row of beachfront properties stood out like a sore thumb.

I expected Frank to tell me I should mind my own business. Instead, he grinned and chugged his second beer. "Let's take a look."

⟋⟋⟍⟍

The gate intended to guard the entrance to my condo complex opened at its usual snail's pace. It was dark now; maybe too late for a fact-finding expedition with a stranger on a motorcycle that had seen better days.

When we arrived at the yellow house, Frank reached into his saddlebag and pulled out a flashlight. The gate from my first visit was still ajar. He slipped through the opening. I followed, swatting at the mosquitoes that were happy to home in on some CO_2 in the neighborhood.

"Is this how you got in?" he said when we reached the entry to the lower level.

I nodded, not knowing if it would be locked or not. Frank twisted the knob and the door opened. He shined the flashlight around the area. "No dead bodies, human or otherwise." He didn't see me roll my eyes.

We climbed to the second level, turned to the left and headed for the unfinished kitchen where Deputy Webster and I met and shared some Vick's VapoRub to ward off the smell of death.

A large brown stain was all that remained of the carcass. Vestiges of the pungent odor that I encountered during my first visit still hung in the air but were tolerable.

"So, the animal was here?" Frank asked.

"And the collar was there," I said, pointing to a corner near where the outline for the kitchen island was marked.

"Anything else arouse your suspicions?"

"Well, yes. Paint cans upstairs that were made to appear used but were clean inside and a mark on the steps going up to the next level. My friend, Jackie Gates said it was blood."

"Jackie? The woman who cleans carpets? She was here?"

"No. I took her a sample and she, uh, tasted it."

Frank laughed. "That's a new one."

"I know. It sounds bizarre. But tell me this. We know the remains weren't Whalen's, but what was it and how did it get in here? Where did the collar come from? Why did Whalen's owner abandon him and how did your friend find him? Why did work stop and why has no one seen the owner recently? Then there's the bathroom upstairs. Who builds an inside bathroom for workers to use?"

And why am I asking you all of these questions?

"Whoa. You are full of questions. Why don't you show me the bathroom for starters," Frank said.

I led him up the back stairway to the room with the sink and toilet. He flashed the light around. Nothing had changed from my first visit.

"No answers here. But this place is filthy. The cleaning woman's been murdered," he said.

I laughed and gave him a playful smack on the arm. "Congratulations. You've figured out the mystery of the abandoned house."

He laughed, too. "You satisfied? I'm starving, but we can stay longer if it makes you happy."

I thought about the locked door across the hall, but my stomach was growling. I would save it for another time. "Sure. Guess I'm ready to eat, too."

During dinner, Frank talked about the history of the island, and the characters that roam the street in golf carts and frequent the Tarpon Bar. It felt like he'd moved on from the day's earlier unpleasantness on his boat, whatever it was.

Eventually, I found myself returning to the topic of the yellow house. No surprise there.

"Am I crazy to think there's something wrong in that place? My instincts are pretty good about things like that. There's a door upstairs that's locked. But anybody from the street can walk in the entrance on the lower level. I've been there twice, and it wasn't locked. Is that normal during construction?"

"Depends on the builder and the stage the house is in. Lots of times doors are left open for easy access by workers. The door upstairs may be locked to keep tools from being stolen. This is Florida. What seems strange to you now may seem normal after you've lived here awhile. Maybe the owner ran out of money."

"And those remains?"

"Probably a sick coyote that wandered into the house and died," he said. "I'd let it go if I were you."

A headless coyote? I don't think so.

"When did your friend give you Whalen?" I asked.

47

"Not long ago. I can't remember the exact day," he said.

"Can we talk to him?" I pushed.

"He left town. Not sure when he'll be back or if he'll be back. That's why he couldn't keep the dog." Frank looked away. Subject closed.

"Maybe you're right. Unless a body appears, I guess there's no mystery," I said, frustrated by his easy answers.

Frank returned his gaze to me and smiled. "The only mystery is when I'm going to see you next. Let's solve that now."

CHAPTER 10

Rain torrents and 50 mile-per-hour wind gusts lashed the island courtesy of a late-season tropical storm sitting in the Gulf. White-capped waves raced across the waters of the North Pass and crashed into my seawall, splashing 10 to 15 feet in the air.

My apprehension with the weather was growing, but I also was wondering why I hadn't heard from Frank. He said he was going out of town on business and would call when he returned. That was five days ago and still no word.

When my cell phone rang, I hoped it was him, but thought it could be Mother wondering if we should evacuate for the mainland.

"Leslie, it's Deb. Oh my God, you're not going to believe what just happened to Phyllis Betz."

"Phyllis? Is she OK?" Phyllis was a local artist who lived a couple of blocks from the beach in a home she and her husband remodeled several years ago. She was a great cook and loved to throw parties. She could be a little spacey at times, but that only added to her charm.

"She's fine. But it'll take time for her to get over what she saw. It was a body. An honest-to-God body. Naked. On the beach. She nearly died. Screamed, of course. There was no one else around except her dog, Max. She's the only one crazy enough to walk in this weather."

My thoughts were racing. Could it be Frank? Oh please no.

"Did she report it to the sheriff?" I asked.

"No. She came home and called me. When we got back to the beach – maybe 30 minutes after she spotted the body – it was gone."

"Gone?" More mysteries and this had seemed like such a quiet island when I first arrived.

"Snatched up by a big wave and carried out to sea again. That's what she and I decided, 'though we can't say for sure. Someone might have hauled it away."

"Maybe it wasn't a body; maybe it was a dead fish," I said. "I think she should contact the sheriff."

"I'm at her house. Come over and bring red wine. I need a drink."

"Doesn't Phyllis have wine?"

"She has white. That's all she drinks, honey. White couches, you know. Her husband's off-island, and she isn't sure when he'll be back. Come over. Now."

Deb was pacing, and Phyllis was sitting on the couch texting when I arrived at what seemed like the tail end of the storm. Max, a cream-colored Wheaton Terrier, greeted me like an old friend – his tail wagging as I scratched behind his ears. He didn't seem at all traumatized by the recent events or the weather.

Phyllis got up and handed me a towel. Deb reached out for the wine.

"What kind did you bring?" she said, adjusting her glasses and then scowling at the $12.95 price tag on the bottle.

"You're being picky? It was the only bottle I had. Uh, Frank and I, uh, drank the rest last week. Wednesday. At least I did. He had beer."

"What? You were with Frank Johnson?" Her eyes widened and her mouth dropped open in surprise. I prepared for an onslaught of questions.

"He stopped by the day after my fishing fiasco and asked if we could have dinner. He said he'd bring the fish. Against my better judgment, I said yes."

"He's a good guy. Don't pay any mind to what I told you about him bein' bad," Deb said. "But you kept this a secret. How come?"

I shrugged. "I know he isn't single yet, but I'm rationalizing that he's separated, so, uh, anyway he's out of town. Tell me about the body, Phyllis."

Phyllis took the towel from me and began wringing it in her hands.

"It was terrible. It looked like one of those zombies on TV. It was blue but faded and white at the same time."

"Male or female?"

"Male. It still had some of its parts," she said. I thought I saw her blush.

50

"You think that would be the first thing a fish would go for, danglin' there and all," Deb said.

The three of us looked at each other and started laughing.

"This is serious stuff," I said, trying to regain my composure. "We have to report it. You want me to call?"

Both women, still chuckling, nodded vigorously.

Even though his office was five minutes away, it took Deputy Bruce Webster half an hour to respond. When he arrived, the rain was letting up. Still, he reeked of wet clothes infused with cigarette smoke. After taking a sniff and crinkling her nose, Phyllis directed all of us to sit around the dining table.

The deputy cleared his throat and pulled out the notebook from his back pocket. "Ya found a body and then it disappeared? What time was that?"

Phyllis paused as if trying to pinpoint the exact minute.

"I usually take the dog out the first thing in the morning so it was a little after 8. I was walking the beach and it rolled up and stopped right in front of me. It was definitely a body. A dead one. And it was a man. I was scared so I came home and called Deb. When we got back to the spot, it was gone."

Although Deputy Webster asked a few more questions about the location, I could sense his skepticism growing. There was no proof, just the word of some female who was crazy enough to be walking her dog on the beach in a bad storm.

"Um. Well, you should've called us first. There's not much we can do when we don't have a body. Habeas corpus, you know."

I had to add my two-cents worth even though I knew the deputy would not be interested in what I had to say. "Maybe it was the missing owner of the house on Oceanview Drive."

The deputy looked at me, his eyes narrowing. "Who said the owner was missing?"

"You said no one's seen him. I call that missing. And you never got back to me about the dead dog and the buzzards. What did you find out?" I asked.

"Didn't have yer number. Some animal wandered in there and died. No proof of foul play like ya thought." He smirked.

"Wandered in? How did he do that without a head?"

The deputy said nothing. *What could he say? And besides that, hadn't I given him my phone number?*

"The case of the headless canine," Deb said, sounding pleased with herself. "That's one for the local paper."

She laughed, but Deputy Webster and I remained silent and glaring at each other. He finished writing in his notebook and admonished all of us to stay out of trouble, or something to that effect, before heading for the door.

"He doesn't much care for you," Phyllis said after he left.

"I get that same feeling when I see him, which has now been two times too many."

I shared the story about the mystery house and my first encounter with the deputy. I told them that the dog Whalen, once presumed dead, was now alive and in Frank Johnson's possession, reportedly given to him by a friend.

"That's some story," Deb said. "No wonder the deputy thinks you're trouble. Sticking your nose into buzzard and body sightings and all that. What's wrong with you, girl? Did someone forget to tell you that this is still a man's world?"

"He'll have to put up with me whether he likes it or not. I'm not going to back off anytime soon," I said.

My companions toasted me.

CHAPTER 11

The children were holding hands, crying. The man was on his cell phone, yelling. "I said a body in a boat on the beach. What don't you understand about, uh, a dead person? Dammit. Don't put me on hold again."

The trio emerging from the shell pathway that wound its way through the beachfront homes on Oceanview Drive to the Gulf nearly collided with me.

The little boy and girl were familiar to me. They had been fishing in front of my condo when Frank and I had dinner together. Today, they wore matching bathing suits with cartoon fish printed on them and looked like they had been at the beach. But instead of big smiles, their reddish cheeks were streaked with dirty tears. The man had on shorts and two beach towels draped around his shoulders. His face looked panicky.

"Can I help?" I inquired.

"My kids were playing around a rubber boat that, uh, washed up while we were on the beach. From the storm two days ago, I'm thinking. I heard them scream and ran to see what the problem was. I looked inside and there was this, uh, you know, this thing. Must have been in the water for a while. My little girl, she's only 4. She'll have nightmares." He wiped the tears out of his eyes with his thumb and forefinger.

"So, you're on hold with the sheriff's office?" I asked, trying to sound sympathetic.

"911," he said. "I guess they're trying to transfer me. Hold on. Yes, yes. Body on the beach. I'm on, uh...."

"Oceanview Drive," I said. "Mid-block near the path to the beach."

"Thanks. Oceanview Drive by the beach path. Ten minutes? Okay."

The man introduced himself as Kent Olden and said he was staying down the street at the beachfront complex with his pregnant wife and two children. I encouraged him to take the little ones home while I waited for the sheriff.

"You don't want to put the children through the ordeal with the boat again."

"You're right. God, this ruins our vacation," he said, scooping up his blond daughter and grabbing his son's hand as he headed at a fast trot toward the entryway to the Seaside complex.

"Deputy. Good to see you again," I said when Bruce Webster emerged from his police car and tossed a cigarette onto a nearby pile of sand.

I'd been sitting on the large rock that marked the path to the beach, wondering how long it would take for the deputy to arrive at the scene. Fifteen minutes by my watch. Not too bad. His time was improving with each corpse sighting.

"The person you want is the man walking this way. His children found the body in a boat. He'll take you there," I said as I walked over to the deputy's discarded cigarette butt, picked it up and stuck it in the pocket of my shorts.

"What are ya doin' here?" he asked. He avoided looking at me as he reached for the familiar pad in his back pocket.

"I just happened to be walking, like I always do in the morning."

"No point in ya stickin' around," he said, half under his breath.

I ignored his comment. I wasn't going anywhere except along with them.

"Sheriff?" The man said as he approached us and held out his hand. "Kent Olden. Staying at Seaside over there with my family."

"Deputy. Bruce Webster. Ya say ya found a body in a boat?"

"Yes. My kids Sophie and Kurt did," his voice broke as he pointed in the direction of the beach and re-lived the moment of discovery. "Over there. It breaks my heart they had to see something like that."

"Show me the body, Mr. Olden."

The man with sunburned shoulders headed for the beach with the deputy behind him and me as the caboose. We hiked across a boardwalk and over a wooden footbridge that led to the sand dunes. Several gopher tortoises munched on the patches of short grass to the side of the path, oblivious to the passing parade. Overhead, buzzards, osprey and gulls soared, riding the thermals.

When we crested a hill, Olden stopped and pointed through the sea grass to a rubber dinghy with a small outboard motor several hundred feet away.

"That's it. The body's inside. Caught up in some ropes."

I pulled out my cell and snapped a couple of long-distance photos. I wasn't sure how much closer I could get before the long arm of the law ordered me to back off.

Deputy Webster was the first to arrive at the dinghy. He stood there, looking at it with his hands on his hips and shaking his head. He flipped the boat over with his foot and then righted it again. It was obvious from his expression that there was nothing extraordinary in or around the small vessel.

"What the hell?" Olden said when he reached the deputy's side. "It was there, dammit."

"Right." The deputy looked at me, his lips squeezed tight. "Is this a joke?"

"Joke?" Olden protested. "My kids are traumatized, and you think this is a joke? I'm telling you, Deputy, it was there. A man, or what was left of him."

Webster shielded his eyes and surveyed the beach. It didn't take a mind reader to figure out what he was thinking. There were no waves to wash away the boat or the body. No people or animals to carry it off. There were only a couple of fishing boats offshore.

He ran his hand through his hair and paused as though unsure what to do. Then he pulled out his cell phone.

"Harry, Bruce here. Listen, I'm gonna need a truck and another pair of hands to meet me at the beach path off Oceanview. Got a rubber dinghy that washed up. Witness said there was a body inside. When I got here it was, uh, gone. The body, if there was one ... what? Yeah. A man and his two kids."

He looked at me. "Mrs. Elliott too. She was on her walk. Okay, okay. But she didn't make the call this time."

The deputy returned his phone to the black leather case attached to his belt.

"Mr. Olden. Give me yer number and address. I'll get back to ya if we have more questions. We're goin' to take the boat away and have it examined. Not much else we can do since there's no body."

"I sure as hell don't know what to make of it," Olden said. "That body wasn't in any condition to get up and walk away."

He put his hand on my shoulder. "My wife said to thank you for sending the kids home. I didn't think of that. Guess I didn't know what to do. I've never seen anything like that in Bayfield, um, Wisconsin."

When the father turned to leave, Deputy Webster looked hard at me.

"The sheriff would like to talk to ya in his office. Now."

CHAPTER 12

As I left Sheriff Harry Fleck's office, I remembered another day in my young life when I was 6 and my parents thought I'd gone missing. It didn't matter that I was off playing with friends and had forgotten to tell Mother. When I got home, my father offered me two options: a spanking or no swimming for three days at the community pool.

Sheriff Fleck, his face red and eyes flashing, had offered me similar alternatives. He even looked like my father. Nose a little too big for his face, curly reddish-brown hair, trimmed short, large hands with a crop of fine hairs sprouting on his fingers. Late 50s.

"I know your intentions are good, but we can't have our deputies running off on wild goose chases," he said from behind his large metal desk.

If I was supposed to feel intimidated, it wasn't working. I'd been around lots of authority figures and I was not impressed by the size of their desks or anything else for that matter. Harry Fleck was small town, and I could see right through him.

"You're saying you want me to stop reporting dead bodies on the beach?" There may have been a touch of sarcasm in my voice. It crept in too often.

"Well, now, Mrs. Elliott, that's the problem. There haven't been any bodies that we can find. Your calls have wasted a lot of Deputy Webster's time for no good reason. We're a small force. You need to mind your business and let us do our job."

I sat up straighter in my chair and raised my voice.

"Seems to me this is my business – as a good citizen," I protested. "It was Phyllis Betz that spotted the first dead body. She asked me to call the deputy. Mr. Olden and his children found the second body, or maybe it was the first one washed up again. I happened to be at the scene when the deputy arrived. And the dog, well…."

"I understand your concerns," he said, interrupting me. "But I'm giving you a warning."

"A warning?" I laughed. "Are you serious?"

Fleck leaned back in his chair, reached for a letter opener and began cleaning his fingernails.

"Nothing written this time. But if this keeps up, we may have to charge you with, um, making false police reports. That could mean jail time and a fine."

When he finished speaking, he looked at me and smiled. A cold smile.

The spanking or swimming conundrum.

"If I created problems for the deputy, I'm sorry," I responded in a controlled voice. "Although I don't think I've done anything wrong. I was just trying to be helpful."

"Consider yourself warned, Mrs. Elliott," the sheriff said, standing.

"It's Ms. Elliott," I responded with a forced smile. When I turned to leave, I saw Deputy Webster standing by the exit, smirking.

⁓⁓

I was still fuming later that afternoon when Deb called to invite me to dinner. Scooter was in the mood to grill, and she thought I should invite the fisherman to join us.

After our first evening together, when Frank told me he was going out of town, I was glad for the breathing room. Now, after a week with no word, I wondered if he wasn't interested. I wanted to believe that would be best for me, but I found myself going along with Deb's plan anyway.

"Call Frank Johnson," I instructed Siri. He picked up after the first ring.

"Frank, Leslie Elliott. Did you have a good trip?"

"Leslie? Oh. Yeah, I did." The sound of his voice was more unsettling than I had anticipated. I hoped he couldn't detect my excitement.

"I was, uh, wondering. This is short notice. It's nearly 4. Deb and Scooter are fixing the fish she caught. She invited me to dinner, and you, if you want to come. At 5:30."

There was silence on the other end. I wanted to retract the invitation and hang up, pretending that I'd never made the call. I must have been wrong about Frank's interest in me. I should have felt relief, but I didn't.

"Just got in. Need a shower. I'll pick you up at 5:20."

I felt myself relax. He didn't say no. "No need to come up. I'll be watching for you. Bye," I said.

As I busied myself cleaning up the kitchen, my mind reviewed the day's events. The body in the boat; the traumatized dad and his children; the warning from Sheriff Harry Fleck and now the feeling of uncertainty from this fisherman who was inserting himself into my thoughts and my life.

What did a friend say when I told him I was moving south? *Even paradise has its dark side.* Was he prescient or just trying to warn me that not everything is as it seems? Hardly ever, in fact.

I was on my way to the front balcony to watch for Frank and his Harley when I noticed the newspaper from the yellow house. It was on the table in the entryway under the paint can. How many times had I walked by without seeing it? I grabbed it and started reading.

The front page previewed the contentious issues of the season: parking and public beach access were the top contenders, as usual. Inside, there was an announcement that a reporter/editor of 20 years had retired. A replacement would be named soon. I needed to remind my journalist friend from up north about the possibilities available to him at the island newspaper. Knowing that he was unhappy working for a Gannett publication, I thought Wes Avery might jump at the chance.

Several pages were devoted to real estate ads. There were photos from the Gallery Centre's final show of the season in May and the announcement of its opening in October. Several shots of fishermen with their impressive catches were bordered by ads for boats, tackle and guides.

I scanned the photos, looking to see if Frank's picture was among them. No one was familiar, with names like Mitchell, Doan, Treat, Senior, Klepser, Thompson. Wait, Thompson? A man with dark curly hair and a goatee was holding a 110-pound shark. The caption identified him as Peter Thompson.

So that's what you look like. If you aren't one of the mysterious bodies on the beach, where are you, Peter Thompson?

I moved on, searching for anything else of interest. Near the end of the last section was another group of real estate listings. There was an X by a small house in the village. *450 Live Oak.* I needed to remember that address. There was also a bank ad with numbers jotted next to it: 104. What was that about?

From outside, I could hear the rumble of Frank's motorcycle. I grabbed a key lime pie from the freezer and hurried through the front door.

Frank had turned off his Harley and was moving my direction. He was wearing jeans and what looked to be the same shirt he'd worn at the art show – the one that showed off his muscular frame. I took a deep breath. "I'm on my way. No need to come up."

He met me with an embrace. We shared the awkward kiss of two people who didn't know each other well.

"This afternoon – sorry. I was expecting another call. Didn't mean to sound rude," he said when we broke apart.

"It was spur of the moment, and you'd just returned from your trip, so...."

"Yesterday. I came back yesterday. Was going to call."

The disappointment from his statement stung. But I ignored it and said, "No problem. Uh, this may sound crazy but any chance we could ride past 450 Live Oak on the way to Deb and Scooter's? I want to see what it looks like."

"Is this another mystery house?"

"It could be." I grinned.

"I'm not sure I should take you there. You're gonna get into trouble. Remember the warning you got from the sheriff today."

CHAPTER 13

Deb Rankin's face was red, her eyelids swollen when she opened the door. "Come on in. Help yourself to a beer, Frank. Scooter's out back," she said, dabbing her wet cheeks with a tissue.

Frank gave her a kiss and seemed eager to escape whatever conversation was about to take place. My eyes scanned the room I'd seen scores of times: well-used furniture, piles of books and art supplies, walls needing a coat of paint.

It was never clear to me how these people who seemed to have such modest means came to own a chunk of the gold-dipped paradise that millionaires and a few billionaires called home several months of the year.

All I knew was that Deb sold the occasional painting and received a small salary for her job at the Gallery Centre. She also tended bar at cocktail parties held during the winter season.

Money wasn't the basis of our friendship, so it mattered little to me how she and Scooter got by – as long as they did. It was the person I cared about. She was bossy but loving, demanding but kind. Quirky at times but with plenty of street sense. Her mouth served as a conduit to her every thought, inappropriate or not.

If Deb was an open book, Scooter, who was eight years older than his wife, was a puzzle. The deep lines on his face had stories behind them. But I wouldn't hear about them from Scooter. He had a maddening habit of keeping information to himself; a man of less than few words.

Over lunch one day, Deb confessed he'd done time in prison for stealing a car in his early 20s. He worked at the marina sometimes. He did occasional construction jobs when the mood struck him. He knew how to take apart a car or motorcycle and put it back together. These days, he spent a lot of time sitting in his back yard, soaking up the sun and staring into space.

He was my friend's husband; I tried not to question what glue kept their marriage intact.

"What's wrong?" I inquired after Frank disappeared through the door that led to the backyard.

"The neighbors. Gordie Fike showed up this afternoon. Said he wanted to talk. Seems they've banded together and want us gone."

Gone? How can someone next door order you to leave your home? I wondered.

"As in they want you to move?" I confirmed, finding her statement hard to believe.

"Yep. We bought this place 24 years ago with insurance money Scooter's folks left him. It's all we have. Now the snowbirds in their fancy new residences think we're an eyesore. Or so Gordie says."

Eyesore was an accurate description of the outside of their house, even though I would never tell Deb that I agreed with her neighbors. There were dilapidated tables and chairs, along with an old Ford truck by the small lake in the back of their property. A riding mower that was half rust, trash cans, ladders and fishing paraphernalia hugged the latticework on the lower level of the house. The patchy grass was mowed, but it didn't appear that Scooter had a weed whacker, or the inclination to use one if he did. A couple of hens patrolled the grounds along with the three-legged, feral cat Deb called Long John Silver.

In contrast, the neighbors' 5,000-plus-square-foot homes soared out of the sandy soil like 21st century palaces, spanning as much as possible of the well-manicured lots on which they sat. Royal Palms lined driveways that were finished in pavers laid in intricate patterns. Backyard pools shimmered blue in the afternoon sun. There wasn't a house in the neighborhood that didn't belong on the cover of *Architectural Digest,* except for Deb and Scooter's.

"What leverage do they have?" I asked.

"None as far as I know. But I'm no lawyer." She blew her nose, discarded that tissue and reached for another. "It doesn't make me happy to know my neighbors hate me and want me gone. It happened to old Sam Zarkas. They put so much pressure on him he finally packed up and got the hell outta Dodge. Got over a million for his house."

"A million? Whew. Did Gordon make an offer for your property?"

"No. Guess the neighbors won't go that far. But he said he'd be happy to list it."

"Did he want to 'make it happen'?" I couldn't help but grin when I thought of the marketing slogan Gordon Fike seemed so enamored with.

"Oh, Leslie. Now yer makin' me laugh. Scooter and I won't sell. Not for any price. Where would we go?"

I looked out the window to where Scooter and Frank were sitting in plastic lawn chairs, having an animated conversation – probably about the neighbors. I wondered if the fisherman was having a heart-to-heart with his friend about picking up the trash.

"Maybe we can get some friends together and, um, you know, help clean it up a bit," I offered.

Deb shook her head. "That's sweet of you, honey. But Scooter calls the shots around here, and he wouldn't stand for anyone touchin' his stuff."

"Well, you guys were here first. The interlopers will have to live with things the way they are, I guess."

"I hope so. But they have money, lots of it, and we don't. It worries me."

It worried me, too.

Deb got up and was about to pour herself another Scotch when Frank and Scooter walked into the kitchen and announced the coals on the barbecue were the perfect temperature for grilling fish.

"If it's all the same to you, sugar, I'd like to drink my dinner," Deb said.

Scooter, spatula in hand, looked at me and started laughing. I wondered what was so funny.

"Your friend, Leslie. Headed for jail. Where's my old prison stripes?"

Scooter's face was now scarlet. And me, well, I'd never heard that many words come out of his mouth at one time. I was also surprised that Frank had provided him fodder for a laugh at my expense.

"You told Scooter?" I said, giving Frank the evil eye I'd learned from my mother. "You might as well share it with Deb."

He had told me the story after we'd driven by 450 Live Oak and discovered to my disappointment that it was unremarkable; a small cottage hidden behind a tall wooden fence that had seen better days.

It seems Frank was in the hardware store that afternoon when Sheriff Harry Fleck walked in and started chatting up the 20-something blond, Ginger, behind the counter. The sheriff often stopped there after getting his afternoon cup of coffee. The visits didn't sit well with Ginger who complained after Harry left.

"He acts like he's single or somethin', and I know his wife. I wish he'd leave me the hell alone," she said.

Frank wasn't so much concerned about Ginger as he was with the comments about me. The sheriff said I was trouble. I'd reported a couple of bodies on the beach – including one today – when there was nothing there. He'd warned me to stop interfering with police business or face jail time.

Frank figured Harry Fleck would pass that tidbit onto others. Soon it would be around town. "People's reputations rise and fall on the words of others. You're new. You don't want a bad rap," he had told me.

"You're saying that the sheriff's out to ruin my reputation? Can he do that?" I asked after he shared the story with Deb.

"Everybody knows him. He's been around a long time. You either want him to like you or not know you. You're known to him and not in a good way."

"Why's he after you?" Deb asked.

"Guess he thinks I'm interfering. I forgot to tell you about the body. It showed up again, at least for a while."

"Phyllis's body?" Deb's puffy eyes widened in surprise.

"Yes, I think. I can't believe it was a new one. A family found it this morning. Poor kids. The dad called the sheriff. When the deputy showed up – my buddy Bruce – I was there. Guess he took offense. We went out to the boat and it was gone. The body that is."

"How come you didn't tell me about this sooner?" Deb exclaimed.

"Because we were talking about your neighbors."

"Fuck 'em," Scooter said as he walked over to the kitchen counter and snatched up the filets Deb had prepared.

"You got any ideas about this, Frank?" Deb asked.

He shook his head and looked off in the distance. "If that body does exist, my guess is you won't be seeing it around here anymore."

Deb and Scooter nodded in agreement. I thought it was an odd thing for Frank to say.

CHAPTER 14

Frank's motorcycle sped down the island's main drag like we were running from the law. Maybe one of us was, I thought as I held tight to his waist and sheltered my face against his back. But which one?

I was still working through his comment about the body not returning. He talked about sharks and fish "making short work of it." Everything was fair game for the ocean's predators. But the body – if there was only one – had turned up twice. How could Frank be so certain it wouldn't make a third appearance? *And besides, it was in a boat! How did that happen?*

The motorcycle veered to the right. After a few more turns, Frank came to a stop and turned off the engine. "We're here."

The shack that was his destination after dinner appeared to have a new coat of paint. The yard was neat and well-tended, in sharp contrast to Scooter's. Someone had planted a few flowers around the front door.

"This is going to be my office. For now, it's storage," Frank said.

I envisioned the fisherman's mother, Georgia, sitting at a small desk, answering phones and trying to respond to the numerous requests for a captain in the late winter and early spring. She was plenty bossy, but I wasn't sure how effective she was as a business manager.

Not my problem, I thought, as I switched my focus from the building to the fishing boat moored nearby. I could make out the word *Dreamcatcher* by the light on a dock that stretched far out into the water. I was hanging over the edge, throwing up, the last time I saw that name.

"Night fishing? I don't think so," I said as Frank reached for my hand and I balked.

"I thought a ride over calm waters to a scrub island about 20 minutes away would be good. Look at the moon and the stars, Leslie. It doesn't get any better than this."

My common sense managed a weak protest.

"What if I get sick again?"

"You won't. I promise."

I shrugged, joined my hand with his and let him guide me down the edged shell path to the dock. He was in the boat without effort and reaching to help me climb onboard. He untied the thick ropes and turned on small running lights in the front and back of the vessel. In a few minutes, we were under way.

I thought back to a time, not long ago, when my friend Tim Fletcher and I had gone sailing on his 43-foot Bristol sailboat. Tim was grounded and in control, as befitted the CEO of a major utility company. Frank, on the other hand, was difficult to read and sent out mixed signals.

"About my getting sick. I was on a sailboat in March, vacationing with a friend in Sarasota and didn't have a problem," I said. A vision of Tim with his white hair and Roman-like features came to mind. I had strong feelings for him even though I had accepted that our age difference and his business responsibilities would probably always keep us apart.

"How big was it?"

"I think, uh, about 40 feet, maybe larger."

"This is a single engine, 24-foot inboard Morgan. They don't make 'em anymore. It moves around in the water more than the one you were on. You weren't fishing in rolling conditions. It wasn't as hot. There could be a lot of reasons. Maybe you liked the guy you were with."

If the fisherman was looking for reassurance that the man on the Bristol wasn't a part of my life anymore, he wouldn't be hearing any details about that relationship from me.

"He's a friend. But so are Deb and Scooter. I haven't decided about you," I said, trying to lighten the conversation. I was glad to hear him laugh at my comment.

Frank piloted *Dreamcatcher* through the dark waters of the South Pass. When we arrived at a large pole sticking out of the water by a small land mass, he lassoed a rope around it and pulled tight.

"Sorry but your feet are gonna get wet," he said as he slipped over the edge and into water that came up to his knees.

"Did you say *feet* wet?" I eyed the surf below and wondered how I could avoid getting drenched.

"Sit on the edge and slide off. I'll catch you."

I did as instructed and landed in Frank's arms. He carried me to the beach, sat me down and pulled me close before I could get my footing. There was nothing awkward about the kiss that followed.

When we separated, he asked me to stay put as he headed into the dense brush at the edge of the sand.

I stared out at the water, focusing on the island lights in the distance. We were alone in this isolated location. If Frank was someone other than I thought, if there was something going on in the mystery house and he was involved, this would be the perfect place for an accident. No one, not even Deb, would think a mishap was anything but an unintended tragedy.

"You cold? You're shivering," Frank said when he returned.

I jumped. I was lost in those dark thoughts that often plagued me and hadn't heard him coming.

"You startled me. Oh my. Where did those come from?" I asked, pointing to the blankets and cooler Frank was carrying.

"I have a shack in the bush. I've got sleeping bags, provisions and other stuff for when Stevie and I camp here. Enough to last for a couple of weeks, maybe a month if the fishing's good. Before I picked you up, I made a run and deposited a couple of things, including this wine."

I was impressed that he'd gone to all that trouble. "Let me guess. Sometimes you come over here to be by yourself."

"Yeah. It's my refuge," he said as though he was sharing a secret with me.

"It's not yours. I mean, you don't own it, do you?"

"I claim squatter's rights; built a little shack. Been coming here for 10 years at least. It has nothing. No toilets. No electricity. It's a piece of dirt and some vegetation in wide-open water."

He spread the blankets on the sand. From the cooler he produced a bottle of white wine and two plastic cups. He poured us each a glass and then stuck his in the sand while he pulled his shirt over his head and tossed it to one side. The moonlight highlighted the patch of fine hair on his chest, danced across his shoulders and down his muscular arms.

"The stars are amazing, even with the moonlight," I said as he rested his arm on my shoulder, took a long drink of wine and then refilled his glass. "There were more visible in the desert when I was taking the shuttle bus from Needles, California to Las Vegas after a train ride. But this is good."

I babbled on about the trip I'd taken several years ago, trying to avoid the silence that might encourage Frank to take further action. When I paused to take a breath, he leaned down, touching my face and caressing my lips with his. It was a gentle connection at first. Just enough to let the electricity between us flow, and then begin to spark.

As our kisses deepened, he lowered me onto the sand. His fingers moved from my face to the buttons of my sleeveless blouse, undoing the first two. An involuntary moan escaped my lips, surprising me. My body was all in, even as my rational mind was pondering whether I should go down this path again, so soon.

As the third button slipped out of its hole, a fierce itching sensation gripped my leg. I pushed hard at Frank and sat up.

"Ouch! Oh!"

"What's wrong?"

"Something's eating me. Lots of somethings." I scratched and rubbed but the itch worsened.

"Damn. Ants or no-see-ums," he said, pulling me up and brushing at the unseen invaders on my legs.

"It feels like they're all over me. Isn't it too late in the season for them?"

"Could be your perfume. I'll get something." He headed for the brush and the shack for what I hoped with a remedy for my problem.

The spoiled mood, the dampened ardor. Legs that felt like they were on fire. I was feeling sorry for myself when I heard the rumble of a boat engine, distant at first but increasing in volume until it seemed that it was almost on top of me.

A bright light illuminated the front of Frank's boat and began crawling across the water to the beach.

"Imira! Look! That's the Dreamcatcher," I heard a voice call out. "Fraaaaank. Oh Fraaaaaankie." It sounded like someone calling a dog. Loud whistles followed.

"You there? You got some girl with you, amigo? Having some fun on the beach? Un poco de sexo? Eh Frankie?" More whistles; summoning and taunting.

I stood up and started to move for the cover of the brush when I saw Frank coming toward me like a running back carrying the ball toward the goal line. He grabbed my arm with such force that he knocked me off balance and onto the sand. "Oomph." I hit with a thud. He reached down and yanked me up.

"Let's go. Now." We took off running. In a couple of minutes, we were at the shack where Frank kept his gear.

"Stay here and out of the moonlight," he commanded as he left me. I intended to do as he ordered, but after a few minutes, I changed my mind and re-traced our path to the beach, taking refuge behind a cabbage palm. My curiosity always wins.

Frank was standing on the beach, arms on his hips, facing the boat that was about 40 feet from the shore. "Amigos. Como estan?" I heard him say. His manner was controlled.

When the light beam moved in the direction of the voice and settled on Frank, he put up his hand to shield his eyes.

"Hey, Frankie. Mejor que tu. Where's your lady?"

"No lady. Just me. Hangin' out. I thought you guys were gone."

"We stickin' around until everything's taken care of, amigo."

"It's here. Like I told you earlier." His voice was steady, confident. *What was here besides me,* I wondered.

"We gotta be sure, Frankie. The boss don't like loose ends. That's what mister...."

"Don't say anymore," Frank interrupted. "Voices carry over water."

"Oh, si, amigo. We don't want other people hearing our business, do we?

"No. That wouldn't be good."

So, Frankie. We see you soon, right?"

"Yeah. Soon." He waved and turned to go.

"Buenas noches y que descances, Frankie."

When the light went off and I could hear the sound of the engine putting distance between the boat and Frank's island, I backtracked to the shack. Frank was not far behind.

"You okay?" he said.

I reached down and scratched at my legs. "These bites are driving me crazy."

"Oh, sorry." From his pocket, he produced a white tube that looked like a large fountain pen. "This will help."

I could feel him watching me apply "After Bite" to both my legs and arms. I knew what was coming. No-see-ums were a curse for tasty folks like me. The itch from one bite could last for weeks, followed by ugly red bumps that took forever to fade.

"Tonight is shot. I'm taking you back." Frank's voice had an edge to it. He threw the towels and the cooler into the building, snapped shut the padlock and led me back to the beach.

"Who were those guys, Frank? Friends of yours?"

"No friends. Remember the men I told you about? The day we had dinner for the first time? They've got a buddy that pays for their trips and joins them sometimes. They were pissed because I didn't have the right licenses for them. Or so they thought."

"Oh, I wondered what they meant when they said their boss didn't like loose…."

He stopped walking and looked at me, hard. "You heard them?"

"I-I was afraid for you. I didn't know what was happening. I was behind that tree," I said, pointing to the nearby palm.

"You followed me when I told you to stay put? Dammit, Leslie, when I tell you to do something, you do it." His hand tightened around mine.

"I don't need you to tell me what to do," I said as I wrested back control of my hand.

"I think you do," he said as he swept me up into his arms, splashed through the water to the boat and hoisted me onboard. He instructed me to throw the rope ladder over the side. I did as I was told even though I was seething inside.

We rode back in silence, first on the boat and then on the motorcycle. At the gate that led to my complex, Frank punched in the code and delivered me to the steps that led to my condo door.

There was no way I was inviting him in. He said he was worried about my safety. I was worried about my safety around him. As far as I was concerned, he could spend the rest of the evening cooling off, alone.

"I had a good time except for the bites and the rebuke. I'm not some child, Frank. I'm capable of handling myself in difficult situations," I said. My voice had an unpleasant edge to it; a sound I knew that most men didn't like.

He shook his head. "Your curiosity's a problem for me, Leslie. First it was the house on Oceanview. Then the bodies washing up and your run-in with the sheriff. You don't listen to others; you have to do things your way. I can't be with a woman like you. My life's complicated enough."

He wheeled his motorcycle about and left me standing alone and angry under the light in the parking lot. It felt like we were finished before we had even started.

CHAPTER 15

Trucks lined the street next to the yellow house on Oceanview Drive. Bulldozers were moving dirt where volunteer pines once stood. A parade of workers marched in and out of the building like ants invading a kitchen after a spring rain. I stood there transfixed – stopped dead in my tracks on my morning walk.

It was the end of October and the summer heat and humidity had magically disappeared, replaced with the mild weather that lures northerners to Florida in the winter months. I reached into my lightweight jacket and pulled out my cell phone.

"Deb. What are you doing?"

"Getting ready for my plein air painting class in a couple of hours. Takin' the artists to the beach again. They love it there, even with the red tide."

"You've got time. Meet me in front of the yellow house on Oceanview."

"You find another body?"

"Yes, lots of bodies. You've got to see this."

I knew my friend wouldn't ignore my summons. She shared my sense of curiosity.

I was replaying the episode with Frank and rekindling my anger with his attitude and abrupt departure when Deb arrived in a red golf cart. She slid to a stop a few feet from me. She was wearing jeans and an oversized sweatshirt that said: *A bad day fishing is still better than a good day at the office.*

I eyed the vehicle, noting that it was rust-free and much cleaner than any of the several parked in the grass around Deb and Scooter's.

"Where'd you get the cart? It looks new."

Deb patted the pristine white leather seats. "From Doris. You know her. The sweet lady with the thick glasses. Said she couldn't see well enough to drive anymore so she donated it to the gallery."

"That was a nice gesture...."

Deb had stopped looking at me and was now focusing on the busy construction site. "What the frick? How long's this been goin' on?"

I shook my head. "Not sure. I haven't walked by here lately."

"When I did a drive-by a couple of days ago, the place was still a mess," she said. "Now it looks like they're back in business. The ratty fence and weeds are gone. There's a Porta Potty by the garage."

I nodded and pointed toward the front of the house. "The doors. See the one on the lower level and on the portico where the buzzards were? They appear to have new locks on them."

"Yep. Amazing. Bet the neighbors are happy," Deb said.

I was sure Mary Sanders was pleased but wondered why she hadn't called to alert me to the activity. Maybe she told Mom to tell me. Mother wasn't always good at relaying messages.

"Wow, look at that," Deb said. "Check out the guy that just came around the corner. Over there. He's a looker."

She pointed to a tall figure with his back to us. He was wearing khaki slacks, a polo shirt and baseball cap and carrying what appeared to be house plans. I guessed him to be 6'2" – close to Frank's height – with a similar build. When he turned around, he fixed his gaze on us, hesitated and then waved.

My knees went weak.

Dark curly hair sticking out from under the cap. Goatee. The picture of him in the local paper.

"Deb, that looks like Peter Thompson."

"Who?"

"The body on the beach. The man who owns this house and has been missing. Whalen's owner."

"Well, he doesn't look dead to me," Deb said. "And he's better lookin' than the body Phyllis described on the beach. Mucho better. Maybe you should call Deputy Webster and let him know that mister, what's his name?"

"Thompson. Peter Thompson."

"Right. Let the deputy know that he's come back to life."

"I think Bruce can discover that on his own," I said, recalling the smirk he gave me the last time we saw each other.

"Oh Jesus, he's comin' over here," Deb said, looking like a kid who'd been caught with her hand in the cookie jar.

"I'm not budging. You go if you want," I said, taking a deep breath.

"I'm stickin' with you, honey." She squeezed closer to me, smoothed her long dark hair and flipped it around one shoulder. I chuckled to myself. No woman, no matter what age, wants to miss a chance to make an impression on a good-looking man.

"Ladies, can I help you?" Peter Thompson looked Italian even though his surname was English and Scottish. A Rolex watch and gold-and-silver pinky ring with an eagle were signs that he had enough resources for his mansion by the sea.

As he got closer, I stuck out my hand. "Hi. I'm Leslie Elliott. Your neighbor from around the corner. I live in one of the condos on the North Pass. And this is my friend Deb."

He shook my hand and then extended his for Deb, who grabbed it, all the while grinning. I swear her face was a few shades pinker than normal.

"I know those buildings. I'm Peter Thompson. I own this. It's not a house yet but it will be, um, someday." His voice was resonant, self-assured.

"I'm Deb Rankin," Deb managed to interject. I'd never seen her so simpering. "Nice to meet you. I think we've seen each other before. You look familiar but I can't quite place you."

"It's a small island. Maybe at the post office," he said.

"Could be. We thought you'd disappeared. Leslie was convinced that a body...."

I interrupted. "Yes, the neighbors were worried. I know they'll be glad to see you."

"We're in the process of cleaning up so the construction site isn't so much of an eyesore. I didn't realize how bad it looked. We're fixing any damage that happened during the delay. We may take another break because of some financing issues, but it won't be as long this time."

"I heard there was a dead animal in there. Guess you had to take care of the blood stains?" I said.

He studied me for a minute, then nodded as if acknowledging a sudden thought. "Elliott. Did you say your name's Elliott? You're the one who reported the carcass, right? I called the sheriff about the bloodstains and the smell, and he told me about your, uh, involvement. Thanks for being so observant. Discovering those birds when you did saved me a lot of headaches."

Now it was my face that was flushing. "Yes, it was me. There were buzzards going into the second floor. I went into your house. It was open and I discovered, well, I thought it was your dog. I left a message, but you didn't return my call."

For a minute, Thompson looked lost. "I'm trying to remember, I'm sure I didn't get your message. I changed my phone number. That may be why. He was a great dog."

"But, he's...." Deb started to say.

I interrupted her again. "Gone. Too bad that he's gone."

"Yes, very sad. I was at the dog park talking to a lady from Canada with two bichons. When I turned around, he'd disappeared. I put an ad in the paper. Tried to find him. I figured he was dognapped."

"When was that?"

"September. Maybe August. You know how the days blend into each other down here."

Deb was keeping her mouth shut, but her eyes were dancing with interest as she watched the two of us chatter back and forth like old friends.

"When I was in your house – and again, I'm so sorry for trespassing – I picked up his collar. Of course, that's how I knew to call you. I wonder how he found his way back to the house and then, uh, died a couple of weeks after he was lost."

"Leslie. May I call you Leslie?"

"Of course."

"I have no idea. But I do miss him," he said, looking over his shoulder at the work going on behind him and checking his watch.

"Um, ladies, thanks for stopping by. I need to get back to work. While I'm here I'm renting a house on Live Oak. 450. Maybe you can join me for dinner. I've got some great South African wines. Bring your husbands, eh?"

"She's not married," Deb said.

"But dinner would be great," I added. "I'm sure Deb and her husband would enjoy it too." I retrieved a card from my jacket and pointed to my cell number.

Peter Thompson said I'd be hearing from him soon.

I hopped in the passenger side of Deb's golf cart. She took off like she was fighting for the lead in a European road race.

"Can you believe that? So much fun. You askin' all those questions. He full of answers and invitin' you to dinner."

"Us. He asked us to dinner. And the answer to your question is no."

"No?"

"No, I don't believe it. I don't believe he lost Whalen at the dog park. I don't know what to think about the house. At least the mystery about 450 Live Oak is solved. Seems he's staying there while his place is under construction."

"What? Well, he didn't seem suspicious to me, honey. He was real friendly, in fact. You're determined to create some sort of a mystery when there's nothin' there. Just a slow builder, a few buzzards and a dead animal. You gonna tell Frank about this? Make him a little jealous?"

I sighed, flashing back to the sense of indignation I felt at Frank's abrupt departure. "No point in talking to him. He said he didn't need someone like me in his life. I guess he wasn't up for my kind of intrigue. And, frankly, I didn't care for his attitude."

A look of concern crossed Deb's face. "Damn. When did this happen? And why didn't you tell me about it sooner?"

"It was Wednesday. After we had dinner at your place. We took a boat ride to some island and ended up in an, well…you couldn't call it an argument. I didn't have much say in the matter."

Deb patted me on the shoulder. "That makes me sad. I know there're plenty of fish in the sea for a woman like you. But I wouldn't toss Frank back in the water just yet."

CHAPTER 16

"Well, I'm not surprised," I heard my mother's voice as I walked up the steps to my condo after meeting the resurrected Peter Thompson. "Who could survive that?"

She was sitting in my living room area, her feet propped up on the ottoman – a glass of iced tea on the table beside her. It wasn't unusual for Mother to stop by my place and make herself at home.

"Who are you talking to, Mom?"

"Myself. I was reading this newspaper clipping someone sent me from home. Friend of mine died. Julia Blackwell."

"Oh, Julia, I'm sorry to hear that. She was a lovely person. Didn't you play bridge with her?"

"Yes, duplicate, for years. She lost her husband about the same time your father passed away. Both from early onset Alzheimer's. It was tragic."

"Wait a minute. Alzheimer's? All these years, I thought Dad died of something else? You never told me it was Alzheimer's."

"Frontal lobe dementia," Mother said, making a sad face. "Same thing; different part of the brain. Horrible. Your father was 57 when I had to put him in the nursing home. Eight months later he was gone – an empty shell of a man."

I knew. I was there, and, besides, Mother had mentioned his plight at least once a month since his death. I thought I had become numb to it but our discussion was making me feel sad again.

"It was tough. He didn't know any of us. What did Julia die of?"

Mother shrugged. "All I know is that she called me about a year ago and said the doctor had taken her vibrator from her. She knew then her life was over."

"What!" I started laughing. Our conversation had taken a different turn. We'd gone from discussing death to self-gratification. Leave it to Mother.

"Her vibrator? My God, wasn't she in her late 70s?" I said, shaking my head at the absurdity of the topic.

"Don't be so quick to judge, dear. The urge never really goes away," she said, looking at me over the top of her glasses.

"But taking away her vibrator couldn't have been, um, fatal."

"No, it was her heart. The doctor said her heart couldn't take the, you know, the stimulation anymore. If you're that far gone, you might as well call it a day."

I was being rendered speechless by the conversation that I couldn't believe I was having with Mother and that had imparted a piece of information that was difficult for me to comprehend. I suppose it could happen. That a doctor would take away a woman's vibrator. It would have been an interesting conversation in the waiting room:

"Oh, what are you here for?"

"To have my joy stick confiscated."

"I may need a drink with lunch," I said. "You want one?"

"I'll have a chardonnay and a chicken salad sandwich in a little bit. I know you have some. I checked your refrigerator," Mother said as she returned to reading her newspaper.

I shook my head and reached for the bottle from the small wine cooler that doubled as a side table. I opened it, poured two glasses, setting Mother's on the table by her and taking mine with me to the nearby couch.

"Says here Julia's last words were about going to the great orgy in the sky." Mother's eyes twinkled.

"Now stop it. It didn't say that. And mothers and daughters don't have these kinds of discussions."

"Don't be such a prude. I have vibrators. Several in fact. I use them at least once a week. How about you?"

Mother wasn't dropping the topic as I'd hoped. I could feel my face growing red. I picked up a magazine and started leafing through it. "I'm not answering that question. Can we please change the subject?"

"I bet you don't have one."

I drained my glass. "No, and I don't have a boyfriend and can't remember the last time I had sex. Are you happy?"

"If you're okay with that sad state of affairs, dear, I guess I am too."

The jingle from my cell phone saved me from further participation in this awkward repartee.

It was Mary Sanders, calling to inform me that Peter Thompson was back in town. He was friendly this time and the two of them had a wonderful conversation – so pleasant that she'd invited him to dinner. She wanted Mother and me to join them, along with some neighbors and Gordon Fike, who, to my surprise, she informed me was Thompson's realtor.

And this was the man who told me he knew nothing about the yellow house when I called him?

"Tomorrow? Halloween. Yes, we'll be there. What can we bring?" I reached for the calendar and wrote *Mary's. 6:30. Take wine.*

"Wear a costume if you have one, but that's all. I'm having dinner catered."

I had a thousand questions for Peter Thompson. Dear Mary had given me the opportunity to ask them. But would he provide the answers or remain hidden behind a mask?

ꙮ

After talking it over, Deb and Scooter realized they'd met Peter Thompson. Deb remembered him from a Gallery Centre trip to a nearby island about a year ago and finally put two and two together after we spoke to him on Friday.

"Why didn't you recognize him yesterday?" I asked as the three of us sat around Saturday afternoon sipping on what Deb called a Frankenstein Reviver. Her tribute to Halloween included gin with lemon and melon liqueurs.

"To be honest, he has that house on the north side of the island and we live on the south side. We're worlds apart, honey. I'd forgotten about him. Wouldn't have recalled his name 'cept that he introduced himself.

"My mind clicked in about 3 this mornin'. I rolled over and tried to wake Scooter. 'I know that guy' I said to him. Scooter mumbled something and was gone again. But I couldn't go back to sleep. I was excited to tell you."

"But the body and the yellow house?" I said, wondering why Deb, who'd been struck by Peter Thompson's good looks, hadn't remembered him.

"Never put it together, honey. Sorry. Seems like he's not the body or even one of the two. And the house isn't so mysterious anymore, is it?"

"I haven't decided," I said.

A soft breeze rustled the nearby palm trees. The three-legged cat jumped on Deb's lap; she began crooning to it as she stroked its matted fur. The smell of Scooter's cigarette curled under my face and threatened to enter my nose. I coughed and scooted my chair out of the way.

"Obsessed," Scooter said out of nowhere. "Frank says."

"Frank? You spoke with him?" I moved my chair closer to Scooter to so I could have a better chance of deciphering his words. But it was Deb who spoke up.

"He dropped by last night. Told us you two had gone separate ways," Deb said. "Course I already knew that from what you said. But I'm not sure I believe it."

"Separate ways? We weren't even on the same path when he left me standing in the parking lot. Said I was – how did he put it – too complicated for him."

"Second thoughts," Scooter mumbled.

"Did you say Frank's having second thoughts?" I asked, leaning in his direction.

Scooter didn't respond. Instead, he stood up, stretched and started walking toward the lake that separated his property in the back from the neighbors.

"Hey, where's he going?"

"That's Scooter's way of sayin' we're movin' into woman talk. He likes you; he likes Frank. He doesn't want to get in the middle," Deb said, as she swirled the liquid in the glass and took a sip.

"There's nothing to get in the middle of, Deb. Frank made that perfectly clear. I don't know the man. He's a fisherman. I used to be a corporate executive. What can we have in common? Did he go to college? Does he read? Or sit around watching television and drinking beer? Does he own a suit? He didn't even have the decency to hear me out before leaving."

"Whoa. You're soundin' a little uppity, missy," Deb said, giving me a look that might have come from my mother. "I'm not sure I like that quality in you."

"So what? It's the truth. Let's go back to Peter Thompson. Tell me what you know about him?"

Deb's frown dissolved into a laugh. She sat her glass on the nearby table and grabbed her long dark hair with two hands, pulling it into a ponytail and snapping a rubber band around it. "He likes 'em young. I know that. And flashy. Remember the TV show, *The Girls Next Door*. Hugh Hefner's little playmates? That first time I saw him, he was with one of those types."

Deb took another swig of her Frankenstein Reviver and continued. "Guessin' she was in her thirties with white blond hair. Puffy lips. The gallery had rented a ferry for a tour of Hermoso Island last year. They showed up about five minutes before the boat was to leave, holdin' hands." She shook her head at the memory.

"She was wearing a white blouse. Had to be custom made to cover her boobies and then taper into that tiny waist like it did. Her skirt – real short – was tight and she had on matchin' heels. Lavender. Everyone on board was lookin' at her. I thought Scooter was going to have a heart attack."

"Doesn't exactly sound like boat attire," I said, interested despite myself.

"They sat at our table with some other folks," Deb continued. "Thompson ignored the rest of us and talked to her the whole way over. Tellin' her she was deep and had amazin' ideas about life. I never heard anyone work so hard to get a piece of ass."

I shook my head, thinking about how many men I'd known whose lives were forever changed by lust. I wasn't against a little now and then but it had to be with the right person at the right time.

"We get to the island and they disappear. Right away. The place is like a little community but there are plenty of nooks and crannies. About the time we go into the restaurant there for lunch, they're back. She must have stopped by the ladies room 'cause she was all put together. He looked bored so he must have gotten what he wanted. In broad daylight. Imagine that. Maybe Scooter and I should try that sometime," she said, laughing.

"He's what, in his early fifties? Single. Good-looking. He's a player. I can see that," I mused.

"Maybe yes, maybe no. Scooter tells a different story. A couple of days after the boat trip, my man was havin' a beer at the Tarpon Bar. Thompson sits down next to him and strikes up a conversation. Scooter was surprised because on the boat trip he looked right through us."

"He had other things on his mind," I said.

Deb chuckled. "Don't most men. The younger ones, at least. The older ones just talk about it on the golf course; about Cialis and those four-hour erections. They all wish."

I reached for my drink, chuckling.

Deb continued. "So, Thompson tells Scooter that he's a widower. He's lonely and wants to find a nice woman. Scooter mentions seein' him with blondie. Thompson blows it off, acts like the woman meant nothing to him.

"Guess his late wife was a big art patron from a wealthy family in Toronto, a respected lady. She was killed in a car wreck a couple of years ago. Scooter said he seemed real sad when he talked about her."

"It sounds like he has a split personality," I said, then swallowed the last of my drink. "I'm having dinner at Mary Sanders tonight. He'll be there. I'll let you know what I think after I've had a chance to talk to him."

I glanced around the back of the house where Deb's husband was walking around the yard picking up trash and throwing it into the bed of the pickup truck. Every once in a while, he would stop and wipe his eyes with a handkerchief from his back pocket. Now he was pushing a rusty hand lawnmower out from behind the house.

"What's Scooter up to?"

"Trying to clean up. It's not in his nature to worry about mess. But this thing with the neighbors has him scared," Deb said. "He's found someone to take the Ford truck. It was his late brother Snake's, but Scooter decided to let it go."

"Maybe this will help," I said, thinking that my favorite couple had a big job ahead of them.

"I hope so," Deb said, sighing. "Wealth buys you fancy houses but seems like around here it doesn't always make you neighborly."

CHAPTER 17

The seven of us sitting around Mary Sander's large walnut table with its pumpkin and mum centerpiece sounded like a chorus from a hospital consumption ward. After a lengthy coughing session, Mary got up and closed the veranda doors.

Mother and I had arrived at Mary's about 6:30. I was wearing a red feathered mask and a black shift with red, gold and turquoise linear designs. Despite his taste for buxom blonds, I was hoping to make a good impression on Peter Thompson. He wasn't my type – far from it – but I wanted to lure some responses to my unanswered questions from him.

"Is there some kind of flu going around?" Peter asked. He picked up the Waterford crystal glass Mary was using from the collection she displayed in an elaborate china cabinet and took a drink of water.

"Red tide," said Jerry Mandino, flashing a knowing grin through his fake pirate mustache. "The first year we moved here from New Jersey there was a terrible outbreak."

His wife, Alice, a slender woman in her fifties, was wearing the low-cut, corseted outfit of a pirate's wench. "There were dead fish all over the beach," she said. "Some big ones. We talked about selling and moving, it was so bad. But we stuck it out and there hasn't been a problem in years."

"Until now," Jerry said, removing the eye patch he'd fiddled with throughout dinner.

The Mandinos lived on the other side of Mary Sanders. Jerry was an investment banker with a sharp mind and a bent toward the occasional off-color comment. Alice, an attractive mother of two grown children, had an infectious laugh and a commitment to physical fitness that I envied.

"Red tide?" Mother asked. "Sounds biblical." She was dressed as a witch, with a long black wig. I could remember many occasions when she didn't need a costume to play the part. I smiled at her fondly.

"It's an algae bloom," said Gordon Fike. "It covers the surface of the water. Fish, even manatees, die from the lack of oxygen. It almost ruined the fishing industry around here several years ago."

A gray mask and the shark fin attached to his back seemed an appropriate choice for the realtor. *Why did he lie to me,* I kept wondering while I watched him at dinner.

"Have you seen the beach lately? It looks like one of the plagues from the old movie *The Ten Commandments,*" he said. "The smell and the buzzards. It's bad for business. Home sales are down."

"So why are we coughing?" Thompson asked. He'd arrived in a Guy Fawkes mask that he removed before dinner. I'd asked him if he felt a kinship with the anti-government activist who tried to blow up the House of Lords in London in 1605. He had just looked at me and turned to talk to his hostess.

"Guess you haven't been here long enough to experience it," Mary said. "It starts with a tickle in your throat and progresses to a nasty cough. Some have troubling breathing. A friend from Michigan only comes here when there's no trace of the stuff. She gets regular reports from Mote Marine. You won't see her this season."

"That's terrible. They should get rid of it," Mother chimed in.

"How do you get rid of a natural phenomenon?" Thompson said, chuckling and leaning back in his chair.

"There's a big question as to how natural it is," Mary said. "Does anyone need more water or wine?"

Thompson shook his head. I got up to retrieve the water pitcher on the kitchen island and stretch my legs, which were cramping from so much sitting.

As I looked around her kitchen at the recipe books and blue and white Spode plates on which she was planning to serve dessert, I could hear Mary talking about the article she'd been reading in the *Miami Herald.* It implied that the state of Florida contributes to the problem when it releases waters from Lake Okeechobee. "The lake's fresh water, filled with fertilizers and other pollutants, goes into saltwater habitats. When the temperatures heat up, all kinds of bad algae thrive," she said.

"So, it can be controlled?" Thompson asked.

"I'd say no." Jerry Mandino said. "It's been around for centuries and the cause is unknown. But these lake releases surely exacerbate the problem."

"So, the environment suffers," I said, returning to the table.

"All of us are suffering, dear," Mother added. "How long does this go on?"

"Until the goop breaks up and those darn buzzards disappear," Mary said. "Oh, I hope this conversation hasn't spoiled dinner. I have some wonderful dessert from the caterer. It's so light. It's lady fingers. Cream and fruit."

"I'm up for it," Jerry said. "And a change of topic. How about politics?"

The groans from the rest of the diners were interrupted by sirens in the distance. Mary, who had gotten up to clear the table, looked toward the noise. "Whenever I hear that sound, especially in a small community like this, I worry that it's someone we know."

I felt a prickling sensation at the back of my neck. I hoped Mary wasn't right.

        ⁀◯⁀

Peter Thompson had spent most of the cocktail hour chatting with Jerry and Gordon about Wall Street and the financial markets, and now that dinner was over, I was afraid he'd escape me and leave. I needed to corner him before the evening broke up. When he got up to pour himself another glass of wine, I joined him.

"I'll take some white. Red sometimes gives me a headache," I said.

He grinned and filled my glass. "We wouldn't want that. A cough and a headache. Not a good way to end the day, eh."

I nodded. "So, how much work is left to do on your house?"

"The incident with the dead animal, er, the dog, set us back. Such a tragedy," he said. "The kitchen flooring's gone now, along with the smell. I was lucky to get workers. With so much construction going on in the area, it's tough."

"Do you have a move-in date?"

"Could take a year or longer. I'm Canadian and there are limits on my time here. Short visits aren't a problem, but if I'm here for any length of time, it creates hassles. I fly in. Land at that little airstrip off-island."

"Oh, yes. I've seen the old hangar there but never noticed any planes. Can you do that? I mean, can you hop in your plane and fly across the border whenever you feel like it?" I was clueless about how freely Canadians and Americans could cross the border between our two countries. It seemed like it was less open than it had been in the past.

"A few regulations, a phone call and a quick trip through customs and you're there. You have a passport?" He flashed a smile my way and leaned in, appearing interested.

"I do. My last flight was on a corporate jet, earlier this year. My knuckles were white the entire time."

"Perhaps I can get you to Canada sometime. I have a pill that will guarantee you a smooth flight. In the meantime, how about dinner? Next week if you're available. I know I said something about you coming to my rental place, but I'm a lousy housekeeper."

I said I'd check my calendar. He promised to call as he reached into his pocket, pulled out a wallet and sorted through a stash of cards until he found mine. "I have a terrible memory. This the right number?"

I glanced at it and nodded. "What do you do for a living, um, Mr. Thompson?"

"You are going to call me Peter, aren't you Leslie? I mean, you've been through my home and bedroom." He patted my arm.

"It wasn't too personal when I was there. No bed and the bathroom needed cleaning." I grinned.

"You got me there. You could say I'm a traveler who occasionally plays at being an attorney, or so my father-in-law says. Found this island when my late wife, Monica, and I were on a sailboat. We bought the property from Gordon over there. He's a good guy. Doesn't talk about my house or me, even though I'm sure he gets questions from nosy neighbors. Anyway, it's sad that Monica will never see it finished."

"I'm sure she would have loved it." I leaned closer, giving him what I intended as an interested but not snoopy expression. "So, attorney. Most lawyers I know don't have time for travel except for business."

"It's not a problem when you're involved in your father-in-law's corporation and your wife has, um, had daddy wrapped around her little finger."

I took a sip of wine. I wanted to learn more – anything he was willing to tell me.

"The old man was very generous when Monica was alive. Since she passed away, he's been hassling me to get more involved with the company. That's another reason why the house will take longer. What about you?" he said.

"There's not much to say. My mother and I moved here several months ago. We're enjoying a leisurely life, volunteering and other things. I spend a lot of time at the gallery. I think we're taking another fund-raising trip to Hermoso early next year. Should be a lot of fun."

"Hermoso?" He raised his eyebrows as if to suggest he'd never head of the place.

"You know, the island with the quaint cottages? Accessible only by water? Weren't you on that trip last year?"

"I was?" Peter Thompson looked at me blankly. "If you say so, I guess I was. I'll look forward to returning, especially if you're going."

ᐁᐁ Cᐁᐁ

"What is wrong with you?" Mother said as I pulled my car into the parking lot by our condos. "You're all fidgety. You have been since we left Mary's house."

"It's nothing, really. Only Peter Thompson acted like he'd never been to Hermoso Island."

"So what? I've never been there," Mother said as we walked down the path that led to both of our condos.

"Deb told me he was on the trip last year. Maybe it wasn't so memorable if he's forgotten it already."

Mother paused when we arrived at the steps that led to my place and gave me one of her famous looks. "Sometimes, dear, I can't figure you out. Since you decided to become a writer, you act strangely. Everything's a big mystery. All I know is that I thought you'd be single for the rest of your life. Now another good-looking man – a widower, in fact – pops up."

"Let's not go down that path again, Mother. I'm not prepared to throw myself at every attractive man that comes along. Besides, he's not my type."

"Testy, aren't we? No matter. I'm getting a headache from all the coughing," she continued as she left me and walked toward her condo. "I'll see you tomorrow. And try to lighten up," she called over her shoulder.

"Good night, Mother."

I had started up the steps to my door when I heard the sound of a motorcycle headed my direction. Frank. I wasn't ready to welcome him back with open arms after the way he treated me, although some part of me was definitely glad to see him.

He'd already let himself in through the gate. When he stopped abruptly in front of me, I could see the worry on his face. "It's Scooter. Deb's been trying to reach you. He's in the hospital."

My cell phone was in the condo. I hadn't thought to take it with me.

"Oh my God. We'll take my car. Give me a sec."

I bounded up the steps and grabbed my purse, the keys and my phone. My stomach was reeling. All thoughts of Frank's arms around me vanished. I envisioned Scooter on a gurney, heading off the island in the ambulance we heard at Mary's dinner party.

"Was it a heart attack?" I asked as I climbed in the driver's side and Frank took the passenger seat.

"Fire," he said and launched into the story.

It seemed Deb and Scooter had too much to drink and fell asleep watching television in the living room. Deb woke up smelling smoke but couldn't rouse Scooter. She ran into the kitchen to get her cell phone and call 911. When she returned, he was gone.

A fire. My mind raced through the possibilities. I had a friend who died after setting his couch on fire with a cigarette. Scooter was a smoker, even rolled his own to avoid paying $5.50 a pack. After a couple of beers and several of those potent Halloween cocktails, anything was possible.

Frank continued: Deb heard Scooter yelling for her to get out, he said he was right behind her. His voice was coming from the bedroom as she ran out. He must have passed out from the smoke. When the firemen arrived, she told them Scooter was trapped in the bedroom. The back part of the house was burning, but they managed to drag him out. She called Frank. By the time he got there, they were ready to take him away in the ambulance.

He looked over at me. "Deb was beside herself. She said to bring you to the hospital."

"Deb's okay?"

"No burns, but she's a mess. Crying and screaming that Scooter's going to die."

"Oh dear. Scooter's going to be all right, isn't he?"

Frank was quiet for a minute and then responded: "I can't answer that question, Leslie. No one will say."

CHAPTER 18

D eb stood in front of the charred structure that had once been her home; her face expressionless and her eyes vacant. I wondered if she would ever fully recover from this tragedy.

After an all-night vigil, Frank and I had lured her from the hospital and taken her to what was left of the house she and her husband shared. Scooter was in critical condition from severe burns to his left arm and smoke inhalation; but his long-term prognosis was good. The doctors had encouraged Deb to leave the hospital for a couple of hours for her own sanity.

"Going in is not a good idea," Frank said when it became apparent that Deb was determined to enter what was left of the structure. "You tell me what you want, and I'll get it for you."

"How the hell do I know what I want until I see what's left," she half shouted. "What's going to happen to us? Oh Lord, we need a miracle."

"I'll check it out first," Frank said and headed for the backyard. I wanted to go with him but felt guilty about leaving Deb alone. I rubbed her back as she stood in the damp morning grass and wept silent tears.

When I could no longer stand not knowing what Frank was doing, I grabbed one of the plastic lawn chairs that wasn't melted and carried it to the shade of an olive tree. I steered Deb to the seat and watched her ease into it. She looked frail, as though she'd aged 10 years overnight.

"Don't worry about having a place to stay. I have plenty of room for both of you," I said.

She nodded, as the three-legged cat hopped into her lap. He purred as she stroked his black and white fur and crooned to him: "Oh Johnny. Good kitty. At least you're okay. What're we going to do?"

At the back of the house, I found Frank nosing around an overturned grill and a blackened patch of weeds that marked a pathway to the burned wooden siding and latticework. They say ashes talk. I wondered if they were telling Frank what caused the blaze.

"My guess is Scooter was drinking and cooking and somehow knocked over the grill," Frank said when I arrived at his side. "It took a while for the coals to catch and then take off."

What Frank surmised made sense, but it felt like we needed a professional opinion.

"I assume the fire department will investigate," I said.

"I'm sure they already have. We don't need to be involved. Let's let them do their job, Leslie."

He gave me a look that was not unlike one from Mother's repertoire of critical facial expressions.

"I wasn't questioning your theory. But now that I think about it how can someone be so drunk that they don't notice when they knock over a hot grill? It could be arson, Frank."

"Another mystery?" he said. If the expression wasn't enough, there was no missing the reproach in his voice. "I'm gonna check on the front of the house. It doesn't look all that bad."

The fire's path was obvious, maybe too much so. How easy would it be for someone who knew that Deb and Scooter liked to drink at night to spread flammable fluid up the side of the house, tip the grill, scatter the charcoal embers and watch the fire crawl across the ground to its target?

Despite Frank's reluctance to listen to my speculation, I could visualize an unhappy neighbor taking matters into his own hands. It would be an easy way of removing this "blight" from his paradise.

ꙮ

Frank had convinced Deb that the house was still too "hot" for her to enter and suggested we talk to the fire chief to see if he had any new information.

When we approached the brick fire station, with its three bays and well-tended landscaping, we found a 20-something firefighter polishing one of the island's two trucks. He hadn't worked the blaze but heard the others talking about it, he said.

"Far as I know it was an accident. Your husband must have knocked the grill over and, uh, not noticed, ma'am," he said.

"My Scooter had a little too much to drink last night, but I don't think he was that far gone," Deb said.

She was defensive. I didn't blame her. The story that Scooter was somehow responsible for burning his own home was going to grow legs. It was easy to blame someone who appeared lazy and shiftless for a certain recklessness. Was no one willing to examine other options?

"I wouldn't know, ma'am. That's what I heard 'em say." The firefighter flashed a sympathetic smile in Deb's direction.

"Are they done checkin' it out?" she said, her finger nervously twisting a strand of her long hair.

"You can talk to the chief when he comes in on Monday. Or the sheriff over there in the admin building. He showed up about an hour ago."

"Maybe I should stay in the car," I said when it was apparent Deb wanted to speak with Sheriff Harry Fleck.

She grabbed hold of my hand. "Oh, honey. I need you and Frank by my side. Harry's not a bad guy. You two just got off on the wrong foot."

Sheriff Fleck was sitting behind his desk wearing a golf shirt. His sunglasses were perched atop his head. A small TV on the credenza behind him was showing the pre-game analysis for the contest between the Miami Dolphins and the St. Louis Rams. The Sunday paper was open in front of him.

The sheriff gave the three of us what felt like a forced smile. "Frank, Deb, uh, Miz Elliott," he said, nodding slightly to me. "Sorry to hear about your house, Deb. How's Scooter?"

Her face melted into a waterfall of tears. "My Scooter's, he's, he's too tough to let some burns and a little smoke do him in."

"Harry, you know anything about the fire?" Frank asked.

The sheriff ruffled through a few papers on his desk and settled on some notes he must have scribbled after talking with the chief. He glanced at them before speaking.

"Firemen think it was an accident, but the fire marshal's comin' tomorrow. I have a feelin' it'll be case closed unless, uh, Scooter takes a turn for the worse. You want me to send Bruce to check it out today?"

I couldn't control the burst of air that came out of my mouth. *Deputy Bruce Webster investigating a fire scene?* "Uh, sorry," I said when everyone looked at me. "I didn't know the deputy was an expert on fires."

The sheriff didn't respond; didn't even acknowledge my comment. "Maybe it would be better if he dropped by tomorrow when he's back on duty. Don't see the need to call him in on Sunday. Have you talked to your insurance agent?" he asked Deb.

She shook her head. "I-I don't think we have one. Our taxes are so high that Scooter said it had to be one or the other. Wind, fire, flood, even health – down here those add up to more than we can afford."

"Sorry to hear that," the sheriff said. He sounded genuinely sympathetic, but I still hadn't made up my mind about Harry Fleck.

Frank touched Deb's back. "It's time to go. If anything comes up, Harry will let you know. Right?"

The sheriff nodded. As we left his office, Deb was crying and I was pondering Scooter's future and the certainty of one, maybe two, long-term roommates. Frank had a look of determination on his face. It felt like there was something he knew but wasn't sharing.

CHAPTER 19

Monday morning and the island's newspaper office was like every other I'd seen in my years in public relations: underpaid folks struggling to meet deadlines and often working overtime to inform their part of the world on the day's events.

As I waited for the receptionist to turn from her computer and acknowledge my presence, I thought of my friend Wes Avery. He was an old-time newspaper man caught in a changing world. It felt like he was becoming bitter. But it wasn't so much world events there were souring him as it was the changes taking place in his industry. None of them good.

I wondered how he was faring in the big city. I missed his weekly calls to my office at the Metro Energy Company, asking, "What's up?"

"Can I help you?" the receptionist inquired, jarring me back from memory lane. She was efficient but not overly friendly

"Hi. Leslie Elliott. I'm looking for a missing dog ad that would have appeared in the paper several months ago. I don't know the date. Where do I start?"

The receptionist knew exactly where I should start. It was also obvious she wasn't going to do my research for me.

"We keep our stories on file, but classifieds? You'll need to look through our old papers."

The woman directed me to a desk in a corner. I put my purse down and watched as she piled three months of newspapers in front of me. Not a big deal since this was a weekly. The problem was staying focused on my mission. I was learning so much about the island and its people that I kept getting distracted.

I'd gone through October with no sign of the missing dog ad when I heard a familiar voice.

"Leslie Elliott. What the hell are you doing here?"

When I looked up, my mouth dropped open. There he was. Wes Avery. The man in my recent thoughts. At 59 and despite his bad habits, he was trim. Actually, slimmer than when I last saw him. And he looked a little more muscular, as though he'd been lifting weights. He kept his gray/blond hair short. His face was rugged – kind of appealing even though every story he'd ever written about problems and heartache in the big city seemed to have left its mark there and in his sorrowful eyes. He was your usual newspaper misfit, and I was damn glad to see him.

"Wes!" I jumped up and hugged him. "I was just thinking about you," I said as I let him go. "If I was a writer, I would say this is too much of a coincidence to be believable."

"Who in the hell cares if it's plausible. I'm damned glad to see you," he said, pulling me back to him and wrapping his arms around me in a bear hug. "Let's get a cup of coffee and catch up, um, if you have the time. I've been intending to call you and let you know I'm finally here – thanks to you and your emails telling me about the place."

I gave him a playful pat on the hand. "Intended? Doesn't get the job done, Wes."

He turned to the receptionist. "My November 13 column's done and, in my files, Helen. You can give it to Randy for the layout. I'm taking my girl, uh, woman, out for whatever we can find to drink that isn't coffee. She hates coffee."

He offered his arm, and we strolled out the office door together.

The grocery store with the flat metal roof and white clapboard siding was the only place in the village that carried fresh meat, vegetables and fruit. It also offered coffee, sweet rolls and lunchtime sandwiches for the hundreds of workers employed by the island's biggest industries: home construction, remodeling and landscape maintenance.

Wes and I grabbed a table under the store's green and white awning. Having him on the island gave me a sense of comfort. He was a bridge between my old and new life. We shared experiences; spoke the same language. I could chat with Deb about art and the activities of the islands' interesting characters. With Wes, it was the news media, corporate America and the dark side of both worlds. I didn't realize until I saw him how much I'd missed all that action.

"I'm in my late 50s and was ready for a change," he said. "Time to make a move before Gannett kicked me out. They've laid off most of the old-timers. I interviewed here a couple months ago and officially started last week. Sorry I haven't called you."

I sat back in my chair, giving my friend the once-over. "You look great. Florida is agreeing with you. And I'm not mad, well maybe a little, that you didn't call me the minute you drove across the bridge, you old reprobate. When I didn't hear back, I thought you weren't interested."

"Yep. I'm here and happy so far. What are you up to these days? Learning to fish?"

"Fishing. Yeah. I tried that and spent the morning hanging over the side of the boat. I'm trying to develop the storyline for a mystery. Inspired by some local events your newspaper doesn't know about yet. I'm curious but not schooled enough in police-like matters. To be honest, I'm naïve about the criminal side of life – or I should say, blue-collar crime?"

"You knew your stuff in public relations. Investigating is a matter of asking the right questions and not being afraid to appear dumb. If you keep at it, one day you'll get the answers. Even the ones you don't want. So, what have we missed?"

I told him about my finds at the yellow house on Oceanview, the bodies that washed up and vanished, the mysterious Peter Thompson and the fire at Deb and Scooter's place on Saturday night.

"I'll follow up on the bodies and the fire with the sheriff. But I think you'll have a tough time connecting the dots," he said. "What do they have in common? It's not even the same people involved."

"There's me! I'm involved in all of them – at least peripherally."

We both laughed, but I was stumped. What did they have in common? I never thought to ask that question until Wes mentioned it.

"So, you were at the paper looking for an ad for a missing dog? The dog that belongs to that guy who's building the house you told me about?"

Although now would have been the perfect time, I decided not to tell Wes that Frank had Whalen. I wasn't ready to go down that path with my friend.

"Yeah. He claims he put it in the paper after the dog disappeared. Last seen at the dog park. This island's not a big place and people here consider their pets part of the family. I couldn't find any ad."

"What does that tell you?"

"Mr. Thompson isn't being honest with me? Guess it doesn't take a brain surgeon to figure out that one. We're having dinner. Tuesday night. Tomorrow. He called yesterday to confirm. I'm trying to figure a way to ask him about it."

"If you plan to confront him, doing it in public's a good idea. Remember, a trapped animal often bites."

I smiled at Wes's manner. I was too old to be his daughter. And, besides, I didn't need a protectorate.

"I'm not going to do anything reckless, Wes. Just dinner with a few questions thrown in."

"Be careful. That's all I'm saying."

I didn't need another warning.

ꙮ

The sound of hammers and saws was punctuated by the song blaring out of someone's radio: *Sex on Fire* by Kings of Leon. Workmen were ripping out burned timbers in the back of Deb and Scooter's house and piling them into a metal trash bin. It seemed that the miracle Deb was praying for had materialized. But how?

Did Scooter hold onto the insurance policy and not tell her? What other explanation was there? These days and in this economy, no one worked for free.

Deb was sitting under the olive tree sorting through papers. She flashed a grin my direction when I strolled up. I wanted to tell her about the arrival of my friend, Wes, but it was obvious she had bigger news.

"Oh honey. I'm not sure how this happened. I won't question the ways of the Man upstairs," she said when I arrived at her side and gave her a hug. I dragged another plastic furniture survivor next to her chair and sat down.

"How's the patient and what's happening here?" I asked.

Deb looked in the direction of the back yard and the blackened path that led from the overturned grill to the house. "He's doin' better, but it hasn't been a full two days and the doc says he's a long way from bein' out of danger. The smoke and all. He doesn't remember grillin' out, but I'm pretty sure we had fish from the freezer. It was those damn Frankenstein drinks. And thanks for takin' me in, honey. It means the world to us."

I gave her arm a squeeze. "Stay as long as you want. I know I'll like the company."

Deb told me she'd returned to the house that morning determined to start going through what was left after the fire. All the junk that resided outside seemed to be okay, but it was mostly worthless. The back of the house, including Deb's and Scooter's bedroom, was ruined by the flames and water damage. Everything inside that hadn't burned smelled of smoke.

"I was ready to call Gordie and tell him to put the place on the market. Hell, the land's worth as much as the house. Before I could do that, these trucks showed up. And Gordie was with 'em."

"You're kidding," I said, questioning if I had heard Deb correctly. "Gordon with them?"

"Yep. You coulda knocked me over with a feather. Said he found some, uh, he called them investors, willin' to pay to have our house fixed up. He was real sorry for what he said about the neighbors. He hoped it didn't worry me." She now had a smile on her face.

"That's not the half of it, though," she went on. "Should take them about a month to take care of it, Gordie says. Everyone operates on island time here. You know, slow. But it's still a real blessin'. He's also got enough money to pay for new landscaping."

"You think the neighbors are funding this?" I found that hard to believe but asked the question anyway. They had wanted her gone and were probably rejoicing in the fire.

"He wouldn't say. No, it was someone pretty special, honey. I don't know who, but they must be God-fearing people who want to help others."

I put my arm around Deb and gave her a hug. "Who wouldn't want to help someone like you?"

But who would do it to you in the first place?

CHAPTER 20

"Someone's walkin' on my grave," my Irish grandmother would say when the winter winds arrived and a trip to the mailbox made her feel shivery.

I wasn't sure what she meant until this very moment. Heading through the darkness to the yellow house, I could feel those same macabre footsteps treading on my bones. I zipped up my jacket to ward off the ominous chill.

Deb had left her burned-out house to visit Scooter in the hospital and tell him about the miracle she'd witnessed: the arrival of a workforce led by Realtor Gordon Fike. I hoped Scooter would take it well. With Scooter, you never knew. That man had more pride than horse sense and was not the kind to accept charity.

I figured Deb would spend most of the evening with him and return to the guest room in my condo late. Mother was at a bridge tournament at the community center. Frank was someplace but not with me. I wasn't sure we'd ever be together again.

I was alone with my bravado, which turned out to be a wimpy companion. More foolhardy than brave.

The large silver flashlight from the kitchen drawer, along with bug spray, a hammer and a screwdriver were in a cloth bag on my shoulder. I wanted another look inside the yellow house before meeting Peter Thompson for dinner.

The gate I'd entered twice, once by myself and once with Frank, was still open. The front area had been stripped of vegetation by a yellow and black landscaping bulldozer that sat off to one side in the front yard. The tattered black plastic was gone from the fence, replaced by blue sheeting. The Porta Potty Deb noticed four days ago was still visible from the street, but was moved close to a large Ficus tree. For shade purposes, I guessed.

Thompson was keeping his bargain with the neighbors.

I took a detour to the right, stopping at the opening for a two-car garage. Beyond that was a separate bay, a taller one, for a boat.

At the back of the boat bay sat a white van with rust on the sides and faded letters that said "Fred's Painting Suppl." There were faint outlines of the missing letters "i-e-s."

I opened the back of the van and peered in. A paint-speckled ladder, two dollies and more stacked paint cans.

Satisfied there was nothing of importance in either garage, I retraced my steps to the lower-level entrance. The door I'd entered before was wide open despite its new lock. Lucky for me. I'm not sure I could have broken in. I stepped inside and flashed my light around. Nothing had changed.

I was moving toward the steps when I heard voices coming from upstairs. My blood turned to ice as I instinctively slipped out the door I'd just entered. The moon was at half strength but still providing too much light. My eyes scanned the lot. The only cover was the bulldozer or the Porta Potty. I made a dash for the brown metal toilet structure and crouched behind it, regretting my choice almost immediately.

"Parece que hemos terminado aquí."

The voices were on the move and coming my way. Were these the same men who talked to Frank that night on the scrub island?

"Sí. Estoy listo para una cerveza y una pequeña siesta."

There was laughter.

"Cuánto tiempo se tarda para moverlo?"

"Nunca se sabe. No es nuestro problema ahora."

Why didn't I study Spanish in school? I recognized *si* and *siesta*. Maybe *problema*. Their work was done, and they were going to take a nap? Someone seemed to have a problem with that?

"Tengo que ir al baño ahora," I heard one of the men say. The door to the Porta Potty squeaked as it opened, sending an unpleasant odor my direction. I held my breath, waiting for the man using the facility and the smell to go away.

After a few minutes, when the sound of urinating stopped, the door creaked again and slammed shut. I breathed a sigh of relief.

"Vamos. Tengo hambre."

"Sí, sí. Estoy listo."

From my vantage point, I could see two men heading for the back of the house. When they disappeared, I skulked back to the lower level. How much time did I have before they returned? They hadn't locked the door. I bounded up the two flights of stairs that led to the third level and my objective.

I reached the familiar hallway in time to hear the sound of a diesel engine Gulf-side. Hurrying to the big room with the windows facing the North Pass, I watched the boat pull away from the dock and head out to the Gulf. *All the time in the world.* I felt my body relax. If only my heart would stop pounding.

When I was 22 and even more impatient than I am today, I used my credit card to get into my brother's locked apartment. I can still see his face when he came home and found me sitting on the couch, watching television and finishing up a bowl of peanut M&Ms.

If the card worked all those years ago, maybe it would do the job tonight on the only door in the house that seemed to stay locked.

I propped my flashlight against the wall and directed its beam to the brass door handle. The credit card from my pocket barely fit into the tiny space between the door and the jam. Jiggling the knob as I'd done those many years ago, I pushed the card hard against the latch.

Jiggle. Push. Wiggle. Push.

"Come on, come on." Nothing happened. I worked on the door for another several minutes. If the card didn't do the job, my plan was to smash through the dry wall with my hammer to reach the lock. During construction there were always reasons to put unexplained holes in walls.

Jiggle. Push. Wiggle. Push. Click.

"Yes!" The door moved. I straightened up and reached out to push it open.

The sound of pressure on the floorboards behind me was the last thing I remember.

"Are you OK?" Through the fog that shrouded my brain, I recognized the voice of Alice Mandino, the woman who lived next door to Mary Sanders and whose company I'd enjoyed at the Halloween dinner party.

"Maybe we should call the police, Jerry," she said to her husband.

"No, please don't," I whispered. My hand went to the back of my head. It was wet and sticky and hurt like hell.

"You're bleeding. You need help," Jerry said. He had lifted my head off the floor and was dabbing the back of it with something. I hoped it wasn't the dirty towel from the nearby bathroom.

"If you call the sheriff, I may end up in jail." I managed to say.

Alice laughed. "Why would they put you in jail?"

"She is trespassing," Jerry said.

"And for the second time," I said, groaning.

Jerry moved me into a sitting position. "Think you can stand?" he asked.

"I'm not sure. Kind of dizzy." I leaned back against his shoulder.

"Uh, oh. We'd better get you home," Alice said.

I had no memory of how I ended up on the floor and no clue as to how Alice and Jerry managed to show up not in time but close.

"How, how did you find me?"

"Jerry and I were taking a walk after dinner. We saw you go into the house and then run back out again and hide behind the Porta Potty. Then we saw a couple of guys come out of the house right after you. When one of them went to take a leak, we started walking that way. In case there was a problem. But they left and you went back inside. We couldn't believe it. I said to Jerry, what the hell is Leslie doing?"

I wish I had asked myself the same thing.

"We were waiting for you when we saw a man in a baseball cap exit the same door you went in. He walked around to the back of the house. When you didn't come out right away, we went inside," Jerry said.

I was contemplating standing up but wasn't sure if I was up to it yet. Regardless of my physical condition, my curiosity remained intact. "Did you see his face?" I asked.

"Not really," Jerry said. I could hear the worry in his voice. "Too far away. Sorry we didn't move faster to come to your rescue. It was like we were frozen in place."

"You did the right thing. Uh oh, there are two of you, Alice."

"You're going to the emergency room," she said.

I didn't protest. I was hoping not to die.

"I'll get the car," Jerry said. "Give me five minutes."

"Geez, Leslie. It was like watching a movie," Alice said, rubbing my back. "You're in, then you're out. Those two guys exit the house and you hide behind the Porta Potty. Then you go back in and another guy comes out. Jerry and I were glued to the spot. He kept saying, 'Fuck, look at that!' It was the most excitement we've had on this island."

I chuckled and then winced from the pain in the back of my head. "Glad I was so entertaining. Have you ever noticed, um, anything strange around here?" *Besides me getting whacked on the head?*

"Other than the off and on construction?"

"Yes, like people coming and going after dark."

"No," she said, shaking her head. "Jerry and I usually go to bed early. You think something funny's going on?"

"Not sure. There seems to be someone who doesn't want me to find out what's in that closet."

"That's easy," Alice said. She eased me off her shoulder and stood up, giving the door a push. It didn't budge. "Um. Locked."

"It was open. I saw it. Before someone hit me on the head."

At the sound of footsteps, we stopped talking and looked at each other. Both of us may have been a little frightened until we heard a familiar voice.

"Hey, it's us," Jerry called out.

"You found her up here?" The other voice was Frank's.

The panting sound accompanying the two men was coming from Whalen, the dog, who was the first of the three to reach me. He started licking my face. I tried to scratch his ears, but the movement made me nauseous.

"What happened here?" There was reproach in Frank's voice. It was becoming a familiar sound.

"I don't know. I had to see, to see what was behind that locked door. I was using my credit card to get in when, when everything went dark."

"Credit card?" Alice stifled a laugh.

"I can't explain it now. It worked at my brother's."

"You're a serial break-in artist?" Jerry said, as he and Frank moved to help me on my feet. "You okay to walk?"

I tried to get up but my legs were like rubber. A wave of dizziness hit me but disappeared quickly when I returned to my sitting position on the floor.

"Um. Maybe not."

"I can carry her," Frank said, hoisting me up in his arms. I put my head against his shoulder and felt safe. "Can you get the dog, ma'am. And, uh, Jerry, right? Can you bring the car closer to the house?"

"I'll do my best," Jerry said.

I lifted my head gingerly, testing it and then quickly returned it to Frank's shoulder. "You warned me, Frank," I said. "Everyone did. I should have listened."

"If there's something going on here, like you seem to suspect, it's no game, Leslie. Maybe now you'll stay away. This could be a matter for the sheriff."

"I don't want him thinking I'm stupid and a trespasser. If you have to talk to him, leave me out of it."

Frank looked grim. "I'll handle it."

After waiting two hours in the hospital emergency room, I was ushered to a gurney where the doctor with a baby face checked me over and pronounced me concussion free. He then shaved a spot on the back of my head and applied 16 stitches to close the wound, advising me to take it easy for the rest of the week.

"I'll try to be a good girl," I said as he handed me two prescriptions.

When he left, a nurse wheeled me into the waiting room where Alice and Jerry were drinking coffee. Frank had taken Whalen home and would meet me at the condo, Alice explained.

"He says you shouldn't be alone tonight. There's a thoughtful man," she said.

"That's nice, but Deb will be there," I said.

"The guy seemed determined to stay with you," Jerry said. "You two can work it out."

I started to get up and Jerry pointed to the wheelchair. "Do you know Frank?"

"Stay put. I'll be your chauffeur. Never seen the guy before but ran into him walking his dog and asked for his help," Jerry said as he pushed me toward the pharmacy. "He said he's a fisherman, right? How do you know him?"

"Let's say we're friends."

"Have you checked out his rod?" Jerry said, his eyes twinkling.

"You'll have to excuse my husband," Alice said before I could respond. "He has no filters. But to tell you the truth, I wouldn't mind being friends with someone that looks like that. He's quite the cutie."

I nodded slightly, setting off the pain and, at the same time, wondering what Frank was doing walking the dog in our neighborhood. His home, he'd told me, was at the other end of the island.

The pharmacy was nearly empty; the three of us waited less than ten minutes get the prescription filled and then Jerry wheeled me to the hospital exit.

"Let's get you home to Mr. Good-Looking," he said, eyeing his wife and then winking at me.

⟳

Frank spent the night, dozing on the chair in my bedroom. Early the next morning, Deb opened my door and peeked in before leaving. I merely waved a hand because I couldn't talk; the pain medicine kept sending me back to la-la land. After hearing from Frank that I'd fallen while boating, Mother stopped by to visit. She seemed happier to see him than she was concerned about me.

"I can fix you some soup and sandwiches. A man like you needs nourishment," Mother gushed after giving me the once-over.

While she and Frank were in the other room, I called Peter Thompson to reschedule our dinner date.

"Fell down the stairs. So clumsy of me. The doc gave me pain meds, which is why I seem to be slurring my words."

"What can I do for you?" he asked.

"Nothing really. I have a friend staying here. I should be all right by, uh, Friday or Saturday if you don't mind looking at a bandage on the back of my head."

"Your lovely face is all I'll see," he said. "How about Friday evening? The Tarpon Bar. If you don't feel up to it, I can bring carry-out to you."

"I'll be ready to get out of here by then," I said.

After hanging up, I fell asleep. When I awoke about 4 in the afternoon, Frank was still in the chair by my bed reading a Brad Thor novel. He looked up as if to ask how I was feeling. My hand reached back and touched the bandage.

"Narcotics. I may live. Thanks for spending last night. You don't need to stay the day. Deb and Mom can check on me."

"I owe it to you. I wanted to do it."

"After your reaction the other night, I didn't expect to see much of you, except with Scooter and Deb," I said.

"I guess I was trying to keep you from harm. But it turns out you are a trouble magnet, and there's nothing I can do about it."

I managed a weak smile.

"You want to tell me what you were doing in that house again?" He offered me a glass of water and helped me into a sitting position.

"It was that locked door. I had to find out...."

"Workman's tools," he interrupted. "That's what was in there. While you were sleeping, I went into the house. They were finishing the kitchen floor where the dog had been. I went upstairs to see if I could figure out what happened. The door was open and there were saws and toolboxes in there. Like I told you before."

"No loose floorboards with gold bullion beneath them?" When I laughed my head hurt.

Frank also didn't react well to my attempt at humor. "There was nothing, Leslie. What's it going to take for you to leave well enough alone? Isn't a bump on the head and 16 stitches enough?"

I was nodding as gently as a I could. Under the covers, my fingers were crossed. "It is, Frank. From now on, I'm sticking to my writing."

CHAPTER 21

The lady behind the desk at the county building oversight department looked more resigned than patient. The day was getting started, but her eyes were already lifeless, weary. *No nametag. No chance for me to give her a friendly personal good morning to boost her spirits.*

She'd probably be on her feet most of the day, this anonymous bureaucrat, with little or no thanks from the folks she helped. I needed to remember to say a kind word before I left.

"How long?" I asked when she handed me a number and pointed to a row of folding chairs across the room.

"There are 10 people ahead of you," the no-name woman said. "It shouldn't be more than an hour."

It was only four days ago that someone had whacked me on the back of the head. Still, when my caretakers announced they had plans for the day, I jumped at the chance to depart my bedroom in search of more information about the mysterious yellow house.

My fact-finding expedition to the county seat started with a 45-minute drive. Faced with a long wait and signs of a developing headache, I was questioning whether this little adventure was a good idea.

I took a seat and pulled out my cell phone, deciding to check out my daughter's Facebook page. Seeing Meredith's sweet face always made me feel good. Social media was an effective way to find out what she wasn't telling me in our weekly phone conversations.

Her postings included photos of her latest boyfriend, a senior from the University of Cincinnati named Austin. She'd mentioned his name and made gushing sounds when she talked about him. What I didn't know, until I saw his photo, was that he had a scenic right arm.

The tattoo started at his shoulder and continued down to his wrist. It was mostly blue with a splash of orange. I imagined what it would look like when he was 80.

I enlarged the photo of Meredith and Austin clinging to each other to make sure my daughter hadn't succumbed to the lure of the needle. She looked clean. I wondered, though, if some vicious-looking snake had attached itself to her ankle and was crawling up her leg under her jeans. We'd have a serious discussion about tattoos when she finally made it to her new Florida home.

After Meredith, I checked out Deb's page, which featured her artwork and a plug for the gallery. Still surfing, I looked to see if Frank had a page. His wife must have created his site several years ago. It included a photo of him with much longer hair, holding onto a large tarpon he'd caught. There was a business phone number but no other postings.

If these people have Facebook pages, why not the owner of the yellow house?

I typed his name into the search bar. There were several Peter Thompsons. When I narrowed the choice to Peter Thompson in Toronto, his Facebook page was an easy find.

I bypassed his background for later study and concentrated on the photos of a woman; a poser with curly brown hair worn shoulder length, ample breasts and a showy smile. A red sports car – a vintage convertible that looked to be a Mercedes – was featured in several pictures. In one, the woman was draped seductively over the hood, with the caption: *Monica's baby.*

Although there were no current postings, I continued to scroll through the site, landing on a photo of three men, shirts off, baseball caps on backward. They were giving the shaka symbol; extending the thumb and little finger on one hand as a sign of *hanging loose.* They were in front of a small plane.

I clicked on the photo and enlarged it to identify Peter Thompson. The photo was too fuzzy to make a positive ID. All three men had facial hair of some type and bore a striking resemblance to one another. Were they brothers?

I checked Peter's profile. No other family members were listed.

"Leslie Elliott?" When the no-name woman behind the counter called my name, I realized I'd been lost in Facebook for more than an hour.

"I'm looking for information on a house in my neighborhood, 392 Ocean-view Drive," I said when I approached her desk. "By the way, what's your name?"

She looked up, surprised, and smiled. "Karen. Let me see what I can find." Her fingers ran over the computer keys.

"Here we go. Owner is a trust. The Monica White Thompson Trust. Principals are Monica White Thompson, Peter L. Thompson and James J. Thompson.

"Construction started more than two years ago after demolition of an existing structure on the property. Looks like their first inspection was a year ago and there hasn't been one since."

"Is it unusual for a house to take so long?" I asked.

"Depends on who's building it. Those guys sitting on those folding chairs with you are in a big hurry to get their places closed so they can move onto the next project," she said. "Some people take their time. I guess because they can."

I wasn't sure how much information she would give me. I was open to anything.

"Is it possible to get a copy of the plans?"

"Sorry. Not here. There should be one in the worksite box. You can look at it, but taking it isn't a good idea. It's there for the county inspectors. Um. Seems like they had some problems with the county over a reported eagle nesting in one of the Australian pines on the property. That could slow things down big time."

"Eagles? I've seen a few of them on the island, but didn't know they could affect construction," I said.

"You have to wait until they've finished nesting and are gone. In my opinion, we don't do enough to protect the critters in our state, including us humans," Karen said.

I agreed with her observation. I'd worked for a corporation that didn't always put the environment first. And then there were Florida's water problems and the red tide.

"Is there anything else? I feel like I should have more technical questions, but I don't know enough to ask them," I said.

Karen smiled. "That's a good one. When you think of what they are you can look us up online. Save yourself a trip down here."

"Oh yeah, your website. I needed to get out of the house, and it was a pleasant drive. You were much more helpful than a computer, Karen. Thanks a lot."

Her dull eyes brightened, if only for a second. Then she reached into her shirt pocket and handed me a card. "Or call me. Anytime. I'll try to help."

"Again, thanks." I grabbed my purse and headed for the exit. I wasn't sure that I'd learned anything useful, but I had a new name to puzzle over: James J. Thompson.

CHAPTER 22

Hard of hearing and suffering from advanced macular degeneration, the octogenarian Doris Selwin had nonetheless managed to attend Deb Rankin's popular morning plein air painting class each Friday without fail.

"Hi Doris. How'd it go?" I asked in a loud voice as I walked into the Gallery Centre around noon. She was sitting by herself in front of an easel and dabbing at a canvas with a long brush that had blue paint on the tip.

She squinted, looking at me through thick glasses. The short gray hairs on her head stuck out, as though she'd poked her fingers into an electric socket. It made her all the more lovable.

"It's Leslie. Deb's friend," I said when I realized Doris didn't recognize me.

"Oh, you sweet thing. A lovely day, but the beach stank to high heaven," she said in a loud voice. "All those dead fish and buzzards. Deb gave me a mask. Can't say that it helped much."

"Yes. The fish are everywhere. What did you paint?"

"The water, the sand and, well, it's a secret. Blue coral."

"Blue coral. Um. Don't know what that is," I said.

"Oh, I saw it years ago in a shell display. And there it was on the beach today. I didn't tell anyone else so I could keep it special for my painting. Some of these hens are copycats."

Doris leaned back so I could get a better look at her canvas. Despite her eye issues, she'd done a good job capturing the dunes with their wild grasses and fragments of shells. Maybe from memory. She had a few pelicans soaring in the background. No buzzards. To the left of a piece of driftwood were four bluish stalks, each about three to four inches long with bits of seaweed intertwined.

"Interesting. Very nice, Doris."

"You don't think they're too blue?" she said, moving her head back and forth to look at the painting from different angles. "They're so unusual."

"Very," I said, nodding my head.

Deb was carrying a couple of easels and heading for the storage closet when she saw Doris and me exchanging pleasantries. "Glad you're here, Leslie. Our artists' meeting's not for another hour. Can you stuff some envelopes?"

"Sure. But come look at Doris' painting. Tell us what you think."

Deb hustled to Doris' side and gave her an affectionate pat on the back. "The grasses look nice. Good brush work. I like how you've draped the seaweed around that bluish thing. What is that? It looks like, uh, fingers."

"Oh no, dearie, it's blue coral," Doris said.

"Really. Blue coral? I've never seen that around here. Are you sure that's what it is? Try to visualize what you saw," Deb said. She disappeared into her office and returned with an iPad. "Did it look like this – like these photos of blue coral?"

Doris squinted again. "Well, I can hardly see those but, uh, not so much. Now when you say fingers, do you mean from someone's hand?"

Deb and I looked at each other.

"This time you get to call the sheriff," I said.

ℓ◯ℓ

Deb pulled the red golf cart Doris had donated to the gallery onto the beach on the island's south side. The tires cut deep into the loose sand as she drove the vehicle across a small mound and closer to the water.

There were no children looking for shells or building sand castles with their grandparents. No sunbathers attempting to cover an abundance of skin with tiny bathing suits. No fishermen with poles stuck in the sand and bottles of beer in their hands.

Dead fish, rotting in the sun, had chased them away.

"This is pretty horrific," I said, stifling the urge to gag. "How did you get your class to stay?"

"After about 90 minutes we cut it short because of the smell. Before that, I gave them masks and menthol. They looked beyond the dead fish and the buzzards to create beauty."

"Right," I said. "And to transform blue fingers into blue coral. So where do we start looking?"

Deb scanned the area, shielding her eyes from the sun with her hand. "The group was in this area. I think I remember seein' Doris over there." She pointed to a flock of scavengers gathered near a small sand dune.

"Those frickin' things give me the willies. Shoo. Shoo." She picked up a couple of shells and threw them at the buzzards. They scattered, and we headed toward a pile of something that Doris wouldn't have wanted on her canvas.

"It looks more like a forearm and hand than it does blue coral," I said, as we approached the bones and rotting flesh. "When Doris saw it, before the birds got to it, the arm part must have been buried."

Deb let out a heavy sigh and reached for her cell phone. "I wouldn't say this in public but since you moved here, honey, a lot of strange things have turned up."

"I can't disagree with you." I was sure this was part of the body that had surfaced at least twice. And didn't the man with the children on the beach say the dead person he saw was missing an arm?

Sheriff Harry Fleck and Deputy Bruce Webster arrived about 10 minutes after Deb's call.

"Where is it?" the sheriff said, looking at Deb and ignoring me.

"Over there." She pointed to the object, which was about 20 feet from where we were now standing.

The two men circled the site, then squatted to get a better look. The sheriff said something that sent Deputy Webster back to the car.

"Who found this?" the sheriff asked.

"My plein air class was out here this morning. Doris, you know her, Doris Selwin? She painted it. Thought it was blue coral. Back at the gallery, Leslie saw it and talked to her about it. We decided it looked more like fingers and came out here to investigate."

"No one else mentioned it?"

"No to me. I don't think Doris recognized it as, you know, a hand because she doesn't see all that well," Deb said.

Deputy Webster returned wearing rubber gloves and carrying a camera and plastic bags. He put yellow crime markers by the mass and took photos from several angles. When he was finished, he placed what remained of the hand and forearm in the bags. I was surprised by this display of professionalism.

"Looks like the deputy knows what he's doing," I whispered to Deb. "Who would have guessed."

"Don't be too hard on him. He's been around a long time. Don't think he makes much money. Lives by himself in one of the apartments in the village. You know, one of those places above a store. Besides, he's a long-time buddy of your friend – ever since the deputy fell overboard while fishing and Frank saved his life. The poor guy can't swim."

"Really? Well, they may be close, but the deputy is going to have to step up his game and get rid of that surly attitude for me to change my mind about him." *The sheriff too,* I thought.

"Looks like we're done here," the sheriff said. "We'll take these to the county. Forensics. I'll call if we have any other questions."

"Do you suppose this is part of the body that washed up on shore?" I could no longer contain myself.

"Assuming there was a body or bodies," he said, clearing his throat. "We have no way of knowing."

"How will we know if you find anything, uh, significant?"

"It'll be in the police report," the sheriff said as he and the deputy gathered up the bags, headed back to their car and drove off.

"Honey, I sure hope things start calmin' down around here," Deb said as she watched the police car depart and then turned toward the golf cart. "I can't take much more excitement. Oh, crap, the meeting. Starts in 20 minutes."

"You go ahead, Deb. I'll walk back. Be there in 15. I need the exercise."

After Deb had gone and I was left to my thoughts, I shielded my eyes and looked out across the beach. Had the sea washed up two bodies and one body part these last two weeks? Or was it the same body, recycled? Was there a killing spree in paradise that no one was talking about except for my friends and me?

A flickering caught my eye. Maybe a tiny sea creature was signaling for help against the onslaught of red tide. As I moved closer, it reflected the full light of the sun.

Nestled against a pink flower blooming on beach vines and not far from where Doris saw the blue fingers was a ring. I picked it up and gasped: gold with an eagle in the center against a background of silver. I'd seen one exactly like it not that long ago.

CHAPTER 23

66 hear you're going out with my husband."

The pompadour-haired artist Janis Johnson was about a foot from my face when she made what sounded like an accusation. It was not an entrée to polite discussion.

I'd just returned from the beach, with the gold and silver ring on my finger, and was preparing to take the minutes for Deb's meeting when Janis moved into my space. I backed up and extended my hand.

"I'm Leslie Elliott. I'm surprised we haven't met before. I've been a volunteer...."

"I know who you are," she said. She refused my handshake and leaned into my space again; her hostility generating heat.

I thought back to my first and only sighting of Frank's soon-to-be ex-wife. At the art gallery opening, standing in front of her scarves, she was defiant but not the aggressor in her conversation with Frank's mother. Maybe she'd gotten up on the wrong side of the bed this morning and decided she didn't like me.

"Not really, uh, dating. We had dinner a couple of times," I said downplaying my tentative relationship with Frank and stepping back once more.

"We're still married," she said, flashing a ring on the third finger of her left hand. "You. Stay. Away. From. Him. Bitch."

The other artists gathered for the meeting – ladies in their 70s and 80s and a few men – grew quiet at the onset of the confrontation, startled into silence by Janis Johnson's tone. When Frank's wife issued her threat, they let out a collective gasp.

If Janis hadn't been so serious, I might have laughed. The word "bitch" was seldom used among the island's polite society and the group reaction was almost comical, like a scene from an English farce. But Janis was in no mood for humor.

"Maybe you should speak to your, um, husband if you have concerns." I scooted to one side and started for Deb's office.

"I don't think you heard what I said." She grabbed my right arm and dug her fingernails into my flesh.

"Ouch! That does it." I reached for the back of her jacket, securing it with my left hand. I stepped into her and moved my right leg against her left one, executing a judo foot sweep that knocked her off balance and onto the floor. I held onto her jacket to keep her head from hitting when she went down.

The gathered artists let out a long "oooohhhhhhhhh" when Janis was felled by my rusty martial arts skills. When I straightened up, everyone in the room was looking at me – their mouths open wide.

"Sorry," I mumbled. Maybe I'd gone too far.

I headed for Deb's office, stopping to look over my shoulder before I entered. Janis had picked herself up and was taking a seat among the others who'd returned to stunned silence.

Deb was on the phone with her back to the doorway. "Skin grafts? What do those cost? Yes. Yes." *Silence.* "Okay. I don't know how we'll pay for them. I'll think of something."

"Was that the doctor?" I said, recognizing concern in Deb's voice.

"He was giving me an update. Seems that Scooter can come home," she said.

"Great news. Both of you are staying with me. No arguments."

"Oh, honey, we can't impose." Tears gathered in Deb's eyes as they often did these days.

"You two can sleep in my room. I'll take the day bed where you've been sleeping or stay with Mother. Didn't Gordon Fike say your house would be done in a month? The three of us can tolerate each other for 30 days, don't you think?" I was hoping that was true. Scooter was not easy to be around and even though Deb was dear to me, I wasn't sure how well we'd do living together.

"Scooter snores loud enough to wake the dead," Deb said, shaking her head.

"We'll have two doors and a living room between us. If he's too loud, we'll stick him in a boat and tie it up by the seawall."

Deb laughed. "You always make me feel better."

"You may change your mind when I tell you what just happened. Janis Johnson told me to stay away from Frank. She flashed her wedding ring in my face and called me a bitch. It was, um, humiliating and humorous at the same time." I chuckled.

"Oh no. When did this happen?"

"Now. In front of the other artists."

"Crap. That woman. What did you say?"

"Not much. Well, until she grabbed my arm and dug her nails in. It's what I did then that surprised everyone, including me." As Deb looked at me inquiringly, I tried to look innocent but had guilt written all over me.

"Okay, okay. I used a judo move from my college gym class and knocked her off her feet. The other artists were shocked as much as anything."

She laughed out loud. "Good for you. I'll have a talk with her," Deb said shaking her head. "Our next exhibit's before Thanksgiving. I can't have Janis creating another scene."

"I can skip the show, opening night at least," I said. "Frank is still married, as I keep trying to remind myself. He belongs to her."

"She's not chasing you away. Besides, I'm the one that introduced you and Frank. If she wants to be mad at someone...."

"Like you need more problems," I interrupted. "We'll work it out. Don't worry."

From her expression, it seemed that Deb was satisfied. Now if I was fortunate maybe there would be no more run-ins with the possessive and witchy Janis Johnson.

CHAPTER 24

The Tarpon Bar had a colorful history that included the ghost of a tragic young woman who roamed the old brick structure with some regularity. She materialized as a chilling breeze in the evening hours. Legend portrayed her as an unhappy spinster.

Mother often speculated I would end up the same way. She was thrilled to learn that I was having dinner with Peter Thompson, the man whose unfinished house was consuming most of my waking thoughts.

She even offered advice on my choice of clothing. She decided a black and red floral-print sheath dress of modest length was perfect. I acquiesced, finishing off the outfit with the gold and silver pinky ring I'd found on the beach that morning. And, of course, the bandage on my head.

When I arrived a few minutes late, Peter was seated at a table at the back of the dining room. In the candlelight, I could see he was buried in his cell phone. Everything about him seemed well managed, from his manicured goatee to his tailored J. McLaughin checked shirt – the sleeves rolled up to expose tanned arms and his Rolex watch.

"Is this seat taken?" I asked, as I pulled out the chair with the worn leather seat and sat down. I shuddered when a breeze caressed the back of my neck. Was it a message from the resident spirit?

"Leslie! How rude of me to miss your arrival. You look fabulous," Peter said, standing up and rushing to my side to give me the obligatory kiss on the cheek. Everyone seemed to know the island routine.

"I was catching up on email. How's the head?" he said, looking concerned.

"Better, um, except for the bald spot in back." I turned to show him my bandage. Why try to hide it? It came from his house.

"You fell down the stairs, eh?" he said, resuming his seat.

"Yes, took a nasty tumble. My flips caught on something and threw me off balance." I scooted my chair forward and reached for a glass of water.

"I've got a dent in my leg from falling off a ladder years ago," I said, setting my water glass down. "You're doing something that seems innocent enough, then bam! You fall and break a leg or, uh, hurt some other part of your body." I was rattling on to hide my initial nervousness.

"You want something to drink?" The fresh-faced waitress who had come up behind me seemed younger than 21. I guessed she was the daughter of the owner. Many island restaurants were family operated.

"What kind of specialty drinks do you have? I'm in the mood for something festive," I said.

She began reciting a list of exotic-sounding beverages.

"Hurricane!" I stopped her. "That sounds good and always appropriate for Florida, but I think I had my first one in New Orleans."

"What's in a Hurricane?" Thompson asked.

The waitress rattled off the ingredients as though she'd described the drink many times. Three kinds of rum, orange and pineapple juice and grenadine.

"Make mine the same. The demon rum can take us down together, eh, Leslie?"

Two hurricanes – a second one for him while I was nursing the first – loosened his tongue. The topics ranged from his love of hockey to a description of his favorite hotel in Banff. He also told me that within the last year he'd been diving around the Mesoamerican reef off the coast of Belize and taken a photographic safari at the Londolozi Game Reserve in South Africa.

"Sounds wonderful, but I'd need a drug that would knock me out for 18 hours to take that flight," I said. He might as well know from the beginning that I was not the least bit adventuresome, except when there was a potential mystery involved.

"Maybe we can find something that would make you feel like spreading your arms and taking to the sky yourself," he said, grinning.

"Don't count on it." I shook my head and took another sip of my festive drink. "I'm definitely a landlubber."

If Peter Thompson wasn't the object of my obsessive curiosity, he might have been an appealing dinner companion. He was likeable and good-looking, as Mother had observed, and he had a travelogue of adventure stories to share.

No questions from him about me. But, then, some people aren't as curious as I am.

Still, I wasn't sure what to make of him. The disappearance of Whalen had me puzzled. The yellow house continued to be a mystery, at least to me. And then there was the dead body or bodies, not to forget the body parts. I'd been sure Peter Thompson was one of the bodies, but here he was, in the flesh, both arms intact.

"Before you got here, I was reading an email from a friend who lives in South Africa. Seems he has a new business. Helping his wealthy associates get their money out of the country."

"Really? Is that a problem? To get money out? Isn't it theirs, or did they bilk it from the poorer residents?"

He ignored my political comment. "Lots of unrest down there, and the government's very strict about what you can remove in terms of assets; only 160,000 rand per adult. That's about $9,600 U. S. You can understand why people there need help."

Peter's friend was a furniture manufacturer, he told me. His designs were modern with clean lines. When customers wanted more than just a comfortable place to sit, he encouraged them to buy Krugerrands, the one-ounce gold coins that cost about $1,900 each in U. S. dollars.

I was going to ask him why, but he kept talking and answered my unspoken question.

The manufacturer would stuff the gold in his furniture in South Africa and export couches, chairs and coffee tables around the world. Once the pick-up had been made, the smuggler would get 10 percent of the value of the deal.

"And also sell his furniture," I said.

"Yeah, you're right. He also sells his furniture."

"Clever but not very honest. I'm surprised he hasn't been caught." I was watching Peter's face closely during the conversation, trying to decide if I liked him or not. He seemed proud of his friend for breaking the law. Maybe a ridiculous South African rule, but the law nonetheless.

"It's a stupid regulation. Like most of them. Anyway, who would suspect an innocent furniture dealer? Think what else you could transport that way."

"Sounds like you have a devious mind, Peter. Are you into transporting illegal items from one country to another?"

His eyes darkened. "I'm into anything that makes me a handsome profit. But, then, you know I'm only kidding, Leslie." His face brightened – night and day. "I'm a very honest man."

Can you really believe anyone who insists they are honest?

"So, tell me about your book," he said, looking into my eyes with sudden if not genuine interest. He then proceeded to talk about himself again before I could clear my throat to speak. "I've often thought of writing but never had the time. You must be very talented."

He reached over and rubbed my hand. The gesture caught me off guard. I tried not to jerk away.

"It's in the development stage," I said, maneuvering my hand to pick up my Hurricane. "Still working on the plot and the characters. A mystery. Maybe I should include the story about your South African friend."

"He might not like that."

"I don't expect my book to be a bestseller. He'll never see it."

"It only takes one slip-up – one person to notice something unusual – for things to go awry."

There was plenty of irony in his comment, although I was sure Peter Thompson wasn't aware of it.

"Say, that's a nice ring you have on," he said.

"I thought so, too," I said, glad that he finally noticed it. "Found it on the beach this morning. Some poor guy's probably looking for it."

"You think it's a man's ring, eh?"

"I do. A pinky ring like yours. It's too small for a man's ring finger, and not dainty enough for a woman. Actually, it's identical to yours, isn't it?" I pushed my hand closer so he could get a better look in the dim lighting. After scrutinizing it for a few seconds, he pulled his hand away and reached for his drink.

"Pinky rings. Dime a dozen."

"I guess they are. Could belong to anyone. So, you mentioned your late wife at Mary Sanders' house. Monica? Was that her name?"

He sighed and looked away. "Yes. She was a beautiful woman. So kind and generous. Killed in an auto accident. Driving too fast in the red Mercedes convertible she loved. I was stuck in traffic for two hours. I had no way of knowing it was because of her. Breaks my heart to think about it."

Maybe it was cruel to press the man for answers about his dead wife. But it felt like a conversation about Monica might reveal some interesting facts.

"You said she died two years ago? Was the house under construction then?"

He looked at me with a blank expression on his face. "I, uh, I'm sure it was."

He reached inside the dark green blazer he'd draped over one of the chairs, retrieved his wallet, unfolded a piece of paper from it, glanced at it and put it back. "She died September 29, 2018," he said, returning the wallet to its pocket. "I know we started sometime that year. Some days, like now, I can't ever remember the date of her death. Emotional trauma, don't you think?"

"I'm sure you're right. Your story is very sad." I paused for what I thought was a respectable interval then continued. "Do you have any children?"

"No children, no pets, nothing," he said. "Where's the waitress? I need another Hurricane and our food."

"And I need to visit the ladies room," I said, getting up from my chair. "Be right back."

No pets. Poor Whalen. How quickly forgotten, along with the death date of his wife and the year they started building the house. Maybe he did have amnesia from grief. Maybe there was something else going on.

On the way back to the table I scanned the room and saw the Mandinos, Jerry and Alice. They were having dinner in a small booth near the entrance. They waved me over.

"How're you doing?" Jerry asked.

"Much better, thanks to the two of you. My rescuers."

"Say, I wanted to tell you. I mean, you asked if we ever saw anything strange at that house. Last night, late, I couldn't sleep. I was talking a walk and saw a white van leaving there. It said something about painting on the side," Alice said.

"Last night?"

"Yeah. When it got to the end of the road it turned left, like it was going off-island. Seemed kind of late for painters to be working."

"Thanks for the update. I'm having dinner with your neighbor. Maybe he'll know something about it."

Jerry laughed. "That guy Thompson? You do get around lady."

I turned toward the table where Peter Thompson was sitting. He was engaged in a conversation with another man whose face I couldn't see but whose stance I recognized.

"Hey. Isn't that Mr. Good-Looking?" Jerry asked. "Frank? Isn't that his name?"

"It is!" Alice enthused. "Wonder what they're talking about? Maybe you, Leslie."

"I hope not. I didn't know they knew each other."

I gave Jerry a pat on the shoulder. "Gotta go. See you soon. And, uh, let me know if you see anything else unusual."

"We'll keep you in the loop," Alice said and gave me a wink.

As I headed back to my seat, my eyes searched the dining area and found Janis Johnson sitting by herself on the other side of the room. I was sure she'd given Frank a blow-by-blow description of the events at the gallery, including the judo move that left her on the floor.

"Leslie. You know Frank Johnson, don't you?" Peter said as I approached the table. "Frank, this is Leslie Elliott. She's a writer."

"I know, Leslie," Frank said, giving me his closed-mouth smile.

"I see you're here with your wife," I said with a hint of frostiness in my voice.

"Doing a little fence mending," he responded.

"Patching things up. That's nice for you." I pulled out my chair and turned my back to Frank.

"Why don't you join us?" Peter said. "Uh, if that's OK with you, Leslie."

"I think Mr. and Mrs. Johnson want to be alone." The minute the response came out of my mouth I regretted my tone.

"Yeah. Maybe some other time," Frank said.

I tried not to watch as he returned to the table where Janis was sitting. Husband and wife having dinner on a Friday night. To the myriad feelings I had about Frank, I added jealousy.

"How do you know Frank Johnson?" I asked.

"He's taken me fishing a couple of times."

"I hear he's a good guide. We were talking about your family, weren't we?" I inquired.

"My family? My parents are dead. I'm an only child."

"No brothers, sisters? Cousins?"

"Cousins. Yeah. A couple of them. Why do you ask?"

"No reason, except that I saw a picture in the local newspaper of someone who looked like you with a fish." I laughed. "I mean he looked like you with a goatee."

He didn't laugh at all so on I went. "But I thought his first name was different. Not sure why I remembered it. James or Jimmy or something?"

The alcoholic haze under which Peter Thompson had been operating lifted like a curtain pulled back to expose the morning light. "Why all the questions?"

I played dumb, like Wes Avery told me to. "Oh, sorry. Was I being too nosy? I just want to know you better."

"Is that why you went into my house?"

"That was because of the buzzards."

"It feels like you're grilling me, Leslie."

"Oh. S-sorry. It's a habit of mine to ask a lot of questions. Drives most people crazy. If I'm making you uncomfortable, perhaps I should leave," I said, putting down my napkin and reaching for my purse.

He grabbed my wrist. "Stay. I find you very attractive. I don't want to ruin this evening. This chance to get to know you better. I was just feeling a little uncomfortable, like you were accusing me of something."

"You know, I've had a long day and my head is starting to bother me. Maybe it's the Hurricane."

"Please." He tightened his grip and twisted my wrist. It felt like a display of power and control, not a sign of affection. I'd been playing cat and mouse with him, but his gesture was no game. I was about to let him know how I felt about men who manhandle women, when I heard Frank's voice over my shoulder. It was low but firm.

"Let go of her wrist." I didn't need Frank's help, but it was nice to have backup.

Thompson dropped his hold and put both hands in the air. "We're good here, friend. Let's not make a scene. You can return to your table."

"I don't think so," Frank said.

Thompson's shoulders stiffened. He looked hard at Frank. "Well, then, maybe you should take the lady home."

The waitress had wheeled up the cart with our dinner orders. When she realized what was happening, her face reddened. "Uh, uh, you still want your food?"

"Bring me the bill, miss. We're done," Thompson said, all the while glaring at Frank.

I stood up, noticing that the other diners were fixated on our table. I could see Jerry and Alice Mandino looking our way. I assumed they were ready to come to my aid again if necessary.

"I have my car. I'll drive myself home," I said to Frank. My wrist ached. I was sure I'd have an ugly bruise as a souvenir of my encounter with Peter Thompson.

"I'll come by after I take Janis home, if that's okay with you," Frank whispered as he ushered me to the exit.

"Why would you want to do that, Frank?"

"There are things you need to know."

CHAPTER 25

I was at the Tarpon Bar long enough to confirm my suspicion that Peter Thompson was a man with many secrets. That was my story to Deb when I walked into my condo to find her drinking a beer and eating a sandwich. I hoped it wasn't the chicken salad that had been sitting in the fridge for at least a week.

"What happened?" she asked, putting down the sandwich she was about to bite into.

"Let's say that Peter Thompson wasn't dazzled by my charm," I said, rubbing my wrist, which by now was deep red. "Guess I asked too many questions between the Hurricane and the main course, which I never got to eat. About his family and, uh, other stuff."

"Why would that upset him?" she asked.

"He said I was grilling him. Maybe I was. As I think about it, I was pretty annoying." I rubbed my wrist. "But that didn't give him the right to act like a jerk, which he did."

"You know, honey, Scooter and I think it's time you moved on from all this drama. There's always stuff happenin' on this island. We try to ignore it and live our lives the best we can," Deb said, taking a swig of beer and then laying her cool hands on my wrist. "Maybe you should, too."

"Maybe I could have moved on from the mystery house, the dog and the washed-up body parts if someone hadn't conked me on the head the other night. And there was the ring I found not far from the fingers on the beach. It matched the one on Peter Thompson's pinky."

"Lots of men wear a ring on their little finger."

"Doesn't it seem odd that they were identical?"

"Whatcha drivin' at?" Deb got up to get another beer from the fridge. I made a mental note to re-stock my alcohol supply, which would dwindle quickly with three drinkers in the house.

"I don't think Peter Thompson is who he says he is. Or maybe there are two Peter Thompsons and they're playing some kind of game. The question is what and why?"

Deb twisted the cap off the beer and shook her head.

"I'm gonna leave that for you to figure out. I got my hands full with Scooter. Can I get you something to drink? You said you didn't eat dinner. You hungry?"

"I think I'll have a glass of wine. Maybe some peanuts. I'll get it. And Deb, can I ask a favor?"

"Anything, honey."

"Please don't tell anyone about my Peter Thompson theory, especially Scooter. Too many people think I'm crazy as it is. Also, Frank's coming by. Says he has some things to tell me. I'm hoping he can shed light on what's been happening. Not sure he'll talk if you're around."

A big grin spread across her face. "I can make myself scarce."

"Let me call Mother and see if she's still up. And, it's not like that, not what you're thinking."

"My mind's pure as my heart. Besides, Ruth's a hoot. I wouldn't mind having a couple of drinks with her."

Mother answered the phone on the first ring. "You're home early. How was the date? Did you chase him away?"

"He said I asked too many questions." I could visualize her pursing her lips, a habit she had when she disapproved of something.

"Do you mind if Deb comes over for a drink? Frank Johnson's stopping by, and I want some time alone with him."

Mother's voice brightened. "That lovely man. He's better looking than that Thompson fellow anyway."

"This is not a date," I protested.

"Tell Deb to bring her pajamas and a toothbrush."

It was past midnight when I stretched out on the couch and closed my eyes, exhausted from the stress of the evening. Frank must have changed his mind about coming over; a part of me was glad.

I was sitting around a campfire. There were others, several Peter Thompsons in various stages of decay, their skins whitish blue with bits of flesh hanging off them. They stood up and began walking toward me, their feet dragging and their arms extended in front of them like monsters from a George Romero film. I tried to scream. There was no sound. I tried to stand up and run. My body was locked in place.

This is a dream. Wake up! Wake up!

My eyes snapped open. I gasped, filling my lungs with air. The room was dark save for a small light on the kitchen stove. A wave of fear washed over my body, paralyzing me.

His voice came out of the darkness and wrapped around me like a blanket on a chilly night. "Easy, Leslie. It's me."

CHAPTER 26

The smell of bacon awakened my appetite and roused me from a bed where the indentation left by Frank's body remained. We had kissed, then talked, and I'd drifted off to sleep. His presence had been non-threatening and comforting.

As I emerged from the bedroom, he looked over at me and said, "Eggs will be ready in a couple of minutes. Hope you like them scrambled." I yawned smiled and fluffed my short auburn hair into place around the bandage.

I walked up behind him, put my arms around his waist and kissed his bare shoulder. Sure, sure. I was headed down a dangerous path. But for some reason, it didn't seem so perilous this morning.

"My mother never was much of a cook. So, my dad and I rustled up meals. You wanna eat on the porch?" he asked.

"Why not? It's a beautiful day." *In so many ways.*

I'd awakened from my nightmare and found Frank wrapped around me, protecting me. We laid there together on the couch, not saying anything, until the terror I'd felt dissipated and my body began to relax.

"That must have been some dream," Frank said.

"Zombies. From the darkest recesses of my mind, and they looked like Peter Thompson."

He laughed. "I'll protect you from all of them."

"Will you?" I propped myself on my elbow, looked at him, searching for something more than a yes. The light from the kitchen barely illuminated his face. His blue-gray eyes looked puzzled for a minute, his mouth set.

"Stay with me," I said. I wasn't sure where she'd been hiding, but the vulnerable part of me was emerging, the part I wanted to keep hidden since moving to the island to seek out a better life and a sense of purpose.

"Is that what you want?"

"Um. Tonight it is," I said, as his mouth covered mine.

I put the placemats and a vase with yellow daisies on the glass-top table on the lanai. Frank arrived a few minutes later with two plates of steaming food; the knives and forks in his shirt pocket.

"What do you need to drink?" I asked, pushing my chair back.

"Sit still. I'll get us some O.J. If that's okay with you?" Frank said.

It was high tide and we could see the manta rays scurrying along the shallow bottom of the pale green water of the North Pass. A hammerhead shark swam by, his fin breaking through the water, a warning to those of us who lived outside the sea.

"That's scary. I've seen people wading out there," I said.

"Hammerheads like the rays."

"If I saw that fin coming my direction, I wouldn't put up a fight. I'd die right there from a heart attack."

Frank laughed and grabbed my hand, kissing each of my fingertips.

"I'd have to rescue you, I guess, even though I'd warned you many times to stay out of shark-infested waters."

"I get the message," I said, wincing at my twisted wrist.

"No, Leslie. I mean it. I would like nothing better than to always be there to save you," he said.

All I could do was smile, even as a tiny question still lingered somewhere inside me. I ignored it.

The small talk continued as the promise of revelation hung over the breakfast table. Frank had said at the Tarpon Bar that he had something to tell me. I didn't want to pressure him, but he hadn't spoken of it the night before and I was by now mighty interested.

When we finished, he pushed away from the table.

"Leslie, I need to apologize for Janis and what she said yesterday," he began.

"It's okay. She's still in love with you. I think I understand why."

"She wants people to think that. One day she wants me back; the next she calls me a loser. Like I told you, it's over between us. Has been for a long time."

"What about Stevie?"

"It's tough to tell what he's thinking. He loves his mother because he thinks he should. But she doesn't spend much time with him. She tells others she gave him to me because a boy needs his father. I took him when I found out he hadn't eaten anything but peanut butter and crackers for two days. She didn't fight me."

"Two days? My God."

"She was off with some guy, and there was nothing in the house for him. It made me sick."

"I'm sure he has a happy life with you and your mother." The picture of the dark-haired Georgia came to mind. I had to check myself from shuddering.

"My mother. Yeah. She takes good care of him and is helpful most of the time. That's all that matters."

"Is that what you wanted to tell me? About you and Janis?"

He shook his head. "It's about the storm."

"The one with the body? What do you know about that?"

He related the story with little inflection. As I listened, I wondered how he could be so cool about it.

He was fishing offshore for bait when he saw the father and the two kids. The father was on his phone. The kids were playing, filling their buckets with sand and building a fort or something. The stuff kids do on the beach.

He saw the rubber boat in the water. It was one of those dinghies people on yachts use to get ashore after they've anchored. He was keeping an eye on it because small craft like that are worth money, and it was potential salvage.

As soon as it drifted onto the beach, the little kids spotted it. They ran over to look inside and started screaming. Frank pulled in his nets and watched. At first the dad wasn't interested. Just kept talking as if he thought the kids were playing.

When he realized they were scared, he was there in a flash. At the time, Frank didn't know what was in the boat. He figured a dead fish or sea turtle. The dad took off walking fast with the kids and was on the phone again; calling the sheriff, Frank assumed.

When the three were out of sight, Frank jumped over the side of his boat and went up to the dinghy, thinking he might retrieve it. That's when he saw the body. It had been in the water for some time. One of the arms was hooked by a rope. The other was missing.

"Right away I recognized the guy. Even though part of his face was gone."

"You could identify the body?"

"Remember the guys I told you about; the ones I took fishing the day we had dinner?"

"The same guys that called to you that night on the beach?"

"Yeah. It was one of them. The guy that pays the bills."

"You think they robbed and killed him? Wasn't he their friend?"

"These guys don't have friends. Anyway, I took the body, put it in my net and got out of there. I could see you coming back. The deputy looking in the boat. The man getting mad."

I could visualize it, unrolling like a scene from a movie. Frank's explanation sounded a bit farfetched, but I guess it had to be true.

"Why didn't you leave the body in the boat?"

"This is too big for Harry and his guys. They're small-town cops. I called a buddy of mine that works for DEA, Drug Enforcement, Miami. There's a lot of stuff going on – not here but further south. I've talked to him before. He said he'd take care of it. No need to notify the locals."

"The hand and arm that washed up has to be part of the body you found in the boat. You said the body was missing an arm."

"The hand and arm?" He looked at me, puzzled.

"Deb and I discovered it on the beach, yesterday, after Doris Selwin painted it on her canvas. We reported it to the sheriff. You need to tell him, Frank. Tell him what you just told me. He'll work with the DEA."

"Sure. I'll talk to Harry this morning. But this has to stay between us. No telling Deb, your other girlfriends or Harry that you know."

I held up my hand as though preparing to swear on the Bible. "I won't say anything."

"There's no need for you to play detective anymore. You can go back to your book and let the feds handle everything."

Now Frank was treading in dangerous territory. Telling me what to do. He should have known better than that. "But the yellow house? The bump on the back of my head?"

"The same guys. They were talking about the house the day we went fishing. Wondering what was in there, planning on checking it out. The DEA will round them up; I gave them their names. They won't bother us anymore."

"You really think the DEA will find them?"

"Absolutely. Trust me."

Trust you, Frank Johnson? My inner voice is telling me to watch out.

"And what about Peter Thompson? I asked. "You think he's involved with something."

"I think he'd like to be involved with you. Do I think there's some great mystery about him? From what I know, he's a lonely guy looking for some action."

"But I found a pinky ring on the beach when we discovered the hand and arm. It was identical to the one Peter was wearing. Identical, Frank."

"You find stuff like that on the beach all the time. It's not a clue if that's what you're thinking."

"How can you be so sure?"

He stood up and kissed me on the top of my head, without providing an answer. "I don't have to worry about you being with Peter, do I, Leslie?"

I shook my head but did not smile at him. *Where did that territorial question come from?*

"They say dreams reveal our true thoughts. In mine he was a zombie," I responded.

My hand went to the back of my head where the large white bandage was. I was falling for Frank Johnson, but I wasn't liking this sudden display of possessiveness. And I wasn't ready to believe everything he told me about the missing body, the yellow house or Peter Thompson.

CHAPTER 27

The bouquet of flowers obscured the face of the gray-haired delivery person. She was barely 5 feet tall; her spindly legs partly hidden behind baggy white shorts. She swayed under the weight of her burden.

"Ms. Elliott?" the woman said. Her voice filtered between white hydrangeas and roses as she stood at the screen door to my condo.

"That's me. Wow. There must be two dozen roses in there," I said as I opened the door for her. "Here, let me take those."

"I got it. This thing's pretty heavy. Where do you want me to put it?"

"Oh sorry. On the kitchen counter."

She struggled to hoist the flowers onto the counter, smoothed her floral print top and then pulled out the pad she'd been clutching under her arm.

Many seniors in Florida needed part-time jobs well into their 70s – the promise of a quiet life in paradise threatened by a dwindling bank account. I scribbled my signature on a form she offered and handed her a $20 tip.

"Oh my. Thank you, ma'am."

"This is a lovely surprise," I said as she turned to leave.

She winked. "It must be love. That's so nice."

I didn't know if it was love. But I knew I had strong feelings for Frank – however confused they were. Given my track record with men, I guess I shouldn't have been surprised that I was falling again, and that he might be less than appropriate for me. What do they say? Hope springs eternal. Hope for love, that is. Or at least something more than companionship.

He'd been gone about three hours. How did he arrange for a beautiful bouquet to be delivered in such a short time and on a Saturday? I pulled the card off the plastic stick.

"Please forgive me for last night. Fondly, Peter."

"What the hell," I said aloud. I wasn't done with Peter Thompson, but after the scene at the Tarpon Bar, I assumed he was finished with me. This was an olive branch. The door to more answers had swung open. Despite warning bells at the back of my head, about where my bandage clung, I picked up my cell.

"Hi Peter. Leslie Elliott. Your flowers took my breath away."

"I was hoping they would," he said. "I overreacted when you asked about Monica and my cousins. Your questions brought back sad memories. Jamie was like a brother to me. He was killed in a boating accident several years ago. I have another cousin – Jamie's brother, Ted – but we aren't that close."

"I'm so sorry. I didn't mean to pry," I said, expressing regret that I didn't feel.

"Why don't we start over? Have dinner with me Tuesday evening. We can go to a bistro off island that's pretty good. Get away from the locals."

I hesitated. Getting away from the locals and my support system to dine with Peter Thompson didn't seem like the wise thing to do – no matter how sorry he sounded about what transpired at our recent outing.

"Dinner's out, I'm afraid for the foreseeable future. My friends. Their house is being repaired after a fire. They're staying here. Deb may need some help in the evenings taking care of her husband who was burned. How about lunch instead?"

"OK. It's a start. I'll get back to you."

"Fine, and thanks again for the flowers, Peter. That was very sweet of you."

I was carrying the bouquet to the dining room table when the ambulance attendant come through the front door guiding Scooter by his good arm. My stomach turned. Deb, who was following the pair, hadn't warned me that even though his arm was the most affected, there were serious burns on other parts of his body.

"Welcome home. So glad to see you," I said, trying to sound upbeat. "You want to sit on the lanai? Or the bed has clean sheets."

Scooter mumbled something I couldn't understand.

"I think he needs rest. Let's put him down, Jerry," Deb said to the EMT and walked ahead of them toward the bedroom. The strong young man got him into bed with no problem.

"You take a nap, darlin'," Deb said to Scooter, stroking his good arm. "I'll wake you up in an hour or so and fix you lunch."

The attendant left with a good-bye to Deb, who pulled out a chair at the dining table and sat down; her shoulders bowed. "The doctor says he has to eat properly and drink lots of fluids. He can't smoke. That'll be the hard one. They've got him on drugs. When he starts feelin' better, he's gonna be a hellion."

I inched my chair closer to Deb's, put my arms around her and pulled her close. My happiness with Frank and my ongoing suspicions all seemed petty compared to the issues she and her husband faced.

"I've made some sandwiches for you and Scooter. Let's go sit on the lanai," I said.

"OK." She let out a giant sigh and stifled a whimper. "I can't begin to repay you for all of your kindnesses, honey."

"It's easy to be a friend when things are going well. Real friendship is about being there when times are tough."

She took a drink of lemonade. "There's no light at the end of this tunnel. Things keep gettin' worse. The doctor says Scooter needs skin grafts on his arm. All I can think about is what something like that will cost." She wiped the sweating lemonade glass with her napkin.

"We can't even afford basic health care," she said softly. "A friend of mine makes about $40,000 a year and pays $300 a month for the cheapest program. It doesn't cover vision or dental or problems with your feet. Her deductible is $6,600 for major medical. Lordy."

Our conversation was interrupted by the screams coming from the bedroom. They were piercing, guttural.

"Fire! Heeeeeeelp! I'm burnin'! Heeeeeelp!"

Deb and I were at Scooter's side in a heartbeat. He was thrashing, his face pale and dripping with perspiration.

"It's okay, Sugar. You're not in the house." Deb tried to soothe him, but he continued clawing at his bandages. "Hold down his other arm, Leslie. He's having a flashback."

When Scooter quieted, more exhausted than comforted, Deb reached into her pocket, pulled out an orange bottle and asked for water.

I returned with a plastic cup, and she took a small white pill from her hand and stuck it in Scooter's mouth. "He had a couple of these spells in the hospital. The doctor said he could have more. It's normal with burn patients, I guess."

Scooter was awake but not with us. Tears traveled across his scorched cheek. My eyes welled up.

"You holler if you need somethin'. We're on the porch," Deb said when Scooter closed his eyes, and his breathing, although shallow, became rhythmic.

"The doc said he has the same thing soldiers experience when they come back from war. PTSD. Scooter's uncle had that. Came back from three tours of duty in Vietnam with the prettiest little wife. He woke up one night and thought he was back on the battlefield and she was the enemy. Killed her. What a tragedy."

My lemonade went down wrong, and I started coughing. Deb reached over to pat my back.

"Sorry, Deb." I wiped my mouth. "That's a horrible story!"

"Well, he wasn't charged," she said. "But it haunted him the rest of his life. He talked about going back to Vietnam to visit her relatives. He never made it."

"That's terrible. So sad." I patted her hand, disturbed for her and by her. "So, Scooter will have these, uh, flashbacks for a long time?"

Deb shook her head. "Looks like life will be a living hell for us for some years to come, honey. A living hell."

CHAPTER 28

Carolyn, the organist with the bouncy golden curls and the generous bottom, lowered her hands to the keys and struck a chord that reverberated throughout the church. Those of us sitting in the front row jumped in unison.

Carolyn's eyebrows shot up and her mouth formed a little bow as if she, too, was surprised at the volume. A clicking sound followed. The chords that emanated from the instrument were softer and more suitable for the small procession that passed by us and headed for the three steps at the front of the church.

A teenage boy carried a six-foot pole with a crucifix. Behind him came a pudgy dark-haired man holding a brass candle lighter. Pastor Billy Cordray in white robe with blue embroidered crosses brought up the rear.

"Look who's lighting candles this time," Mother said in a voice dripping with judgment. "It's the acolyte Gordon Fike. He wants everyone to think he's some sort of saint. But I know the truth about him."

"What do you...."

"Good morning and welcome to the Island Church where love and light are ever present." Pastor Billy had a voice as big as the smile on his face. He was beaming, as though he'd just concluded a personal audience with the Lord.

"Thank you, Father, for this amazing day and the opportunity for all of us to be together to hear your precious words. Let us now sing our first hymn together, *Come Thou Fount of Every Blessing.*"

We rose in unison as the organist played the first stanza. Gordon had disappeared from my view and was sitting somewhere behind the organ. It was surprising to see him in such a prominent role. I didn't want to be judgmental like my mother. Maybe he was a devout Christian.

"*Come, thou fount of every blessing, tune my heart to sing Thy grace.* What do you know about our man Gordon?" I sang to my mother. "Calls for songs of loudest praise."

Mother looked at me and chuckled. "I saw him with the woman with the pompadour at the store the other day," she sang back to me.

"*Praise the mount! I'm fixed upon it.* Were they together as in one?" I crooned.

"*Sorrowing I shall be in spirit.* Yes, they were, they surely were."

"*Yet from what I do inherit.* You can tell me yet today."

Mother and I raised our voices: "*Come, my Lord, no longer tarry....*"

"You may be seated." The pastor cleared his throat. "Do we have anyone who needs prayers from the congregation today?"

This was the reason I'd come to the church; I wasn't a regular like Mother. I raised my hand, stood up and turned to face the others. "You all know about the fire at the Rankin's house. Scooter's out of the hospital, came to stay at my place yesterday, but is going to need a lot more treatment, including skin grafts and your prayers."

There was murmuring among the crowd. A voice from behind the organ spoke: "I know the Rankins will need financial help. I'm wondering if we can take up a collection for them today, pastor."

"Uh, er, well, it's highly unusual," the pastor said. "But in the spirit of Christian giving, I'm sure it will be fine. Thank you for your suggestion, Brother Gordon."

"I'll match whatever is contributed," Fike added.

I leaned toward mother and whispered. "Maybe you want to change your mind about our friend."

She pursed her lips and shook her head.

When the service ended, Gordon was standing at the door with a basket on his arm. As the congregation filed out, they tossed $10s, $20s, several checks and loose change into the container. I handed him two $20s, which was all I had in my purse.

"What a nice gesture, Gordon. Is it possible, um, can I come by your office tomorrow? I have something to discuss with you."

"Sure." His face beamed. Was he hoping I'd changed my mind about buying a house?

"Can you take this money to Deb and Scooter?" he said, thrusting the basket at me.

"How much?"

"Maybe $1,500," he said. I thought I saw a tear travel down his cheek, but I couldn't be sure. Gordon never struck me as the kind of man that could muster sympathy for anyone except himself. Yet here he was doing another act of kindness. Why did I keep being so wrong about him?

With his matching check, I had $3,000 to deliver to my friends. It was a drop in the bucket for what they needed, but I hoped it would lift Deb's spirits.

ee) Cee

"I about died when you started singing questions to the hymn," Mother said as we headed back toward our condos. "It reminded me of one of my favorite Alfred Hitchcock movies."

"Not *The Birds*?"

"Oh no. The one with that handsome Jimmy Stewart and Doris Day. They're in a church just like we were. They spot the villains and start singing to each other. It's a wonderful scene."

I was a big movie fan but I couldn't place the classic Mother was referencing. "I don't think I know it," I said.

"*The Man Who Knew Too Much*. You young people seem to think the only good movies are the ones with sex – raw sex I might add, not romance – or those special-effects disasters that cost millions to make. Give me the old movies with their subtleties. I can dream up my own fantasies."

"I'm sure you can. So, do you think you could conjure up a movie scene between Gordon Fike and Janis Johnson? You said you saw them together."

Mother started laughing and then covered her mouth – a habit she had when she was tickled about something. "Really, dear, you are so funny. I never knew that about you until we moved here. You want to know where I saw them? It was in the grocery store parking lot. They were having quite an argument."

"What about?"

"It sounded like money to me. She wanted some and he wasn't giving her any was the gist of it."

"Is that what they said? She was asking him for money?"

"Well, uh, that's what I assumed," Mother said. "I couldn't hear all that well. But they were quite animated. He was looking for answers and she wasn't giving him any, or maybe it was the other way around."

She shrugged as if it didn't matter, then shuddered.

"I don't understand what a wonderful man like Frank Johnson ever saw in that woman anyway. The hair. The tattoos. Disgusting."

"I'm sure it was, uh, an evolution on her part."

"More like a revolution. Revolting. So typical of young people these days. I'm glad our dear little Meredith isn't involved in any of that."

I thought of Meredith's new boyfriend and his richly stenciled arm. "Me too."

It was clear Mother had seen something. The question was what.

ꝏꝏ

Scooter was being led to the lanai by Frank and Deb when Mother and I arrived home after church. Along with his bandages, his cheeks glistened bright red from the ointment he was wearing.

The compassion Frank was showing his friend, Scooter, touched my heart, as did so many things about the fisherman.

"How was church?" he asked.

"We asked for prayers for Scooter," I said hesitantly. I wasn't sure about Deb and Scooter's religious beliefs. But surely no one could object to having devotions said on their behalf.

"That weasel Gordon Fike was the acolyte, uh, candle lighter, if you can believe that," Mother chimed in. "There's something about him I don't like."

"Oh, Mother. Everyone takes their turn at lighting the candles. Besides, it was Gordon that encouraged people to…." I stopped. I was sure Deb wouldn't want Scooter knowing that the congregation had chipped in to help pay his expenses. I put my fingers to my lips.

"Deb, can I talk to you in the second bedroom."

"Sure thing, honey." Deb was in her early fifties, but Scooter's burns, the fire and the situation with her wealthy neighbors were taking a toll on her face. I was sure I hadn't seen dark circles under her eyes before. Crow's feet and the tiny lines around her mouth had claimed new territory.

"How's it going? Scooter feeling any better?" I inquired when we were finally alone.

"This thing has sucked the life out of him. Me, too. Sometimes I-I-I wish the fire had claimed him." Tears gathered in her eyes. "Lord help me for saying that."

I put my hand on her back and rubbed it gently, hoping to provide the comfort that comes with human touch. "You don't want to see him suffer. None of us do. But I have something that may make you feel better."

I told her about Gordon's generosity and gave her the $1,500 in cash and his check for the matching amount.

Deb's face crumpled and her tears flowed freely. "Oh, honey. I'm overwhelmed. The people on this island are special. What else can I say?"

I put up my hand as if to confirm that I had nothing to do with the money. "It was all Gordon. He deserves the credit. He brought it up in church, and the pastor agreed that taking up a collection was the right thing to do."

"Then I owe him big thanks. I'll call when Scooter's asleep."

When we emerged from the second bedroom, Mother was leaning on the kitchen counter, a glass of lemonade in her hand. She was eyeing the large bouquet.

"Where did these flowers come from?" she asked. "There was no card."

I glared at her. Mentioning the flowers with Frank standing there was something the old unpleasant Ruth would have done.

"Peter Thompson. He apologized for Friday night. Said he wanted me to go out with him again. I told him no," I responded. After all, I had nothing to hide.

"I hope we've seen the last of him," Mother said.

Frank looked at me and raised one eyebrow.

CHAPTER 29

The white bungalow that housed Waterside Properties brought back memories of my resignation from Metro Energy and the move to Florida. Tim Fletcher's niece, Ginny, was with me, helping me find someplace to live on this beautiful island when we first caught sight of the small real estate office.

It wasn't even eight months ago that I'd purchased the condo. It felt like several years had gone by.

I could picture Gordon Fike on that hot day: *The door opened and a corpulent man with thick brown hair and a neatly trimmed mustache emerged. A large dolphin charm was attached to a gold chain around his neck. The same creature was affixed to a gold ring he wore on the little finger of his left hand.*

Another pinky ring. Peter Thompson had said they were plentiful, not special. Guess he was right.

The receptionist, Dollyene, had shoulder-length black hair, rosy cheeks and big teeth. She greeted me with a hello that was far too cheery for a Monday morning. "It feels like the red tide's getting better. I don't think I coughed once yesterday," she said.

I pictured the dead fish that were piling up on the beach and threatening the island's tourist business. Hotel crews were working hard to remove them. Some locals were burying them in sandy graves by the water. But everyone was having trouble keeping up.

"When I was at the beach Friday it was still plenty strong. Seems like there are more buzzards every day," I said.

"Maybe you're right. I try not to notice. You lookin' for Gordie?" She checked her watch and glanced at the calendar. "He should be here in 10 minutes or so. He doesn't have any appointments today."

There were a couple of chairs next to Dollyene's desk; brushed nickel frames and tan vinyl with a few cracks emerging. I sat down, wondering why Gordon didn't have a nicer office. Maybe he wasn't as successful as I thought.

On the walls were photos of the realtor with large fish, mostly tarpon, several maps of the island and ads for lavish homes with fancy price tags. I zeroed in on a faded picture of Gordon with Frank Johnson and a woman on a boat that looked like the Dreamcatcher. I hadn't noticed it when I was there the first time, shopping for my condo. Of course, I hadn't known anyone when I was first coming in here so there was no way I would have recognized the people on the boat.

Now I did. It dawned on me that the woman was Janis. She had a mane of silver blond hair and no tattoos on her arms. Her waist was tiny. 24 inches or less. She had perfect teeth, like a row of little pearls in her mouth. She was wearing a red bikini that revealed slim muscular arms and ripped abs. I was on the lean side but not a fan of working out. I never looked that good in a two-piece bathing suit and hadn't worn one since I was in my twenties.

Frank hadn't changed much except for a few more lines on his handsome face. In the photo, his hair was longer and pulled back in a ponytail. He was standing off to one side and looking out to sea.

At 40 pounds lighter, Gordon was another surprise. A large cigar, a stogie, was clenched in his teeth. His arm was draped around Janis. If I didn't know better, I would say that Janis was with Gordon, not with Frank. That might explain what Mother saw in the parking lot. There was, or had been, a relationship there – what kind I didn't know.

I got up and moved closer to get a better look. "Who took this photo, the one of Gordon with the Johnsons?"

"Uh, I'm pretty sure it was Mrs. Fike: Jennifer. It was taken about 15 years ago. When they were still married."

"A Mrs. Fike? Never thought about him being married. He seems like the perennial bachelor," I said.

"He is now. Jennifer left him about 12 years ago. It may have been because of Janis. I think Gordie had a thing for her and it didn't sit well with Jennifer. At one time, they always hung out together. You won't see them together now, though.

Gordie and Frank hate each other. Guess I shouldn't be telling you this," she said, putting her hand to her mouth like she'd been caught revealing a confidence.

"It's a small island and tough to keep secrets. If you didn't tell me someone else would."

"Beautiful morning," Gordon said as he breezed through the door. His hair was wind-blown. "Nice to have convertible weather back, isn't it Leslie? You're here bright and early. What can I do for you?"

He directed me to the room around the corner and stopped to ask Dollyene if she had anything for him. The two chairs with tan vinyl in front of his desk were more presentable than the ones in the reception area. I pulled one out and sat down, thinking about how I'd noticed none of this when I first came in here.

On the walls, certificates thanking the realtor for his sponsorship of local events were interspersed with photos of Gordon and more fish. There was a beach scene print by an artist whose name I didn't recognize. In the corner was an artificial plant that needed a good dusting.

When he finally sat down and looked at me inquiringly – big smile – I said, "It's about Deb and Scooter. They, uh, Deb really appreciated the money. She didn't tell her husband. I don't think."

"She called last evening and thanked me. It was the least I could do"

"You've already done so much. I'm reluctant to ask for more, but Scooter's in terrible shape, Gordon. They need money for his treatments. Plenty of it. I was hoping you had some ideas. I mean, someone told me that you do fund-raisers, spaghetti dinners, on the island."

"Yes, for scholarships and other charitable reasons. The winter residents are generous. I might be able to raise another $10,000 when the season kicks into high gear."

"That sounds like a lot, but they don't have health insurance. I don't think I'm speaking out of school, but $10,000 won't cover his burn treatments, let alone the skin grafts and follow-ups. I've thought about a GoFundMe page on Facebook. It's tough to ask for money when you're sitting on an expensive piece of…." my voice trailed off when I realized what I was about to say.

Gordon reached for the calculator at the edge of his desk and scooted it closer. His fingers traveled quickly over the keys.

"I'm not sure they'll go for that," I said, leery that he was speculating on what they'd get for their place. "They love that old house and the land around it,"

"It's the only solution, Leslie. They have to sell that house. And what better time? When the workers finish, it'll be in prime condition…at least most of it. It won't take much to get the rest there."

As I'm shaking my head, he continued. "The house itself could go for $650,000, maybe more, but with the additional land it's worth over $1 million. I'm positive we could make that happen."

"A million? You think? It's amazing what outrageous prices you can get for property on this island." I paused. "Can the lot be sold separately from the house?"

Gordon's brow furrowed. His fingers remained on the calculator. "I need to check the property lines. But if so, the land could go for, uh, say, $500,000, in that neighborhood. Let's see. Realtor's commission at six percent, that's $30,000. Throw in $2,000 for surveys, fees – maybe a little more."

He cleared his throat. "The people who contributed to have the house fixed up will want their money back. That's a reasonable request, don't you think?"

Apparently, Gordon had financed the restoration of Deb and Scooter's property using investors to whom he'd made promises. If the house was sold, they could get their money back. I don't remember Deb telling me so, but my guess was that Gordon hadn't mentioned it to her either.

"That's another $150,000 plus interest. Giving them, uh, about $275,000. That should pay their bills with some left over."

"And they can keep their home?" My enthusiasm for the idea was growing.

"A happy ending for everyone," he said.

"How soon can you check the property lines?"

"I'll get the surveyor on it today. And there's always the possibility of moving the house over a couple of feet. Won't be that expensive since the workers are already there."

I was glad for what seemed like a practical resolution to the Rankins' problems. Pitching it to Scooter might be tough but, in the end, he'd have to go for it. Wouldn't he?

I jumped in again. "It's none of my business but in the outer office, when I came in, I saw the photo of you, Frank and Janis, um, taken by your ex-wife. I didn't know you hung out with the Johnsons."

Gordon sighed and shook his head. "We were close then. Not now, although I feel protective of her."

"Interesting times when we're young, don't you think? I imagine the island was a different place then, 20 years ago," I said.

"Quieter. More casual. It also had big drug problems. Not anymore. Those days are gone. Back when I was a teenager, dealers would pay ten grand for kids with boats to make runs. That was more money than my dad made in a year. Lots of poor kids were tempted. We talked about it amongst ourselves after school. But I, um, didn't have a boat or access to one."

I nodded. "I can see how you might be tempted. Easy money. And the young seldom think about consequences. Did you know Janis in high school?"

He smiled as if conjuring up a pleasant memory. "She was a couple of years behind me. God, she was beautiful. So talented with her art and all. The attitude and the way she looks today? Breaks my heart. Frank's to blame."

"Frank? Why do you say that?"

"She needs to be taken care of, to have nice cars, a beautiful house. Frank didn't do that for her. When she saw how others on the island lived, the people from up north, it affected her like it did many of us. I understand how she felt; she deserved more – and, well, still does."

I wasn't sure why Frank was being blamed for Janis's materialism. He seemed a hard worker. Surely, he tried his best to provide for her and their son.

"I'm sure he tried to make a good home for her." My words echoed my thoughts.

Gordon said nothing as he stood up and checked his watch. I'd moved into painful territory, and he was ready for me to leave. I rose and extended my hand.

"Thanks for everything, Gordon. I'm afraid I haven't given you the credit you deserve for being a nice guy."

"I'm one step up from a used car salesman in most people's minds," he said, shaking his head. "It's a tough rap to beat. You won't hear any objection from me if the word gets out that Gordon Fike isn't such a bad guy after all."

"I'll try to make that happen," I said, thinking that I hadn't heard anyone say that about him. Maybe he was being too hard on himself.

～○C～

The GoFundMe page and the potential for crowdfunding on Facebook was a spark in my mind when I first mentioned it to Gordon. During my short walk to the newspaper office, it became a full-blown idea. I was hoping my reporter friend Wes Avery could help me with that and some other things I had in mind.

Even if the Rankins agreed to sell all or part of their property, they might need more money. And if they didn't decide to sell…well, with them nothing was certain.

The weekly newspaper's newest family member was leaning over the balcony smoking a cigarette when I started up the stairs that led to his second-story office.

"Didn't you tell me you were giving up that filthy habit?"

"Yep. It seems like a good idea every time I tell someone I'm quitting. Just can't pull the plug on these things," he said, looking at the smoldering cigarette between his first and second fingers.

"It must go with the job," I said.

"Quite a few bad habits do. So, Snoop, what do you have for me?"

"Several things I think you'll find interesting."

We sat down on a wooden bench on the balcony, and I shared with him the story about the blue fingers and arm on the beach. I didn't mention what Frank told me about handing over the body to the drug enforcement officers.

"Gruesome finds are always news," he said, taking another drag. "You think it's linked to the other bodies you told me about?"

"I'm certain it is. But the sheriff will say he's never seen those bodies so it would be impossible for him to make the connection, which I guess is true. But he can't deny the hand and arm on the beach. Deb and I were witnesses."

"I'll ask him about the bodies anyway. Just because the sheriff didn't see them doesn't mean they weren't there. We'll alert beach walkers and get the buzz going," Wes said.

My next piece of information was about the fire at Deb and Scooter's place on Saturday. The paper was planning on running a small piece on it and quoting the fire chief who was attributing the blaze to owner carelessness.

"Wes, their bills are going to be huge and they don't have any insurance," I said.

"How's that possible?" he responded. "Isn't it mandated?"

"Mandate is not a word that Deb and Scooter use or understand. I need to talk them into letting me do some crowd funding on Facebook. If I decide to do it and they go for it, can I count on you to publicize it?"

"Sure, why not."

"There's something else. I saw a photo of Peter Thompson with a big fish in the September 4 issue when I was looking for the missing dog ad. Do you still have a digital copy?"

"Helen will know."

We stepped inside, and after greeting the receptionist at the front desk, I posed the question to her. I hadn't paid much attention to her before. She had dark curly hair, pulled into a knot on top of her head. Her large glasses with dark frames, very much in style, gave her a scholarly appearance. I was correct in my first assessment of her. She was efficient.

She explained to me that the paper would have saved the digital image and the PDF of the page. There were also copies of the papers in a storage facility. If a photo is dropped off at the office, it's scanned and returned to the owner immediately. If it isn't used, the digital file is deleted.

It took five minutes for Randy, the man in charge of the paper's layout, to pull up the file for me. There was Peter Thompson with the fish and his silver and gold pinky ring on display as he held up the catch.

His hair was tousled and his goatee a little longer than it appeared at dinner Friday night. Other than that, he looked like himself.

"Can you blow this up a bit? The face is what I'm interested in."

The photo was surprisingly clear when Randy enlarged it. A gold earring. A small mole by the side of his nose. I didn't remember any of those facial marks. I could check them out the next time I saw Peter.

"What's that to the left, a little behind the fish? Looks like someone else in the background. Can you focus on that?"

"Can't get it any wider. The photo's cropped," Randy said.

"You think you might have the original, the photo as it was submitted?" I asked.

It was Monday afternoon. Randy was a one-man shop and busy, with a deadline looming large. He looked at Wes as if to ask if this was necessary.

"It's important," Wes responded.

"OK. Gimme some time."

He rummaged through his files, pulling out folders and tossing them onto his workspace. It took several minutes to go through all the photos. Wes was the one who found it.

"You're an angel," I said, squeezing his arm.

Randy grabbed the 4x6 picture, scanned and enlarged it. When he was done, Wes and I looked it at each other in triumph.

There was Peter Thompson. Standing off to one side, wearing a baseball cap and a big grin, was the second person in the picture. He was the mirror image of the man with the big fish.

CHAPTER 30

Scooter and Deb's angry voices carried through the screen door and out onto the parking lot. I was wondering if I should go inside or stay far away when I saw my mother motioning to me frantically from the balcony outside her condo.

"What's all the noise about?"

"It's your good friend, Gordon Fike," she said, a note of panic in her voice. "He called to say that someone's interested in their house and lot. Said he wanted to talk to them. I was over there, with some cookies, and heard the whole thing. It got plenty heated."

Dammit. Why didn't he wait for me?

It wasn't two hours since Gordon and I hatched the plan that I hoped would solve my friends' financial woes. Gordon obviously didn't understand the art of the spin like I did. If we'd delivered the news the correct way, I was confident we wouldn't hear many protests from Scooter. Gordon had blown it.

"From the look on her face, it seemed Deb liked the idea," Mother said. "But when she told him, Scooter exploded. I don't know where the man summoned up the energy to react like that."

"It's too late to worry about that now," I said, stealing myself for the confrontation that was sure to follow my appearance. "Here I go. Keep your fingers crossed that I make it out alive."

My head was still buzzing from my discovery at the newspaper office. I was sure I'd seen the faces of Peter Thompson and his cousin, Jamie, one of the three named owners of the yellow house. But further investigation would have to wait until I'd taken care of my friends and their issues.

The palms of my hands were sweaty. I'd stuck my nose in their business. My intentions were good but as my father used to say: *The road to hell is paved with good intentions.* I could feel the fires of damnation smoldering in my condo where Deb and Scooter were waiting for me.

"Hello," I shouted as I walked up the steps and through the door.

"We're on the porch," I heard Deb say. At least she was still speaking to me.

"Sorry I didn't leave a note," I said, strolling into the screened area and sitting down on a bench near the Adirondacks. "I had several errands and didn't want to wake you."

"You saw Gordie," Scooter said. His words emerged like a growl. His teeth showed white. He pulled a cigarette out of his shirt pocket in defiance of my sign that said *Thank you for not smoking.*

"I did."

"Givin' us a bed don't mean you can butt in," he grumbled.

Deb grabbed the cigarette out of his hand. "The doctor said no."

"Fuck this. Won't stand for it," he said, looking away.

I took in a gulp of air and let the words flow. "I love you, Scooter, but you're being pig-headed. Think of Deb and what she's going through. Gordon Fike's willing to work with you, maybe help take care of your financial problems. You should listen to what he has to say."

"We do thank you, honey. But this is between Scooter and me," Deb said. Her voice was saying what she knew she should for her husband's benefit. I could see a different response in her eyes. She liked the idea.

I shrugged. "There are options. Your life could be better."

Deb put her arm on Scooter's shoulder and began stroking his back gently. The three of us sat there, looking out at the North Pass and the buzzards soaring overhead. It was an awkward silence.

"Maybe we should find someplace else to stay," she finally said. There was no conviction in her voice.

"Don't be ridiculous. I was planning on moving to Mother's condo in a couple of days to give you and Scooter more room. You're not going anywhere."

Scooter rose from the chair and hobbled to the door that led out of the lanai to the strip of beach and seawall below. Clinging to the railing, he moved down the steps, groaning with the effort. In a few minutes, the smell of cigarette smoke drifted through the screens.

"This surely is a mess," Deb said. "I don't fault you for trying to help, honey. I welcome it. Scooter, well, I don't know what to do with him."

"Gordon said he could divide the property and sell the land only, if that would help. That would leave you the house and about $275,000 for medical bills," I said.

"He told you that?"

"Yes, and even if your house sits too close to the property line, he said it wouldn't cost much to move it."

"He told us he had a buyer for the house and the lot. Didn't say anythin' about the other," Deb said.

What a colossal creep, I thought. "Give him a chance. This could fix all your problems. And if you need privacy from your neighbor, you can plant a row of areca palms. They grow like weeds," I said.

"Yes, honey, I know that." She thought a minute. "You call him. Tell him Scooter and I'll meet him at his office."

I didn't know if dragging Scooter to Gordon's office was a good idea. "Is he strong enough to handle this?"

"Maybe not. But he's doin' it whether he likes it or not. And, honey, you call Frank and see if he can come with us. We'll go in there together. United. Maybe Scooter doesn't know it right yet, but you two are the best friends we have."

ee)Cee

"Frank Johnson fishing charters. How can I help you?" The woman's voice was clipped, efficient sounding. My opinion of Georgia Johnson was not that favorable. But, to be fair, I'd only had those few minutes with her the night I met Frank.

I hesitated. "Is this Mrs. Johnson?"

"Yes. Who's this?"

"Leslie Elliott. We met at the art show a couple of weeks ago. I was serving champagne as you came in the door."

"Don't remember you. You want to book a fishing trip?" She had one mission and it wasn't small talk about her son's whereabouts.

"I was hoping to speak to Frank. I thought this was his cell?"

"Rings over to the home phone if he doesn't answer. Haven't seen him all day."

"Did he have a charter?" I asked.

"Nope. He had one Saturday. Nothing yesterday or today."

"Some friends of mine have a meeting with Gordon Fike, the realtor. They want Frank...."

"Ach." The disgust in Georgia Johnson's voice was obvious. "I can tell you right now that Frank won't have anything to do with that man."

"If he calls, will you give him my message please? Tell him that Leslie needs to speak with him right away."

"What's your last name?"

"Elliott. Leslie Elliott."

"Your number?"

"He has it. Thanks for your help Mrs. Johnson. Goodbye."

It was nearly 4 p.m., the time of the meeting with Gordon, and I still hadn't heard from Frank. I avoided calling his number a second time for fear that I would have to deal with Georgia again. Maybe we didn't need him there after all.

"What's wrong, honey?" Deb said as we walked toward the Waterside Properties office.

"Nothing. Don't know where Frank is. That's all."

Scooter had refused our help and was laboring to get out of my car on his own.

"Should we?" I glanced in his direction. Perhaps we were putting too much stress on him. Maybe he shouldn't be out and about at all. The fire was a week ago and Scooter had serious burns. My sense of guilt conflicted with my need to be firm in helping the Rankins find a solution to their financial problems. It wasn't my business but that wasn't stopping me.

"Nope," Deb said. "He wants to go it alone. Let him see what that feels like."

"What did you have to do to get him to agree to even talk with Gordon about this?"

"D-i-v-o-r-c-e. Like the old country song by Tammy Wynette. I told him that if he didn't shape up, I'd leave him. We both know that isn't true. But I wanted Scooter to chew on it a bit. So, Frank can't make it?"

"I haven't talked to him all day."

"He'll turn up. Must be off-island."

"He'd tell his mother, wouldn't he?" I mused.

"You spoke to Georgia? Lordy. That woman."

"I called Frank's cell and she answered. Said his calls were forwarded to her. She doesn't even try to be helpful. Must be great for business."

Deb snorted as we walked into Gordon's office, where we found him on his computer. If it was physically possible, his eyes would have registered dollar signs instead of pupils. We sat down in the brushed nickel chairs, watching the realtor shuffle papers and waiting for the third member of our party to arrive.

"How are you feeling?" Gordon asked when Scooter finally joined us, entering the room like every step was a dagger through his heart.

"Fuckin' fine. Get on with this," he said, settling into the small metal chair with some difficulty.

"Oh," Gordon said, his face turning red. "Well, uh, I think, you'll like what I have for you." He produced several documents, neatly stapled, each with a summary on top.

The first offer was for the house and lot: $1.2 million as is, so the work could stop and Deb and Scooter would walk away with more than $1 million in their pockets. The second offer was for the lot, which ended up being 100 by 105 feet. The Rankin's house could remain where it was. The offer was $500,000. The proceeds were about $300,000 after repairs to the burned structure, Gordon's commission and other expenses.

The potential buyers, a young couple from out of town, wanted to build on the same street where their friends lived. However, they understood the circumstances and were willing to scale down their new home if they couldn't get the two lots that made up the Rankins' property.

"Like I told Leslie, there's plenty left over to cover your medical bills either way," Gordon said as though we were co-conspirators in the real estate deal. I wished he'd shut up about me.

"You two need some time to decide?" he asked Deb and Scooter.

"Whatever you fuckin' want," Scooter said, glaring at Deb.

"But we can keep the house, Sugar. You'd like that wouldn't you?" she said. She patted him gently on the part of his arm that wasn't bandaged.

"Won't be the same," he said half under his breath. He stood up slowly and walked over to the window. His back was to us, but I could see his fists go to his eyes. His shoulders shook. There was no sound.

Deb stared at him. It was only a minute or two but felt like hours.

"We thank you, Gordie and Leslie." Her face was pale, but her voice determined. "Scooter and me aren't interested. We'll wait for another miracle. Doesn't seem this is what the Lord intended for us."

I was surprised by their stubbornness. But when I turned to see Gordon's reaction, the dollar signs in his eyes had vanished and rage had taken their place.

CHAPTER 31

The intimacy we'd shared gave me a small sense of ownership in Frank's well-being. It had been almost four days since I last saw him. When I didn't hear from him by lunchtime on Thursday, I was feeling a little frantic.

I hesitated, then dialed his cell phone. The recorded answer said to leave a message. "Frank, it's Leslie. Please call when you get this."

Deb and Scooter had gone to the doctor. There were so many *honeys* and *sugars* floating around the condo on Tuesday, I was glad to be moving in with Mother. Theirs was a bleak and uncertain future, but they didn't seem worried. I wanted to talk to them about social media funding, but my enthusiasm had waned. If they didn't care, why should I? And Scooter was such a crab, why start talking about charity?

When the clock on the kitchen microwave switched to 1:30 and there was still no word from Frank, I grabbed my purse and headed for the car.

Harry Fleck was not in the sheriff's office when I walked in. Instead, Deputy Webster was sitting at Fleck's desk, smoking a cigarette and reading a magazine with a deer head on the cover. I wasn't a hunting fan but not surprised to see that the deputy was. Hunting was embraced in Florida as a sport and source of food. As a person who couldn't even bear to kill a spider in the condo, I tried not to judge.

Despite the ill-will that existed between us, I hoped the deputy would be a willing participant in the search for the man who once saved his life.

"Mrs. Elliott. Another body wash up in yer neighborhood?" His voice was dripping with sarcasm.

"It's Frank. Frank Johnson. He's gone. Missing." Tears tumbled out of control, down my cheeks. A sob escaped my lips. I didn't want to fall apart in front of my nemesis, but I didn't seem to have a choice.

What happened next was uncharacteristic and fast. Deputy Webster snuffed out his cigarette and was up and helping me into a chair in a matter of seconds. He grabbed a wad of tissues and put them on my lap. He patted me on the back.

"Frank Johnson? Missing? When was the last time ya saw him?" His display of genuine concern was quite different from his usual detached manner.

"Sunday night. We had dinner together."

"Knowing Frank, that's not so long. He's disappeared before, tellin' me he likes to hop on his motorcycle and feel the power of the engine between his legs, carrying him off to where life doesn't weigh so heavy on him."

The deputy looked at me as if trying to convey a message. I got it that the fisherman liked his privacy, but I didn't find his assessment of Frank's loner ways comforting.

"We're close, Bruce. I left him messages. He wouldn't, he wouldn't ignore me."

"Did ya speak with his mother?"

"On Monday. She didn't know where he was. Hadn't seen or heard from him either."

The deputy checked his watch and looked at a sheet on the sheriff's desk. "I'm off in 45 minutes. If ya can wait, we'll look for him together."

"You'd do that? Look for him on your time off?"

"That's my job, and Frank's my friend. Now ya go get yourself some coffee 'round the corner. I'll be by in a bit."

I nodded, took another tissue from the box on the sheriff's desk and left the office, marveling at the side of Bruce Webster I'd never seen before. Another changeable character on this island. Why didn't they just stand still and be one way or the other? Or why didn't I give them more leeway before jumping to conclusions? Maybe it was me, not them.

When he picked me up outside the grocery the deputy was wearing pressed khaki shorts, a shirt sporting maritime symbols and maps and brown leather sandals that looked new. He was clean shaven and smelled of lime.

In his own independent "Cracker" way and, despite the seasoning of his face, Bruce Webster was not a bad-looking man.

"I've known Frank Johnson since he came here. May have some ideas about where he is," he said as we climbed into the car marked *Sheriff.*

We headed south and turned onto a dirt road, stopping at a cottage that was similar to Deb's but even more rustic. The deputy hopped out and knocked at the door. A woman emerged, in her early 40s, with long black hair braided in the back.

She was beautiful in an earthy sort of way. She looked to be Native American. The afternoon sun illuminated a slender figure through her loose-fitting dress. I wondered if she was close to Frank.

"Just a minute," I heard her say. "Gator! Come talk to Deputy Bruce."

Gator? Frank's first mate? I laughed with relief. This was Gator's house and the woman must be the teenager's mother. Gator will know where Frank is, I thought. I opened the car door and headed for the others.

"Do you remember me?" I said when Gator joined his mother.

"Yes, ma'am." He lowered his head. "I sure do. This is my mother, Jewel."

"Your Gator's a hero," I said turning to the woman. "He cleaned up after me several times after I got sick fishing. It was rough that day."

"All part of the job, ma'am," Gator said, flashing a shy grin in my direction.

"Son, have ya seen Frank lately?" the deputy asked.

"Yeah, last week. Can't remember what day. Said he wouldn't need me until later this week. Gave me $100." He reached into his pocket and pulled out a bill folded into a small square.

"Gator. Why didn't you tell me about that? That's for your school fund," Jewel said, reaching for the money.

The boy drew back. "Frank said it was jus' between us, Mom. For me to take my girlfriend to the movie, if we can figure out a way to get there."

"Like ya have a license to drive," the deputy said, narrowing his eyes at the youngster as he'd done several times with me.

"Who was he fishing with?" I asked.

"Maybe the guys, the ones that speak Spanish. He doesn't take me when he's with them."

My mind flashed back to that night on the beach with Frank and the men who warned him about "loose ends." My thoughts moved on to the house at Oceanview Drive and the episode with the locked door. I replayed Frank's confession that he took the body from the dinghy, the body he identified as one of the men who had no friends.

If Frank was with those men, the worst was a possibility. My heart climbed into my throat.

"Let me know if ya hear anythin' or if Frank contacts ya," the deputy said, looking at me. Was he reading my mind? "We have some other places to check."

Jewel placed her hand on her chest. "Oh Bruce. He has to be okay. We count on him in so many ways."

"We'll find him," the deputy said, giving her a pat on the shoulder and a kiss on the cheek.

Our next stop was the building Frank used as a storage unit. The deputy looked through the small windows, saw "nothin' here" and moved onto the dock where Dreamcatcher was moored.

There was no outward evidence of foul play aboard the fishing boat. Still, the deputy boarded it and gave it the once-over.

"I'll try to think positive, that he's on his motorcycle somewhere," I said when Bruce Webster gave me a look that said the boat was a dead end.

Whalen the dog rounded the corner of our next stop and greeted us by jumping up and putting his paws on the passenger side of the sheriff's vehicle.

"Down boy. Down. Don't scratch the car," I said. He backed off, his tail wagging and his tongue hanging half out of his mouth.

Frank's cottage looked better than I imagined it would. It was small but well-maintained, with coconut and foxtail palms lining the brick path to the front door. Flowering bushes hugged the house, displaying reds, pinks and yellows against the cream-colored cottage with brown shutters.

Georgia Johnson was outside washing the windows. When we pulled up, she looked over her shoulder but continued cleaning.

"Mrs. Johnson. I'm here to ask ya some questions about yer boy, Frank." As the deputy walked toward her, Whalen bounced alongside him, licking his hand.

"He's not here," she said. She pushed a few black hairs back from her face, dabbing at her forehead with the same cloth she was using to clean the windows.

"When was the last time ya saw him?"

"Saturday, no, Sunday. He gave me some money, like he always does on Sunday."

"Is Stevie here?"

"In school. He won't know anything. No point in asking him."

The deputy handed her his card. "If Frank comes back, let me know or have him call me."

She said nothing but nodded and turned her back to us.

As we pulled away, I noticed Frank's motorcycle parked by the side of the house. I pointed and told Bruce. He just nodded. Apparently, he'd seen it, too.

"We've got one more stop. It's a long shot but maybe we'll get some answers," the deputy said. He looked in the mirror, smoothed back his hair and pulled a mint out of his pocket.

The one more stop was a pale pink residence off-island, maybe two bedrooms, with a smaller wooden structure in back. A painting of a seductive-looking mermaid was sprawled across the area over the one-car garage. In the yard were wind catchers and colorful statues of frogs and jumping dolphins.

"Stay in the car," the deputy said, not unkindly.

He pushed the doorbell several times, then opened the door and walked in. I could hear his voice, as if he was calling someone. Through the picture windows that gave me a clear view to the back of the house, I watched him go outside and head for the building in the backyard.

She met him halfway, throwing her arms around him. He put his hands on her buttocks and pulled her close. They lingered over a kiss. When they separated, she reached up and smoothed his hair behind his ears. So, that was why he got cleaned up and put on a fresh shirt. Not for me.

Janis Johnson and Deputy Bruce Webster. My mouth stayed open as I watched them talk and stroke each other's arms. *Was there no man on-island she wasn't connected with?* At one point, Janis' body stiffened, and the look of defiance returned to her face. I assumed they were discussing Frank. Or me.

Not long ago. she was threatening me to stay away from her husband. Today, it appeared she'd staked her territory on another man. And what about the heated discussion Mother had witnessed between Janis and Gordon Fike in the grocery store parking lot? The lady with the pompadour was complex.

The deputy pulled a cigarette from his pocket, lit it and handed it to her. She took several drags. He checked his watch, said something, and she nodded. When she started to return to the building, he reached out and smacked her bottom. She laughed. I'd never seen Janis laugh.

"Frank's wife lives here," the deputy said when he returned to the car. "Said she hadn't seen or talked to him since Friday night. Guess they had dinner at the Tarpon Bar."

"I saw them there," I said. "I was with Peter Thompson, the man whose body keeps washing up on shore and then coming back to life again."

The deputy looked at me for a few seconds and then returned my remark with a grin that exposed that one missing tooth.

"We're done for today. I gotta think about this some more. Don't ya worry. He'll turn up," he said as he dropped me off at my car.

Alive, I thought. *Please let him turn up alive. Not another body on the beach.*

CHAPTER 32

" I need (crackle) do something (crackle) tomorrow." The voice on the phone
was barely audible and broken at intervals.

"Frank! Where are you?" Was it possible to feel relief and anxiety at the
same time?

"The key (crackle) from Scooter (crackle). Instructions with (crackle)…Gat…."
The phone went dead.

"What key? Where?" I asked the emptiness.

I was relieved to hear his voice but scared for him at the same time.

"You need somethin', honey?" Deb's voice came from the lanai where I'd found
her and Scooter watching the sunset after my day with Deputy Webster.

"That was Frank," I said, walking in their direction. "Thank God, he's alive.
But that's all I know. The cell connection was terrible."

"Glad to hear he's okay," Deb said as though I'd just announced the time.
Scooter grunted.

The breezes from the Gulf stirred up the waters of the North Pass, bringing
a chill into the lanai. Across the way, the lights on the docks danced in the waves.
There was the faint outline of clouds, but they were barely visible on a moon-
less night.

Deb asked no questions. I had no answers, but I wondered why she wasn't
curious about Frank's disappearance. I wasn't considered a real island resident yet.
Maybe that's why I didn't always understand their tribal ways.

"I'm gonna get my sweater," Deb said getting up from her chair. "Scooter,
sugar, you need anything?"

He shook his head.

"What's going on? Do you know something I don't? Frank said something
about a key, Scooter. Do you know where he is?"

"Nope. Knowed he was alive," Scooter said as he took another sip of beer.

I didn't say anything for several minutes, trying to keep my anger from building. When I finally spoke, my tone was biting. "Why didn't you tell me? I was worried sick and you...."

"Frank goes away." It was Deb speaking behind me. I turned around. "Sometimes days, sometimes weeks. Doing man's business. That's why he needs Georgia to take care of Stevie. It's his nature, honey." Deb had on her fleecy cardigan sweater with a fringe collar and was carrying a small object that she handed to me.

"The key you were askin' about. We've had it for a couple of months. Kept it in Scooter's billfold for safekeeping. Guess Frank wants you to have it now."

"What's this for? Is there anything else?"

Unidentified keys in the back of my desk drawers always drove me crazy. You didn't want them but you couldn't pitch them. Now here was another one. I wasn't getting any help from my friends as to its importance. Frustration was setting in.

"Frank said to use it if anythin', uh, funny happened or one of us heard from him about it. That's all."

"How can we use it if we don't know what it opens? And how'd you know he was alive, Scooter?"

"Felt it in my bones."

"That makes everything all right then, does it? You and your all-knowing bones."

Scooter gave me a strange look but said nothing. He and Deb had chided me on many occasions for being suspicious and nosy about the yellow house and its owner. Now they were participants in their own intrigue and were okay with that.

The group fell silent again. Sometimes, like tonight, Deb and Scooter got under my skin. I needed to quit talking about it and move into Mother's condo to protect what was left of the strained relationship between the Rankins and me.

"Paper," Scooter muttered out of nowhere.

"What? Oh yeah, honey, the piece of paper. When Frank gave us the key there was a piece of paper that went with. Instructions, I think. I'm not sure what happened to it."

"Burned up."

"Oh, it was in our bedroom and was destroyed in the fire?" Deb said, translating for her husband.

He nodded. "Hope it wasn't important," Deb said, turning to me. "But, knowing you, honey, you'll figure it out."

Great. Now I'm the Amazing Kreskin, the mentalist who can hold items in his hands and glean information from them about their owner.

I held the small key, turning it over and looking for an indication of what it might open. Frank had said Gator's name or at least it sounded like he said it. Maybe Gator knew the answer. But why would Frank entrust a kid with something that must be important?

Perhaps it had something to do with Dreamcatcher. I was determined to find out, but I had to wait until tomorrow. This time I was following Frank's instructions.

Gator's mom was eager for her son to be helpful when I called early the next day. The boy was still asleep, she said, but he'd skip school and meet me at Frank's boat.

On the way, I stopped by the fisherman's house. I was glad to see that Georgia and Stevie were gone. Whalen's bark greeted me from the backyard where he was tied to a Foxtail Palm. When he spotted me, he jumped about, knocking over his water and food dishes.

"Settle down, Whalen, er, Buddy. Whatever they're calling you these days."

Whalen didn't care about his name or who I was. He wanted freedom.

"You're coming with me. I may need your help," I said, pulling out a dog leash I'd picked up at the convenience store.

Maybe Georgia wouldn't object if the dog was missing, but Stevie would be distraught. Wherever the key quest took us, I'd better be back before school was out. Just in case, I scribbled a note and laid it on the dirt sticking out from under the dog dish.

The dog and I took off for Frank's' boat, with me driving and Whalen hanging his head out the window, the wind baring his teeth. Gator was waiting for us, his young face reflecting my concerns. When we got onboard, I held up the key.

"Frank asked me to get this from Scooter. Do you have any idea what it opens and why we need to take the boat?"

The youngster looked at me as if eager to be helpful. "Frank said if anyone asked me about a key, I was to take them to the island. That's all he said. Is that enough?"

"To the island? The one about 20 minutes from here?"

He nodded. "My mom said he's alive. That's right isn't it? I don't want nothin' to happen to him."

"He'll be fine, just fine." Was I reassuring the boy or myself? Gator cast off and headed toward the open water with me holding onto the dog and trying to keep my stomach in line.

The South Pass was unusually still, with streams of pale green running through the dark blue water. I watched the other boats skim past us. Most were fishermen looking for hot spots to help clients pull in the big ones. Frank should be out there, among them. Not gone. Not part of the mysteries I was working so hard to uncover. Or manufacture – I still wasn't sure which.

When Gator piloted us toward a beach with a mass of palm trees and a large pole sticking out of the water, I thought the area looked familiar. I couldn't be sure. The only time I'd seen it was in the moonlight.

"I'll anchor here," the youngster said, tossing the rope ladder into the water. He was over the side in no time, along with Whalen who leapt off the craft like a cliff diver. It took me a little longer to climb down.

"Should we put him back on the leash?" Gator asked, glancing at the dog who'd quickly paddled ashore.

"Let him run. Let's see if he finds anything."

As if on command, Whalen took off, vanishing into the underbrush.

The two of us followed the dog's path and within a few minutes arrived at Frank's fishing shack. The dark green structure, which looked sturdy enough to withstand strong winds, rested on pilings two feet off the ground. I reached for the key in my pocket and slipped it into the padlock. It clicked open, allowing us to step inside.

That was too easy.

"You been here before?" I asked Gator.

"Once. Last year. I spent the weekend with Stevie and Frank. It was my 16th birthday. Frank let me drink beer." The teenager blushed.

Everything looked in order. There were boxes stacked in one corner, rolled up blankets and pillows in another. Fishing poles were propped up against a bare wall. A fisherman could survive on the island indefinitely.

"It doesn't feel as though anyone's been here the last day or so," I said. "Let's check outside."

A rustling in the nearby underbrush was followed by the appearance of the dog. The pristine animal we'd released into the water 20 minutes earlier was no more. His muzzle and front paws were black with dirt and sand.

In his mouth he carried a bone about 18 inches long. The stench coming from his direction matched the skunk-like odor in the house on Oceanview Drive the day the vultures arrived for breakfast.

"Geez. Where'd he find that?" Gator said. His eyes widened to the size of silver dollars.

A chill worked its way up my spine to the back of my neck. "Looks like a radius or ulna, a bone from someone's arm," I said, remembering my high school anatomy class as we walked toward the dog. "Give it to me, boy. Come on."

Whalen's tail wagged as he tracked my movements. When I was almost close enough to grab the bone, the dog took off running. He stopped 20 feet from me, his body shaking with delight at the pursuit.

"We are not playing a game here, dog," I said.

"Don't think you'll catch him until he wants you to, ma'am."

"I'm sure you're right. Let's see if we can figure out where Whalen found that thing."

The dog pranced alongside us as if he was the one in the know. Within a few minutes it was obvious which direction we should travel; the smell made for easy tracking.

The shallow grave was 100 yards or so from Frank's fishing shack. The exposed body was loosely wrapped in plastic with the right arm missing and part of the left gone. Whalen was a thorough grave digger.

Gator's face turned white. "Holy shit. Oh, sorry ma'am. It's not…."

"Frank? No, no. That body's been around for some time." I put my hand on the teenager's shoulder. "You okay?"

He nodded, but I could tell he wasn't.

"Frank told me about this. Said he found it in a boat on the beach. Guess he brought it here for safekeeping until he could notify the drug enforcement police," I said.

I lied to protect Gator's innocence and Frank's guilt. It was obvious Frank didn't tell me the truth about handing the corpse over to his DEA friends. I didn't have time for anger. That would have to wait.

"We can't tell anyone about this, Gator. Frank wouldn't want us to. He knows what he's doing. You understand? Not your mother or the sheriff or the deputy. Not your buddies at school."

He shook his head. "You want me to, to cover this up again. I mean, Frank buried it so maybe he wouldn't like it being uncovered."

Gator reached into his back pocket, pulled out a red bandana and tied it in back so that it covered his nose and mouth.

"Good idea. I saw a shovel in the shack. You're sure you can handle it?"

He nodded, and we backtracked. Whalen trailed along, carrying the bone like he'd won first prize in a sporting trial.

"Phew dog. We have to get the bone away from you and back in the ground," I said as I opened the door to Frank's shack once more. "And you'll need a long swim before we get back on the boat."

After Gator left with the shovel and the dog trailing along, I surveyed the inside of the small building. It was 12 by 12. With the boxes rearranged, three people in sleeping bags could fit in there.

"Damn you, Frank. I'm no detective. I need some help here," I said aloud. Maybe this was his idea of a joke. *She thinks she's so smart, let's see if she can find what I've hidden.*

Starting in one corner, I worked my way through the contents of every box, unrolled every blanket and felt my way through each of the pillows. Nothing.

The wooden floor didn't appear to be hiding a separate compartment. Still, I got down on my hands and knees and examined every board. Nothing loose; no new nails. The walls and a frame around the small window in back offered no clues. There was nothing on the ceiling except for unpainted bead board.

What am I missing? It has to be here, whatever it is. If not, why would Frank tell me to get the key from Scooter? And why would he instruct Gator to bring anyone with a key to this island?

I stood back by the door to get a panoramic view of the room. The only thing I hadn't examined were the three photos on the wall. The first was of Stevie when he was about 3 with a little potbelly, a mop of dark hair and a quizzical look on his face. The next photo was of Frank, with longer hair and a large tarpon. The third photo was of a much younger Georgia Johnson and an unsmiling child that I assumed was Frank as a boy.

Georgia must have been in her thirties, with the same dimple in her chin that she'd passed onto her son. Frank could have been 10 or so when the photo was taken.

A photo of Janis with her long blond hair and ripped abs would not have been a surprise – the Janis that Frank and maybe Gordon fell in love with before rebellion claimed her. But Frank's mother, Georgia? Why would his hideaway include a picture of the woman whose bossy ways drove him to visit Scooter and Deb several times a week?

I removed the photo from the wall and turned it over. Nothing obvious. No note with further instructions pasted on the back. But the cardboard backing did seem thicker in the middle. I remembered seeing a screwdriver in Frank's tackle box. I grabbed it and pried the metal staples off the frame, releasing the cardboard. A piece of white paper fell to the floor. A small key was attached, along with a number: 104.

I'd seen those three numbers before.

CHAPTER 33

"Don't tell anyone what you saw on that island," I warned Gator for the second time as we prepared to depart the Dreamcatcher with a much cleaner version of Whalen in tow.

The dog had given up the bone in exchange for canned meat I found among Frank's stash. The cabin also contained a bar of soap, which Gator and I used to scrub Whalen in the Gulf waters. He was not happy about it but withstood the process with some attempt at doggy dignity.

Back at Frank's dock, I watched Gator tie the boat to the dock and noticed that he seemed different. Quieter maybe? Why wouldn't he be affected by what he'd witnessed? I was sorry to have played a part in this apparent loss of innocence. *It comes to all of us at some point: that recognition that evil exists and can touch our lives.*

I thanked him and said I'd let him know when I heard from Frank. "And don't worry. Everything will be okay." I seemed to be saying that a lot these days even though nothing was okay, not really.

When I arrived at Frank's cottage, I was relieved to see that Georgia's car was still gone. I could return the dog, and no one would be the wiser.

"Guess it's back to captivity for you," I said. Whalen looked at me with sad brown eyes. I filled his dish with water, scratched behind his ears, gave him a pat on the rump, grabbed my note and headed back to my vehicle.

The key in the front seat of my car was smaller than the brass ones with the rounded head used to open boxes in the island's post office. It was slightly larger than the one to the padlock on Frank's shack.

I parked in front of the island bank. After what I remembered seeing in the local paper I'd picked up at the yellow house – the numbers 104 scribbled near the bank ad – it was an obvious first stop.

Norma, an attractive middle-aged woman with a deep tan, was my go-to teller. She was well-organized, sweet and always interested in whatever story I had to share.

"Hey there, Leslie. You been out on a boat this morning? Your hair's all, uh, messed up."

"Been exploring the mysteries of the sea." I ran my fingers through my hair. "Better?"

"Um," she responded. "What can I do for you?"

I reached into my pocket and pulled out the key and the piece of paper with the number on it. It might have been more persuasive if Frank had written 104 on a bank deposit slip and signed his name. The number and my bravado were all I had.

"This is Frank Johnson's key to his safe deposit box," I said as I scooted it toward Norma.

"You two seeing each other?" she said, casually.

"We've gone out a couple of times."

"He's a nice guy. Good looking, too. Let me look that up for you," she said, leaving me for a minute and then returning. "That's Frank Johnson's box all right. You have the right number and everything, but, uh, your signature's not on the card. Just Frank's."

"What does that mean?"

"I can't let you open the box."

"But he gave me the key and the number. He's out of town and needs something from the box. I said I'd get it for him. I, um, don't want to let him down."

Norma nodded as if understanding my dilemma. "Let me talk to the manager."

I was proud of myself for figuring out that the key fit a safety deposit box even as I recognized it wouldn't take a genius to reach that conclusion. But in my moment of triumph, Norma and her boss were potential roadblocks.

Rita, the black bank manager, emerged from her office and headed my way. She had a serious look on her young face. She offered an efficient hello, while giving me the once-over. We didn't know each other well.

"This is your lucky day, Friday, the 13th," Rita said, barely cracking a smile. "I have a note from Frank Johnson in my files, which says that if anyone comes in with the key and that number, I'm to give that person this letter."

"A letter? Not the box?"

"I'm not sure how you got the key, but I'm going to respect Frank's wishes, as I told him I would. But I can't let you open the box. Sorry. Rules are rules."

"You all know me. I have the key and the number. What if Frank was dead? What would happen then?"

"The executor of his estate would be in charge. If he didn't have his key, we'd have a locksmith present and would open and examine its contents then," Rita said.

"Oh. I see. When did he give this letter to you?"

"Couple of weeks ago. Guess he had this planned and knew you'd be coming in. Like a scavenger hunt and this is your next clue," she said.

"I'm pretty sure this isn't some kind of game." I took the letter from Rita, thanked her and Norma and left the bank. Outside, I sat down on the bench beside the bank entry and opened the envelope. I wasn't sure how to feel about anything, especially Frank.

If I'm missing for more than a month or found dead, take this letter and the key to Michael Land, attorney in Venice, Florida. He will know what to do with it.

ᘒᘒ◯ᘒᘒ

"Michael R. Land, attorney at law," the person on the other end of the phone was barely audible. Another scratchy connection.

"You said this is Mr. Land's office?" I wondered if my hearing was starting to go, and I wasn't even 50. Too many rock concerts at a young age.

"Yes. How can I help you?"

"Uh, what?"

"HOW CAN I HELP YOU?"

"Oh, sorry. We have a bad connection. I'd like to make an appointment to see Mr. Land. It's about a letter...."

"You want him to write a letter for you?"

"What?"

"YOU WANT HIM TO WRITE A LETTER?"

"Sorry. I need an appointment."

"HE CAN SEE YOU 2:30 MONDAY AFTERNOON."

"That works." I gave her my name, spelling it slowly, and my cell number.

I'd arrived at my condo and gone immediately to the front balcony to make the phone call to the attorney and grab some clothes to take to mother's. When I finished, I went back inside, wondering where Deb and Scooter were.

The wind was blowing in from the west, carrying with it the smell of decomposing fish, cigarette smoke and the sound of my houseguests' voices. I reached inside the kitchen cabinet and pulled out a lavender room scent, sticking it in the wall socket to mask some of the foul odors filling my condo.

I could hear Deb and Scooter's voices from below my lanai. I ventured out to the porch and saw them sitting on beach chairs near the seawall. I decided against joining them. I needed time to process the dead body and the key findings.

I started to leave when I heard Scooter say: "Told Frank. The key. Wasn't tryin' to snub us. She'd know what to do. Didn't want to burden us."

"Now, Scooter. It's not that he doesn't trust us. He figures she's smarter than we are, and he's right. You know that," Deb said.

Scooter grunted but made no further comment. It was nice to hear Deb stick up for me.

"Did he say when he'd be back?" Deb responded.

"Coupla days. South America. Don't want anyone knowin', 'specially Leslie. She's got that, you know, 'magination. Would worry. Anyone who knows Frank figures he's off agin, like he does now and then."

"Did you tell Deputy Bruce like Frank said to?" Deb asked.

"Yeah. Fishin' trip."

"What about Gator? Didn't the boy go with Leslie this morning. Somethin' to do with the key?"

"Called Jewel. Gator didn't say nothin' about the trip. Jus' something about the dog."

"You wanna 'nother beer, Sugar?" I could hear Deb's chair creak. "I'll get a blanket. Then we outta think about dinner. Speakin' of missin', wonder where Leslie is, and if she discovered anythin' interestin'?"

I turned and headed for the front door, grabbing my purse. A Cracker conspiracy. Don't tell Leslie anything. She'll figure it out on her own. Let her worry while we go on keeping secrets and living our mundane lives.

I walked to Mother's condo. I wanted them gone. All of them out of my condo and out of my life. Deb, Scooter, Frank. Why did he call Scooter and not me? Why didn't he tell me he'd be home in a couple of days?

Maybe there was a good reason, I thought as my mind went back to the scrub island and the dead body. Was I being used to cover up a murder?

I wiped away angry tears as I climbed the steps to Mother's condo. I rapped on the door, pushing it open before Mother could answer.

She was watching Fox News and drinking a glass of wine.

"Oh my," she said as she turned to look at me. "You look like something the cat dragged in. What's wrong, dear?"

"Everything. I'm moving in with you."

Once I was sure Scooter and Deb had gone to bed, I returned to my condo, picked up the few clothes I needed, my make-up and toothbrush. I scribbled a note saying I was staying with Mother for the interim and would be in touch later. I put it by the coffee pot. Deb consumed about six cups a day, so I was confident she'd see it first thing.

The grudge I was starting to harbor against the two people I cared about and had taken in during their time of need would go away in time. Today I was nursing a feeling of betrayal. Maybe they were trying to protect me, but it felt like they'd closed me out of their secret circle.

I wasn't sure I'd be so quick to forgive the man who said I should trust him, the man to whom I'd given part of my heart. He'd sounded urgent on the call to me. But maybe he expected me to hold onto the key until I'd heard something definitive from him. If he knew he was coming back, why didn't he let Scooter keep the key and retrieve it when he returned?

The unanswered questions made my head spin and my heart heavy.

CHAPTER 34

The sign on the door of Michael Land's law office said to knock before entering. I did as instructed and waited for what seemed like an interminable length of time. A gray-haired lady, who looked to be in her early 80s, opened the door and yelled at me: "TAKE A SEAT, MR. LAND WILL BE WITH YOU SHORTLY."

I chuckled to myself once the door closed. She of the shaky voice had answered the phone when I called to make my appointment and assumed I was hard of hearing because of our bad connection. Once she noted it on the calendar, she was trying to accommodate my impairment.

"Shortly" turned out to be a 30-minute wait in a tiny area with three orange chairs and a matching couch, circa 2000, a few magazines touting the advantages of living in south Florida and no current news. I checked my cell phone, caught up on messages and was starting to get restless when a man I presumed to be Michael Land opened the door.

"Yes, thanks, Mother," he said over his shoulder. "Ms. Elliott? I'm Michael Land. Please come on in."

He was a slender man, balding, scars from teenage acne on his face. If his mother was in her 80s, Land appeared to be in his 50s, maybe even late 40s. Perhaps he was a late-in-life child who still relied on his mother's help.

What did my father use to say? *You take care of your children from the day they're born until the day you die.* I wasn't sure about my generation, but the millennials seemed to be taking that concept to a new level, at least in southwest Florida.

There were two rooms in the law office space. Grace Land, whose name was on a plaque on her desk, shared her area with a copy machine, a printer, several bookcases and a couple of filing cabinets. Her son's office was larger, with more bookcases and better appointments. A big mahogany desk sat atop a thick oriental rug of reds and blues. The navy upholstered chairs with mahogany arms and legs were much nicer than the ones Gordon had in his real estate office.

On the bookcase behind Land's desk were several photos of himself with celebrities, including the governor, a state senator, a TV personality I knew from the local news, and golfer Tiger Woods.

I had spent all day Saturday and Sunday thinking about the questions I might have for this man who Frank Johnson had hired as his lawyer. I wondered how much he'd tell me. Attorney/client privilege were words I heard and typed often when I worked for Metro Energy. Would he invoke that sanctity and answer my questions with silence?

"Nice to meet you," he said. "Are you able to hear me all right? I can speak louder if not."

"When your mother and I talked on the phone we had a bad connection, which is why she thinks I have hearing issues."

"Oh," he said and smiled. "It's so common down here because of so many retirees that she's used to it. My mother's a good soul. She wants to keep busy even though she just turned 80. Nobody does a better job for me. We have a partnership of sorts."

"That's very nice for both of you," I said, wondering how Mother and I would fare working together.

"What can I do for you?" Land said, leaning back in his leather chair and putting his fingertips together in a contemplative pose.

I reached inside my purse, fished out the key with the piece of paper and placed it on the desk. My plan was to be honest without telling the attorney about the body on the island. I was invoking my own privileges.

"Frank Johnson called and told me to get a key from his friend Scooter Rankin. It was Thursday that this happened. There was no indication what the key unlocked, only a note that said *Gator*. He's the teenager that works as Frank's first mate."

"Yes, I've met Gator a couple of times when he was with Frank," the lawyer said.

"Okay. Well, he and I went to the island where Frank has a shack. The key unlocked the padlock on the door. After going through the things he has stored there, I found this second key attached to a note card with these numbers. It was hidden in the backing of a picture frame."

No comment from Land.

"I took it to the bank, figuring it might be the key to a safety deposit box. They said it was, um, Frank's. But they wouldn't let me open it because my name was not on the signature card."

The lawyer nodded as if to indicate he was hearing what I was saying. I continued.

"Instead, they gave me this letter, which they said Frank gave to them about a week ago." I reached in my purse and pulled it out, handing it to the attorney. "You can see what it says. That's how I ended up here."

While he glanced down at it, I went on. "I don't know what you are allowed to tell me...." My voice trailed off as I studied Land's expressionless face.

"What information would you like from me?" he said.

That was a good start. I took a deep breath. "Everything. Everything you know about Frank and this key and the security deposit box. I mean, as much as you can tell me."

"I'm prepared to be honest with you. Frank gave his permission, as my client, to answer any questions the bearer of the letter might have. Would you like a glass of water or coffee, first?"

"Water would be fine. Thanks."

Land got up, opened the door to a small refrigerator in the back of his office then placed a plastic bottle of water in front of me on a coaster. I took a drink, then another deep breath.

"What's in the box?"

"According to Frank, there are keys to four other safety deposit boxes, along with two envelopes. The first envelope contains his will. The second contains a list of his wishes, separate from the will, regarding how he wants his possessions distributed; the house, the boat and what to do with the money. I have copies of both in the event of his death.

"For all practical purposes, he's not a wealthy man. His business barely makes enough to support his family, keep up the boat and provide some financial assistance to Gator and his mother. But he does have resources."

"He supports them? Gator and his mother? Is that because, uh, Gator is his child, his natural son?" I could feel a lump growing in my throat.

A bemused smile crossed Land's face. "Why would you think that? Frank has never claimed paternity and, knowing him as I do, I think he would. Apparently, he feels a responsibility for the two of them. I don't know why."

"Can we go back to the money? I mean, do you know how much Frank has in the safety deposit box? And is there more in the others?"

"I can't say for sure, but he told me he has in excess of $3 million dollars stashed in all four."

"Three million?" Despite my best efforts to remain calm, the news sent my insides into a tailspin.

"You said he wasn't a wealthy man. Is he a bank robber?" I laughed and noticed it sounded hollow.

"I thought you knew." His voice was matter of fact, as though I'd inquired about the time. "He's involved with drugs."

The Spanish-speaking men on the boat. Were they his contacts? The men with no friends. Murderers. And Frank was part of that?

My mind was hearing but refusing to process Land's words. I couldn't believe Frank was involved with drugs. He didn't live in a big house or have fancy boats or cars. He was a father. He must know what drugs can do to kids. How they can destroy people's lives.

My emotions were like a roller coaster. How could this man I cared about be nothing more than a low-life scum who dealt in death and destruction? I felt cheapened by our intimacy.

"Why?" When I responded to his drug comment I sounded like Land's mother. My voice was soft and shaky.

"I'm sure Frank has reasons for what he's doing."

"What am I supposed to do with the key and this, uh, information?"

"You can't do anything but be aware of it. If something happens to Frank, he dies or goes missing for a prolonged period of time, then you come to me. There are procedures in place for opening the boxes and distributing the contents, per his instructions."

"But when the boxes are opened, the bank people will know, I mean, they'll figure out there's something wrong when they see all that money," I said.

"They will only know the contents if the box goes unclaimed and they have to call in a notary public and a locksmith."

"And when did Frank tell you about himself, about the drugs?"

"The first revelation about his drug involvement was several months ago. A week, ten days ago he called and said you might be the one coming to my office. He said if something happened to him, he could count on you to handle the aftermath."

"He expects me to be complacent in his illegal activities? He must not think too highly of me," I said, feeling the fury inside me growing.

"On the contrary, he said you're an amazing woman."

"I guess he doesn't know me very well." I stood up and extended my hand. "Your honesty was painful but appreciated. Thank you, Mr. Land."

"Call me if you need any help," he said.

When the door to Michael Land's office closed behind me, I felt I was experiencing another dream like the one with Peter Thompson and the zombies. But based on what the attorney had just told me, it was the fisherman who had become my worst nightmare.

CHAPTER 35

Peter Thompson's phone message was brief and entreating. "Love to take you to lunch today, tomorrow or any day that works for you, Leslie. Call me. Um, this is Peter."

If Frank was a drug dealer, what was Peter Thompson?

The information I'd just gotten from Frank's attorney made me even more determined to uncover Peter's secrets. It was obvious that night at the Tarpon Bar that Frank and Peter were not friends. I guess drug dealers didn't have to be chummy to conduct business together.

"Peter! Sorry I didn't answer your call. I was in a meeting with an attorney. So nice of you to invite me. How about tomorrow?" I tried to hide my wariness with false enthusiasm.

"Terrific. How'd you like to have lunch in Key West?" he said.

"Key West? Isn't that a bit of a drive? About eight hours?"

"Try flying. We'll be there in an hour."

"Oh, yes, I forgot you have a plane."

I swallowed hard. My fear of flying could be tolerated on those rare occasions when the stakes were high enough. In this case, they were. Still, getting into a plane, no matter what size, was not on my list of favorite things to do.

"I should warn you. I'm prone to motion sickness."

"No problem. I've got something that will make you feel right as rain during the flight," he said, laughing.

"Peter, I'm not into drugs or anything like that."

"This is a little something that takes the edge off, eh. It's harmless. Trust me."

If I thought Peter was a criminal, why would I trust him? I didn't, but I was willing to take him at his word that this was going to be a short flight to Key West for lunch and an opportunity to ask more questions at some point during the day.

"OK. Sure. When?"

"Tomorrow. Like you said. The sooner the better. By the time we return, you'll love flying. And maybe you'll decide I'm not such a bad guy after all."

"I'm sure that's the case." *I wasn't sure at all.*

ꙅꙅ)Cꙅꙅ

Calm. That's how I was feeling as I contemplated putting my life in Peter's hands. I carried pepper spray in my purse, a habit I'd picked up when I was working late for Metro Energy and had to walk to the parking lot several blocks away in the dark.

After the incident at the yellow house, I'd also ordered something more potent – a pepper spray gun. It was a vicious-looking instrument that fired pellets containing tear gas and ingredients designed to dissuade the most persistent attacker. It looked like a real revolver. I wasn't sure I could use it except in the direst of circumstances. Still, it was comforting to have it nearby at night.

Peter wouldn't try anything while we were flying. If we were going to Key West as he said, we'd be surrounded by people. If he had something unseemly in mind, there was always the purse spray.

Before departing, I decided to have a little chat with my reporter friend Wes Avery.

When I arrived at the newspaper office, I discovered he'd gone for coffee at the nearby market. Newspaper folks needed to blow out the cobwebs several times a day, he once told me. Stopping by the market was his way of doing that. I wondered if he was also becoming a regular at the Tarpon Bar.

His first column had appeared in *The Island Sun* on the same day I'd found Frank's safety deposit key. Friday the 13th. It was Wes's self-proclaimed lucky day; not necessarily mine.

Word had spread quickly about the new reporter. A crowd of folks gathered around his table at the market. He was shaking hands and handing out his cards. Now that he'd been discovered, I figured it would be several months before Wes had to pay for his own coffee.

I worked my way through the crowd, saying hello to folks I knew, and sat down beside him. The crowd drifted back to their seats.

"Snoop," he said. His eyes twinkled. "How are the mysteries progressing?"

"Not well. Remember when you told me I might not like some of the answers to my questions. You were right."

"Oh? Well, life isn't all peaches and cream," he said.

"You learn that in the newspaper business?"

"Yes, I did. I sure did. Every day. What's up, kid?"

"I'm not ready to tell you yet. But I want to give you a heads up about Peter Thompson. You remember my telling you about him, the Canadian, the mystery house on the north end?"

"Yep. The man with the look-alike cousin? Did you discover some new dirt on him?"

"Not yet. I wanted someone – you – to know that I'm flying down to Key West with him tomorrow."

"You're flying to Key West with someone you suspect may be involved in criminal activities? Leslie, you're out of your mind." Wes took a large sip of coffee, all the while shaking his head.

"I think I'll be safe. But if I don't come back, you need to go to the sheriff and tell him that I've disappeared. And that Peter Thompson is to blame."

Avery downed the rest of his drink. "I'm not sure what I can say except, don't do it, Leslie. If he's as bad as you think he is, you could be putting your life on the line for some ridiculous idea you've gotten into your pretty head."

"Don't patronize me, Wes. This idea in my head is based on facts, some facts, at least."

"Facts?"

"A reliable, um, source said there was drug dealing going on around here."

Wes straightened up in his chair. "Drugs. Have you notified the sheriff?"

"Not yet. And you can't say anything to him."

"It's not your job to track down drug dealers. You have lost your mind."

"I'm not tracking them. They've come to me. It will all make sense soon. Let me do this. Please, Wes. You're the only person I can confide in."

"You are naïve, lady. But I've seen you in action before and it does seem that you can take care of yourself. Take your cell phone and call me if you have any problems with that guy. Not that I'll be close enough to help."

I stood up and wrapped my arms around him. "Did I say that I love having you on this island?"

"You just did. Now go on before I get maudlin. And check in, middle of the afternoon. Don't leave me worrying that you're floating in the ocean somewhere after being dropped 8,000 feet from a small plane."

When I got home, I wrote a note to Wes about Frank's attorney and put it and the key in an envelope where Mother or the deputy could find it if something happened to me.

CHAPTER 36

Peter Thompson's plane – white with red and blue trim – was a Piper Chieftain with two engines and a Garmin system that would get us to Key West with no problem. At least that's how the Canadian described our flight as he helped me onboard.

I surveyed the interior with its four beige leather seats, two small tables and a little plaque with the date 2001 on it. It was pristine, but the area smelled of disinfectant. I hoped the overpowering fragrance wouldn't trigger my motion sickness. The back of the plane appeared empty, as though seats had been removed.

The perfect aircraft for hauling drugs across the border.

As if reading my mind, Peter pointed to the empty space and gave me an innocent enough explanation: "My late wife, Monica, and I often stashed our racing bikes in the back and she had, well, more luggage than any four women put together. If you feel like buying something large in Key West, we'll have room to haul it back."

"So, is, um, 20 years old for a plane? You know, in dog years that's 140."

"What? Oh, yeah." He chuckled. "Leslie, you can be quite amusing. We're going to be fine. It's well maintained. Only had one problem. A fuel truck clipped her several years ago. But that was fixed, and she's been great ever since."

I nodded, settled into the co-pilot seat and found myself facing a panel of controls – at least two dozen dials against a shiny wooden background.

"I hope you know what all of these are for?" I asked, voicing my growing uneasiness.

"I could fly this baby blindfolded. And have felt like I was doing that a couple of times up north. I've never had an accident; never even come close. Of course, the first time could be the last." He winked at me. "But I do have a parachute."

Do I? I thought with Wes's question ranging in my ears: *Have you lost your mind?*

At this moment, I was certain the answer to the latter was yes. I was about to embark on a trip in a small plane with a man whose identity was a question mark; a man who had shown me his rougher side on our first outing together. My insides wanted to crawl out of my skin and ooze down the plane's steps to the safety of the runway below.

"You look a little nervous. You want something? I have the miracle pill."

While my brain screamed "NO!" I heard my mouth say, "Sure." Against my better judgment, I reached out and accepted his offering. It looked innocent enough, but then so had Lucy in the Sky with Diamonds – LSD – dropped on a sugar cube back in the days of Timothy Leary.

"There's a bottle of water beside your seat. We'll give it a minute, and then I'll take off."

There didn't appear to be a bathroom on the plane, so I drank just enough to help swallow the pill. Then I sat in silence while Peter checked his cell phone. I'll be all right, I kept telling myself.

"How long does it take to fly from here to Canada?" I asked, when I could feel a sense of calm settling in.

"About three hours. Does that question mean you'll be flying with me up north? You'd love it – and so would I."

"Let's get through this first. I think I'm ready to go."

Peter flipped several switches. The roar of the twin engines could be heard inside the cabin. I liked the sound. If one engine went, there was a spare.

Even though my mind wasn't embracing the idea of being 10,000 feet about the ground, my drug-numbed emotions didn't seem to care anymore. I soon had a clear view of the Florida Keys: tiny green footprints on a bright blue landscape. Within an hour, we were landing at the Sugar Loaf Shores Airport in Key West.

"Duval Street. Anyplace close to Mallory Square," Peter instructed the cab driver as we climbed in the back seat. "That wasn't so bad, was it?" he said, grabbing my hand and patting it.

"You're a good pilot. Lots of practice, I guess. The, um, medicine worked like a charm, whatever it was."

He didn't provide specifics. "There's more where that came from. And if you're interested in something a little more fun, I have a supply back on the island. In my rental house."

Party drugs at 450 Live Oak. What a surprise.

The pink cab sped down the narrow streets. Although the neighborhoods were picturesque, the community had a seedy feel to it, like the residents were more interested in having a good time than keeping up appearances.

A trolley approached, filled with people in shorts and t-shirts. iPhones were waving in the air as they snapped photos to share with their friends on Facebook. The driver's voice rattled through the palm trees lining the street. "...community was hit hard by the storm surge from Hurricane Wilma in 2005...." His voice faded as the vehicle squeezed past our cab.

"Looks like it hasn't recovered much," I observed. Peter was checking the messages on his cell phone again.

"Uh, what?"

"Nothing. I was just remarking on how some fresh coats of paint are needed here."

"You're right. But then it wouldn't be Key West. Enjoy it, Leslie. Don't be so critical." *He was right to admonish me. Quaint and historic didn't always mean pristine.*

"How's this?" the cabby said as he deposited us in front of a Baskin-Robbins ice cream shop on Roosevelt.

Peter reached for his wallet, then helped me out of the cab and continued holding my hand as we headed southwest toward a colorful building with the symbol of a yellow rose.

"I hope you like Cuban food," he said. "This place is one of my favorites."

The slender, dark-haired hostess at El Mason de Pepe guided us to a table of four, stepping over two baby chicks and their mother en route. She placed large menus in front of us. "Please don't feed the birds," she said as she departed.

Peter excused himself, and I was left alone with a large rooster crowing nearby and a menu that felt overwhelming.

"I like this platter." The woman sitting about three feet from me leaned my direction and pointed toward a photograph of a plate heaping with potatoes, beans, meat and plantains. "My husband and I shared it today – as we always do."

"Well, it looks good to me," I said. "Thanks. I was a bit lost."

"You with the cruise ship?" she asked.

"Me? No, I arrived here by cab from the airport."

"We're from Ohio. We take this same cruise every year and eat at this same restaurant. Silly, but it's our tradition."

I remembered someone on my island telling me that the cruise ships had destroyed Key West. The daily dump of people onto the streets had changed its personality and not for the better, she said. The shops, once known for works of local artists, now catered to tourists looking for cheap souvenirs and inexpensive food. I wondered if she and I were being too critical, as Peter had mentioned.

"Here comes my husband. Enjoy your meal," the woman said. She rose from her chair and headed for a slender man wearing an Ohio State cap, just like the one Meredith had given her father, my ex.

I was studying the menu when I heard Peter's voice.

"Leslie. Sorry it took me so long. I ran into Raul, my friend Raul Pinelli. We haven't seen each other for some time."

A man with graying hair, combed back from his face and a thick salt-and-pepper mustache stepped out from behind Peter. He reached for my hand and offered a bow in my direction.

"Hola linda. Un placer conocerte. A pleasure to meet you, madam. You said she was lovely, but…." He put his fingers together and kissed the tips, ending the gesture with a flourish.

Raul was wearing a cream-colored shirt with elaborate embroidery down the front. There were two cigars in his shirt pocket. His dark eyes were expressive, flirty.

"Peter. How did you woo this beautiful woman to our fair city? And why haven't I met her before."

"I'm just getting to know her. Don't get any ideas. I hope you don't mind, Leslie, but I asked Raul to join us. He can tell you a lot about Key West. And Cuba for that matter. We're about 105 miles from Havana."

"How do you two know each other?" I said, taking a sip of the ice water the waitress placed on the table.

"We've done business together," Raul said.

The way he looked at me caused me to have second thoughts about the sleeveless blouse I was wearing. The front dipped to the top of my bra. Mother might have approved, but I was suddenly uncomfortable. I untied the sweater I had around my waist and slipped it on, buttoning it up to my throat.

"Oh, and what kind of business is that? Are you an attorney, too?"

Raul grinned at Peter. "No. I'm a simple man with, um, muchos intereses negocios. Many business interests."

"After lunch we'll have several hours to tour the island, if you'd like. Raul can be our guide. Where should we go?" Peter said, reaching over and giving me a territorial pat on the shoulder.

I looked at my watch to cover up the flinch of my shoulder. It was nearly 1 o'clock. A tour could take several hours. I hadn't discussed our departure time with Peter, but I assumed we'd leave about 4 p.m. I was certain that with Raul in the picture, the trip would not be a fruitful one. There would be no real opportunity to ask questions, at least not until we were on the plane again.

"Hemingway's house. Should be fun to see that. Then we should head back, don't you think?"

Raul nodded. "A great writer. A man's man and a Cuban at heart."

The tour of the Hemingway house began in the parlor, with its pink settee and photographs of the author, his boat and fishing expeditions. A Hemingway cat lounged on a glass-topped table as tourists snapped pictures of his famous paw and its extra toe.

The final leg of the tour was a visit to Hemingway's writing sanctuary at the top of what looked to be a garage. "Two people at a time," the guide instructed. Peter and Raul didn't appear interested, so I climbed the stairs by myself and agreed to meet them out front.

The sanctuary was a large room with a tiny viewing area, marked off with a velvet rope across the door. There was a round desk adorned with an old-fashioned typewriter but no chair. *Did he write standing up and with a hangover*, I wondered?

A bookcase filled with literature, but whose writings I couldn't tell, took up most of the back wall. A rattan chaise lounge with green fabric and white fringe and a matching chair and table provided the only seating area. Light filtered in through two floor-to-ceiling windows on the far side of the room, reflecting on the wooden floor.

There was no way for a tourist to enter the room and receive inspiration by touching those things the master once used. *Or did he actually use them?* Where those items his or were they randomly collected bits and pieces from the shops in one of Key West's back alleys? My heart wanted to believe they were his, my mind was skeptical.

When I joined my male companions, they were standing along the fence that surrounded the large white house with green shutters. The cigars from Raul's shirt pockets were now in their mouths, the smoke curling about their heads.

"How was it?" Peter asked.

"Surreal. When you think about the man who once lived there and how he committed suicide, it makes you realize how transitory and sometimes sad life can be."

"Live everyday like it was your last. Is that what you're saying? Wise words, bella linda," Raul crooned.

"Something like that." I held out my hand, eager for this interloper to be on his way. "It was certainly nice to meet you, Raul. Perhaps if you visit Peter on our island, we'll have a chance to see each other again."

Peter cleared his throat. "Um, well, Raul will be joining us on the flight home. He's looking for a new boat, and I was telling him about a couple of prospects at our marina. Hope you don't mind."

"Why should I? It's your ride," I said. As hard as I was trying to appear nonchalant, my thoughts were roiling. This was a wasted trip, with too many people and trolleys in Key West. And now any chance to question Peter on the return home was gone.

When we climbed into the plane, I slipped into one of the seats in the back, wishing I had my Kindle with me. Raul was Peter's new co-pilot.

I watched the landscape below race by until I felt my eyelids getting heavy. When I opened them again and checked my watch, 45 minutes had passed. Raul was sitting across from me, staring at me and giving me the creeps.

"Nice nap, Leslie?"

I stretched, moving a bit away from him and wishing he'd return to the co-pilot's seat.

"Peter and I've been talking about you."

"Oh. And what did he have to say?" I yawned.

"Peter tells me you're a woman of great curiosity."

"I've been told that," I said, studying him. Every hair in place. Well-groomed. Manicured nails. I only knew one other man that wore nail polish; a small fellow with meticulous personal habits who owned a shoe company in Cincinnati and had a yen for professional baseball players.

"He says you've been in his house looking around. And when the two of you went out to dinner, you asked a lot of questions."

"I guess I did. My friends like to say I'm far too inquisitive." I laughed to diffuse the tenseness growing in my chest.

"As a new friend who thinks you are a very special lady, I would say that you should *ten cuidado,* be cautious, as you say in English. People who get involved with things that don't concern them can put themselves and their loved ones in harm's way. I see no reason for you to worry. But you must keep yourself safe, my lovely."

He punctuated his words with an exaggerated smile. Was he trying to tell me his warning had teeth?

CHAPTER 37

When Peter drove to the gate of my apartment complex, he punched in the numbers without asking for confirmation. He couldn't recall the date of his wife's death, but he could remember my gate code. I might have been flattered by this simple act, if Raul's warning hadn't scared the shit out of me.

"These are quite nice," Raul enthused from the back seat. "You say your mother lives here too?"

"She's not here often. Rarely in fact. She often visits her sister who lives in Arizona. She likes the weather there better," I lied.

"Let me walk you to your door, Leslie," Peter said. "I'm afraid our luncheon trip turned into business. So sorry. Hope you'll forgive me and let me take you out again soon."

"No problem, Peter. I understand how these things happen. Such a coincidence that you and your friend happened to connect in Key West. Did you say he's buying a boat here?"

"Looking at one," Raul chimed in.

"Which one is that?"

"Didn't I tell you she's full of questions, Raul. There are a couple. One is a 50-foot Sea Ray Sundancer. Nice boat. The other one is a 48-foot *Kadey Krogen*. Twenty years old. I think you know the seller. It's Gordon Fike. My realtor," Peter said.

"Gordon? Didn't know he has a big boat like that. But then I don't know him that well."

I checked my watch. It was nearly 7 p.m., and I was eager to grab a bite to eat and get to bed early. Whatever Peter had given me to relieve my anxiety on the flight had worn off, leaving me tired and out-of-sorts.

"Thanks again, Peter. Raul, um, nice meeting you. I don't need any help getting to my door."

I exited the car before Peter could comment further and headed toward the end of the building, passing my condo and then Mother's. When I was a safe distance away, I turned and waved, waiting for Peter to depart and drive through the gate.

Mother was watching a black and white movie with Bette Davis and Miriam Hopkins when I entered her place.

"Did you change your mind about Peter Thompson? I can't believe you, who hate flying, agreed to go on a small plane." She continued watching but reduced the volume.

"The flight was okay. Small planes might not be as safe as the larger ones, but you have a feeling of more control," I said.

"And Key West?"

"Needs work."

"That's nice."

I rolled my eyes and headed for the shower.

My bed was a fold-out couch in Mother's guest room. Like the second bedroom in my condo, the room had a sliding door that led to a porch overlooking the parking lot. I'd left the door ajar to get some fresh air. Around midnight I got up, slid it all the way open and stepped out onto the deck. I couldn't sleep. My mind kept flashing Raul's Cheshire cat grin.

The moon was little more than a sliver, barely a presence in the big sky overhead. The light by the entryway to the condo complex was missing, broken by some kid with a shell and a good right arm, I guessed. In the dark, the stars popped like bright dots. I searched for the ones I knew. Orion. The Big Dipper.

The breeze from the Gulf was cooler than I expected, so I slipped back into the room, grabbed the blanket off the bed and threw it around my shoulders.

Outside again I took a deep breath, trying to clear my head. So much had happened since I moved to the island with Mother. Not much of it was good. Well, except for a couple of new friends. I mulled over Deb and Scooter for a while as I sat on the bench next to a potted palm and pulled the blanket tighter to ward off the chill.

Then I had to think about drugs and Frank. I tried to wrap my mind around that connection. I didn't want to believe it, couldn't believe it. But Attorney Michael Land had said it with such matter-of-factness it must be true.

The figure was halfway between the entryway and my condo when I saw it creeping along the edge of the 10-foot sea grape hedge, skirting the asphalt parking lot. It moved deliberately as if trying to avoid detection.

I scooted to the edge of my chair and felt a chill that had nothing to do with the temperature outside. Was it Raul or Peter coming back to make me pay for my curiosity? The adrenalin rush was instantaneous.

My cell phone was in the bedroom. There was also the new pepper spray gun. I was uncertain what I should do. If I got up to retrieve them, I'd lose sight of whoever it was. If I'd been on my own porch, I'd have a better chance of recognizing the figure. But here, two doors down, with my view obscured by a bottlebrush tree with its bushy red flowers hanging down, it was difficult to see.

The figure stopped at the bottom of my condo, looked both ways, then bolted up the steps. *Oh my God! Deb and Scooter.* I ran into the bedroom, grabbed the phone and went back onto the porch.

"Siri. Call 911."

"I'm really sorry…." the computerized voice responded. Then a beep and nothing.

"Damn you, Siri." I punched in 911 and put the phone back to my ear. It was dead. I'd forgotten to plug it in when I returned from Key West. The photos I'd taken and a day without recharging had done it in.

I tiptoed into Mother's bedroom and snatched her phone off the nightstand. Even without knowing her password, I could make an emergency call. I stopped before punching in the numbers. By the time the police got there, it might be too late.

Back in my room, I stuck Mother's phone in my pocket and the pepper spray gun in the waistband of the shorts I had slipped on.

A glow coming from the back of my condo filtered through the kitchen window to my entryway, casting just enough light for me to find my way up the steps. The front door was open but the noisy screen was a concern. It managed a few complaints as I pulled it back, slipped in the opening and eased it back into place.

I could hear voices and what sounded like a commotion, a scuffling. I had to save my friends. Had to hurry.

From the kitchen, I could see the intruder. His body was backlit by the light in the bedroom. He was facing Deb and Scooter, who were wearing the oversized Tampa Bucs t-shirts they often slept in. They didn't appear frightened, but I wasn't close enough to read the anxiety on their faces.

The adrenalin surging through my body carried me across my small living room in a flash. I pulled the pepper spray from my waistband, hoping it would pass for a real gun. I clutched it in my sweaty hands, standing about 10 feet from the stranger.

I'd read the instructions but never tested the dangerous device. I worried that my lack of knowledge and poor aiming skills might send the spray onto one of my friends.

There was only one course of action. I held the gun in both hands and aimed as best I could, spurred on by audacity and memories of the thousands of cop movies I'd seen.

"I have a gun and I'm prepared to shoot," I yelled. "Drop your weapon and turn around!"

To my surprise, all three people in the room gasped.

"Jesus, Leslie. Don't shoot. It's Frank." It was Deb's voice that issued a warning as she jumped off the bed and moved toward the lanai. Frank disappeared behind the door. Scooter scrambled toward the safety of the headboard.

"Oh my God. Frank." My nerves buckled my knees, pitching me forward. I grabbed onto a nearby chest with carved palm trees to steady myself.

"It's okay. It's not a real gun," I said in an attempt to calm my friends. I could hear what I thought were sighs of relief. Or maybe frustration with me.

Frank, sporting the start of a goatee, sat down on the edge of Deb and Scooter's bed and unzipped the black leather jacket he was wearing. With his dimpled chin hidden, he looked like a different man. He focused his gunmetal eyes on me and asked a familiar question: "What the hell were you thinking?"

"I-I saw you go in the door to, to my condo. I-I thought you were going to try to harm Deb and Scooter, thinking it was me."

"Why would I want to hurt them or anyone?"

"No, not you. I couldn't see that it was you. I thought it might be, uh, someone else. A Spanish-speaking man I met with Peter Thompson today. Raul somebody. He said my curiosity could put my family and friends in danger."

"Raul?" I watched the color drain from Frank's face, then saw him recover quickly.

"You've got one crazy friend," he said to Deb and Scooter. "I've never met a woman with such an imagination."

Everything about him right then sounded artificial to me.

"Smoke," Scooter said. "Going outside."

He struggled out of bed, his nightshirt exposing a bandage wrapped around one of his legs, and limped toward the lanai.

"I may join you, Sugar, and bring a couple of shots of whiskey along," Deb said shaking her head. "Frank, you take this girl back to her mother's. And see if you can get that weapon away from her before she hurts herself and everyone around her."

Frank nodded and stuck his hand out. "Give it to me. I'll take care of it," he said.

I shook my head vehemently. I wasn't about to hand over my weapon to anyone – especially a man I knew to be a drug dealer.

CHAPTER 38

M y mind was rehearsing what I should say, contemplating what I should do. I'd worked hard to diminish Frank during the eight days he was gone. Thought of him as smaller, less attractive, less desirable. He was the worst sort of criminal. A drug dealer.

"You want something to drink?" I asked, opening the refrigerator at Mother's condo and looking through jars of olives and white to-go boxes to the back. "Mother has a couple of bottles of beer. Bud?"

"Yeah. I need one."

Now that he was back and standing three feet away, my desire for him was resurfacing despite my best efforts to keep it at bay. I removed the screw top and handed him the bottle.

"What was that all about, Leslie?" he said.

About you being a fucking drug lord, I wanted to say but held back. Michael Land had changed me with his revelations, and even though Frank didn't know why, he could see the difference.

"Couldn't sleep. Was sitting on the porch when I saw somebody, like I said, sneaking into my condo like some criminal."

"If you thought I was an intruder, why didn't you call 911 instead of taking matters into your own hands?"

"The sheriff's office is 10 minutes from here on a good night. Deb and Scooter could be dead by the time he arrived. That's what I thought. Besides, my battery was gone. By the time I found Mother's phone, I worried it would be too late."

"You said Raul. You thought I might be Raul." He gave me a severe look. "What did you mean?"

I turned my back to him and began putting dishes away from Mother's drain rack. I was seething as I told him about the trip to Key West and the meeting with

Raul Pinelli. I couldn't see his face as I shared the details of the day, including Raul's desire to buy a boat and the warning he'd given me on our return flight. But I assumed his expression would be one of disgust – with me.

"I thought you were done with Peter Thompson. Didn't we talk about you staying away from him?"

I turned to face him. "What's this we? I didn't agree to that. And stay away from him because he's what? Dangerous? A drug dealer? A criminal? A man who ruins people's lives for profit?" I could feel my anger rising.

"That's what you are, Frank. That's what your attorney told me. And the body. Gator and I found the body. Really nice for your friend Gator, let me tell you. You said you'd turned it over to the DEA. Another lie."

Frank smiled. Like the arrogant son-of-a-bitch that he was. "You talked to Michael Land?" he asked me. "Good. Were the instructions easy to follow? I didn't want to give too much away."

I read his look as smug. Maybe he had plans for me to join his drug business. He set down his beer and reached for me. I backed away, now against the refrigerator. "Your attorney told me you're a drug dealer. That you have millions of dollars stashed away."

"He said I was a drug dealer?"

I thought back to the conversation between myself and Michael Land. Maybe I'd heard him wrong. "I think he said 'involved.' What's the difference?"

He grabbed my hand. I pulled away, but he came close. I let him guide me to the bedroom. I didn't want our voices waking Mother.

"You've wanted answers, and I'm ready to give them to you."

We sat down next to each other on the bed. His face was barely visible in the dark room. I made no move to turn on a light. I didn't want the sight of him to detract me from his message. His lies. Whatever he was up to.

He told me he had been a cop in a small community in the northern part of the state. One evening, he and his partner, Don McKechnie, were investigating a drug deal when it deteriorated into a shootout. A 14-year-old, riding his bike home after playing video games with his buddies, was killed in cross fire. When the investigation was done, at the parent's request, it was determined that the bullet that ended the boy's life came from Frank's gun.

"His parents said he was a good boy who'd just brought home a report card with five A's and one B. They were tortured by what happened; blamed me. I may have been doing my job, but I'd taken their son's life. I can still see his face; he looked asleep. But only inches below, his chest was covered with blood…that I still have on my hands."

Suddenly I was full of compassion. I wanted to kiss him. Hold him.

He paused, rubbed his eyes and then went on to explain that police counseling didn't work, so he quit the force and did odd jobs on a yacht anchored in Tampa. When his boss sailed to our island, Frank jumped ship. He worked and saved enough money for a down payment on a fishing boat, the Dreamcatcher, and went into business for himself. Several years later, he married Janis and Stevie was born.

I was now holding his hand, stroking it. He didn't pull back.

About six months ago, Frank's former partner called. He was working for the DEA and wanted Frank to do some free-lancing. The agency was worried that operatives out of Miami were moving into the smaller communities on the west coast of Florida.

"Here's your chance to save some kids' lives," his former partner said to him.

"It was the only thing that could bring me back. This island's the perfect location. Laid back and with a sheriff who's good at handling misdemeanors, a nice guy, but doesn't have the skills to deal with, um, cartels and their henchmen.

"I made it known on the island that I was interested. Talked about my willingness to pick up some extra cash and pretty soon they contacted me."

"They? Who?" I asked.

"The names would be meaningless to you. We're putting the case together, and I don't want to blow it. We're after the big guy. That's where I was this week. Meeting with one of his seconds. Talking about expanding our operation even further. Trying to get him to leave South America and come here to scope out the area with me and the others."

"Is that man Raul?"

"All I can say about Raul is stay away from him and from Peter Thompson."

"You've already told me that several times. So, so the money. The $3 million. That's drug money?"

"My cut for the last three and a half months. That's how much volume we have. I put it in the safety deposit boxes with letters explaining everything and implicating some of the people involved. I don't consider it mine."

He looked at me and shook his head. "I can understand how people get hooked on it. Not on the drugs but the money. It flows in like the tide, Leslie; so easy and effortless as it fills your pockets with dreams."

I was so relieved I could barely understand what he was talking about.

"When you find yourself thinking about it – wanting that easy life – you have to picture the faces of the people whose lives are ruined by drugs. I force myself to think of that poor dead kid every day. I've resisted the urge to take a penny, even though no one would notice or care. It's equivalent to what the DEA would pay me in rewards and is pennies in the big picture, but still...."

"I understand," I said, rubbing my hand across his back. "But why the game with the key, Frank?"

"Game? Before you came along, Scooter and Deb were the only people I could trust. Them and my attorney. That's why they had the key, knew about the shack, the picture of mom and the bank. I wrote it all down for them. They don't know about the drugs or how much money. They didn't ask any questions. It's not their way."

They didn't ask any questions because they got instructions with the key. Why was I the one that was being tested?

"Then you came along. You're stronger, smarter. I could see that right away. A little reckless, but the one to take charge if something happens to me. Not Scooter or Deb."

"Why all the subterfuge? Why didn't you tell me straight out? Why didn't you have me put my name on the signature card at the bank?" I was trying to figure out what Frank was up to. It wasn't ringing true.

"That was my plan. Things heated up before I could get everything under control," he said. "It was your interfer...." He stopped and looked away.

"My interference?" *Oh, blame me for not having your act together.*

"I needed more time to get the details worked out. When I realized I didn't have it, I wanted you to have the key and the instructions. I didn't think you and Gator would find the body. I feel bad about that."

"I just got the key. Scooter and Deb didn't have the instructions. Said they burned up in the fire."

"Damn. No instructions? I'm not sure how you figured everything out without them. You are amazing." His eyes registered admiration. Or at least it looked that way to me.

"Leslie, I'm flying by the seat of my pants here and dealing with dangerous people. You gotta cut me some slack. Thank God, I've got you on my side. You are on my side, aren't you?"

I nodded. I wanted to be mad at Frank. But I'd thrown a wrench into his plans. Now he was trying to deal with things the best he could. I was willing to take some responsibility for the confusion.

"Of course, Michael Land also has the information. But it might take months for it to come out if I was killed and no one found my body. Regulations and stuff. By that time, how many people, drug users, kids, could die?"

"Can you tell me about the house? Peter Thompson's house? I was clobbered on the back of the head there. I owe Peter Thompson for that one."

He was silent for a minute as if weighing what he was going to say. "It was me, not Peter. I hit you on the back of the head that night."

I was ready to walk away again. He was making me nuts.

He did it to protect me, he said. There were drugs in the locked closet – drugs he'd put there. It was a convenient hiding place since work in the house had stopped. He couldn't risk me finding them. I listened to the words coming out of his mouth, touching the back of my head as he spoke. The wound, still healing, was warm and sore when I put my fingers there.

"Man, you hit me hard. It felt like there was anger in that blow," I said.

He touched my arm lightly. Not sure how I would react, I guess.

"Maybe there was. You were making things difficult," he said. "But I'm sorry for that. It had to be convincing. My mother's car was parked down the street. I was getting ready to take you to the hospital. I didn't care if you knew it was me. When I ran into Jerry, he and his wife made it easy for me to stay undercover."

"There are still too many unanswered questions. What about the body? Or was there more than one?" I asked.

"It won't be long before I can tell you everything. Not now. No more questions. I'm beat."

It was nearly 1:30 a.m. My body was also begging for rest, but my mind was alert. There was no way I could go to sleep.

Frank removed his shirt and patted the bed. "Come closer. I've missed you," he said.

"Leslie." His voice was no more than whisper. "Let me stay here with you."

I turned to this man whose face was like a thunderbolt through my heart when I first saw him. I let him enfold me in his arms. My head leaned against his shoulder; my fingers traveled through fine silky hair on his bare chest to the back of his neck. The smell of Dial soap and aftershave mingled into a familiar fragrance that felt like home.

CHAPTER 39

Did the clock really say 9:12? *No Frank. Wonder when he left? And if I ever see him again ...* I left that thought alone and bolted out of bed. I had a 10 a.m. appointment for a facial. I glanced at myself in the bathroom mirror. Hair and face a mess. Dark circles from the late night listening to Frank's revelations. It looked like I'd been on a bender. Minerva, the aesthetician, would understand and be helpful.

My cell phone rang. I didn't recognize the number but answered anyway.

"Ms. Elliott?"

"Yes."

"Willy from the paint store. Sorry it took me so long to get back to you. Lots of construction going on. We've been busy."

"Willy. You called me back." I was stunned to be hearing from the man who'd given me a hard time when I took the empty paint can to him almost a month ago. I laughed. "Good for you."

"Tih. S. Tih," he said, trying to say what seemed unpronounceable.

"What?"

"The man that bought the paint cans, empty ones. Fourteen of 'em. Said he needed 'em to divvy up paint for the workmen at his house. Dated back eight months ago, which is why it took me so dang long to find it. The invoice. I remembered when I saw it. Thought it didn't make much sense at the time. But a sale's a sale."

"Tih? S. T-i-h? Is that what you said?"

"Yep. Something like that. It's kind of scribbly. Got the receipt here if you want a copy."

"Thanks, Willy. I'll be by later. I appreciate your time. Can I pay you?"

There was a pause. A mumbled voice. In the background, I heard someone say "bottle of Jim Beam."

"No. Jus' a thank you."

"I'll be by later." *After a stop at the liquor store.*

ꙮ

"Relax, Leslie. You seem tense, and, um, your face is a little pink." Minerva, the soft-spoken woman giving me a facial, wrapped a towel around my auburn hair and placed a sheet over my body.

"My friend is growing a goatee."

"That explains it," she said, laughing. "We'll fix you right up."

A switch clicked, filling the room with piano music; soft tones, gentle rhythms. Behind the notes was the sound of waves. I envisioned the Gulf water kissing the white sand and depositing shell fragments and bits of seaweed here and there. I tried to keep my thoughts from going to corpses and body parts.

"Ummm." The involuntary sound coming from my lips accompanied Minerva's warm touch on my face. Round and round. Her fingers worked to smooth out the tiny aging lines establishing themselves on my pale skin. Another cream followed.

What's that aroma? Ah. Lavender. Spice.

Frank had smelled like spice last night, and there was the fragrance of lavender from the soy candle I'd been burning in Mother's guest room since I'd been staying there. They mingled into a scene of two bodies. Stop. It hadn't gone that far, but Minerva would be horrified if she knew where my mind was.

"This may sting a bit," she said as she applied a thick liquid to my face. "It has cayenne pepper and you're a little tender."

A vision of a dark liquid, boiling, rolling and folding into itself replaced the scene of Frank and me together.

"Whew, that *is* strong," I said.

"It'll cool down when I put on the neutralizer."

As the black heat tortured my skin into suppleness, my mind moved on to the dark forces at play on this little island.

Who was S. Tih? Some workman at the yellow house? Or a drug dealer I hadn't met? He couldn't be the kingpin. That person was in South America – or so Frank said.

222

What had Wes Avery said to me when I told him about the mysteries of the island? *What's the connection?* The only answer I could think of at the time was me. But there had to be something or someone else involved besides Frank and perhaps Peter or was it Jamie Thompson? Maybe it was this Tih person.

The cast of characters drifted in front of me like computerized mug shots. S. Tih materialized as a faceless silhouette with a question mark. I was sorting through them and barely aware that Minerva had moved to the end of the table until she grabbed my big toe and gave it a squeeze. She traveled to my calf, pressing with her knuckles to remove the tightness.

"It is possible for you to do that for the next hour?"

She laughed and kept on pushing and rubbing as my mind drifted into a sun-dappled forest with a little stream. Frank and I were walking through it holding hands.

When she finished with my legs, she returned to my face. The heat from the pepper was followed by a cooling cream that must have been the neutralizer. As the tingling in my skin diminished, I allowed my mind to return to the faces of crime. They were like cards being swirled and shuffled in a magician's trick. *Connections, connections. What are the connections?*

Minerva rubbed something lighter on my face that I recognized as sunscreen. The last application. My hour was almost up. I opened my eyes.

"I always hate it when these sessions come to an end. You have a busy day ahead?" I asked.

"Unless I get some walk-ins, you're my last client. I'll have plenty of time to check out the local newspaper. I like looking at the real estate sections. Not that I can afford any of the houses, but I have my dreams, and I like to go to open houses."

The facial room was still darkened, but the light bulb that switched on in my head sent a flash of illumination through me.

"Oh, my God!" I sat up and looked at Minerva with an expression that must have been scary to witness.

"Are you all right?"

"Yes! Oh yes. I think I know who S. Tih might be! Thanks to you."

"Glad to help," Minerva said, shaking her head. "You can pay out front and make another appointment if you want."

"I'll be back. That's for sure."

⁋

Wes Avery was chatting with the newspaper's receptionist when I burst in the door like a reporter with a scoop yelling "Stop the presses!"

"Whoa. It's the cat with canary feathers still hanging from her mouth," Avery said as he looked at me and laughed. Helen, the receptionist, appeared startled.

"Are you busy?" My breathing was labored from my dash up the 18 steps to the newspaper office. My cheeks were still tingling from my cayenne pepper mask. "Can you spare a couple of minutes?"

"Anything for you, Leslie. Whatever it is must be good."

"I think it is, Wes. Do you have a chalkboard in your office?"

"I have a bunch of post-it notes and a blank wall."

"That'll do. Before we start, please promise me that this conversation is off-the-record and not to be confided with anyone. Swear, Wes, or I'll leave, and you'll always wonder."

He shook his head. "You're something else. I swear."

As Wes watched, a look of amusement on his face, I scribbled the names of my cast of characters and began sticking them in a line to the left on the wall. Then I wrote a list of the incidents: the mystery house, the dead dog, the bodies and body parts on the beach, with dates, and attached them to the smooth surface. Finally, I set up a category for miscellaneous and included such things as the pinky ring I found on the beach and the empty paint cans.

I told Frank that I wouldn't tell a soul what he shared with me. I intended to keep that promise. But how could I keep my friends and family safe if I didn't know everyone who was involved in these illegal activities?

"Can we do some brainstorming?" I wrote the word "motive" on a note. Under that I stuck the word "money."

"Obvious, right? That's what drives all criminal activity," I said.

"And passion or, um, sex," Wes said, shaking his head.

"I'm focused on dollars for now. So how can you make big money on our little island?" The answer seemed simple enough. But I was trying to collect my thoughts.

"Most peple make it before they come here and sink it into property," Wes answered. "Not me, of course. I'm just a working stiff, which is why I rent an apartment above the bank."

"Right. Right." This wasn't about Wes, although I was sympathetic to the plight of newspaper people in a shrinking industry.

"And you've seen the police runs. Small stuff like fishing tackle, maybe a golf cart or two during spring break that's recovered later in the drink. No big crime wave in our neighborhoods," I said.

"True. I guess that leaves the drugs you mentioned before." He laughed. I didn't.

"Unless criminals are into kidnapping some rich person, what else is there?"

Wes shrugged.

"Here's my theory. Peter Thompson comes here with his wife, Monica. They start building a house and get to know some people on the island, go fishing and stuff like that. He invites his cousin Jamie to come down and join in the fun. They could be twins they look so much alike. It's easy for them to visit the place because Peter has a small plane that he flies back and forth from Canada.

"Monica, who lives off Daddy's money, is killed in a car accident. Peter isn't used to working all that hard and is in danger of being cut off now that his wife is gone. I'm only speculating about the money because I don't know his relationship with his father-in-law. Other than his one off-hand remark that the two of them were not best friends.

"Anyway, Peter talks about his need for money to a friend on the island and they hatch up a plan. The house, under construction, serves as a relay station for drug transfers. Peter's in no rush to complete the residence because his wife's dead, and he no longer cares if it gets built or not. Besides, it's obviously the perfect cover. He even has someone report an eagle nesting in one of his trees to cause more delays.

"A boat, carrying drugs, comes up from someplace – South America or Mexico. They bring the stuff to the old dock behind Peter's house and unload it, storing it in a locked closet on the third level.

"Peter transports it to his plane in the empty paint cans I found, the ones that had a powdery substance that I discovered when I opened one of the cans in my kitchen. I thought it was drywall dust and so did the guys at the paint store when I took the can there."

"A powder? Did you have it tested?" Wes asked.

"The guys at the store accidentally emptied some of it on the counter and then blew it off into the air. You had to be there. It was a comedy of errors."

"Peter Thompson's your man. Drugs and money. Simple enough." Wes said, folding his arms and looking proud of himself.

"Maybe yes, maybe no. I think somewhere along the line Peter Thompson stopped playing ball with the drug dealers and his island contact. He was flying the drugs to Canada and, in his mind, taking a lot of risks. Maybe he wanted a bigger cut. That's when they decided to send him a message by killing his dog and leaving its remains in the house.

"I thought you told me the dog wasn't dead." Wes scratched his ear while he studied my notes on the wall.

"It isn't. But someone wanted Peter and the drug guys to believe it was." He looked at me blankly. "It was some other dog," I said in exasperation. "Don't be so dim!"

"Ahh," he said.

I continued. "Mary Sanders, his neighbor, said she saw Peter with the dog all the time. But when I had dinner with him that night, it was as if Whalen never existed. And, as we know, he didn't advertise that the dog was lost."

Wes was now all eyes and interest.

"I think Peter was angry about what he thought was Whalen's death, and so he challenged the drug dealers. They killed him and dumped his body in the Gulf, figuring the sharks in the area would take care of it."

I took a deep breath. "It was Peter's body that washed up on the beach twice. The hand and arm also belonged to him."

"Where's the body now? You told me the sheriff had the arm but nothing else."

"Uh, probably lost at sea." I was trying not to lie to my friend as I also did not want to reveal anything that would connect Frank and his mission to the events I was describing.

Wes got up and closed the door. He reached for the pack of Marlboros in his shirt pocket, opened his window and lit up.

"Now that their messenger was gone, they had to find someone else. Jamie Thompson could step easily into the role of his cousin. They were like brothers. They had similar temperaments. Jamie knows how to fly. If no one in Canada is aware that Peter is dead, well, Jamie can play the part, at least for a while."

"OK. But how did the drug dealers know Jamie?"

"I don't know for sure. But we did see that photo of him with Peter, the one that ran in your paper. He was no stranger to the island or to Peter's friends."

"With Peter gone, who's the local connection?" Wes said.

"The people who've lived here most of their lives aren't wealthy. They're fishermen or they work in the local stores or have some other job. They're sitting on gold mines because, somehow, they managed to inherit or buy a piece of land years ago when it had little value.

"They look around them and see people who will always have more than they will: big houses, fancy boats, money to burn. Some of them," I continue, "like my friends Scooter and Deb, don't care. They just want to be left alone. But others hunger for the wealth and prestige."

Wes chimed in. "That sounds like our local realtor with the new Mustang convertible. That guy's always hustling to sell property. He runs all kind of ads in our paper. Tried to get me to do a profile on him the other day. I said I'd think about it – did for two seconds – and then rejected the idea.

"You have to admire get-up-and-go, but Gordon Fike's over the top," he added.

"Exactly, Wes. It was Gordon Fike who sold Peter Thompson the land to build his house. I think it was Gordon who connected Peter and the drug dealers. I'm sure of it. He could get a cut without taking too much of a chance. It was Gordon who ordered Whalen the dog killed as a message to Peter when the Canadian got out of line. When the drug dealers killed Peter, it was Gordon who lined up Jamie, almost a dead ringer for his cousin."

As Wes absorbed this, looking at the Post-it notes, I was thinking of "S. Tih". An illegible signature on the receipt for 14 paint cans had to be G. Fike. Besides me, he was the one person that had a connection to all the others. It had come to me on the facial table when Minerva mentioned house hunting. I was sure I could confirm it when I picked up the copy of the receipt Willy had waiting for me and compared it to the signature on my real estate documents.

"You're saying Fike orchestrated the whole thing. How would he know drug dealers?" Wes asked.

"He told me in his office. When he was young, there were dealers all over this island. Used to offer high school kids with access to boats thousands of dollars to run drugs for them. The dealers even used that little airport off-island. When the wealthy folks started buying up property, it became unseemly for the place to traffic in drugs – at least as openly as they had in the past."

I was so excited I could feel my adrenaline level surging as I talked.

"Gordon told me he never sold drugs, implying that it was because he and his friends didn't have access to a boat. But we know he's a boat owner now. His *Kadey Krogen* is for sale."

Wes shook his head. I couldn't be sure if he thought my imagination was on hyper drive or that I might be making sense.

"You don't think he makes enough money selling real estate?"

"When the crash happened several years ago, property values plunged. They're just now getting back," I said. "For a man like Gordon, who's impatient for the good things in life, the market upswing isn't happening fast enough."

Wes still looked bewitched, so I continued.

"Then there's Janis Johnson. Frank's wife. I think Gordon's been in love with her a long time. I'm sure he figures she can be bought. He told me himself how she liked fine things."

Wes snuffed out his cigarette, closed the window and returned to his desk. "Who set fire to your friends' house?"

"I'm convinced it was Gordon, but I haven't figured out why or how since he was at Mary Sanders' dinner party when the fire started. I also don't know why he showed up with the money to have it repaired."

"Maybe a change of heart?"

I shook my head in response. I wasn't convinced that Gordon had a heart.

"Where does your boyfriend fit into this scenario?"

I bit my lower lip. I'd listened to Frank and bought his story. But I couldn't be sure if he was telling the whole truth. He never mentioned Gordon.

"It's one of those questions, like you said. I'm not sure I want the answer."

Wes sat down in his chair and surveyed my scribbling. He nodded a couple of times and then smiled. "This is great stuff. Tied together nicely. Now where's your proof?"

"Proof?"

"That's what I said." Wes stood up, checked his watch. "Speaking of. Gotta check the paper proofs. Until you find the smoking gun or someone steps forward and confesses, Leslie, this is nothing more than an interesting conspiracy theory that no one is going to swallow."

I hated to hear those words coming out of my friend's mouth, but I knew he was right. And while I was proving that Gordon Fike and his buddies were the bad guys, I also hoped I would be confirming to my satisfaction that Frank was as innocent as he claimed.

CHAPTER 40

The cottage that housed Westside Properties, office of the island's drug king, was my next stop after I left Wes. I was like a kid with her hand in the cookie jar; I couldn't stop myself from wanting more.

Before leaving, I'd made my reporter friend swear he'd keep my theories to himself, unless something happened to me. At some point he'd have the scoop. He agreed, but I knew it would be tough for him to keep a secret for any length of time. Newspaper people are born storytellers. They love to be first with the news; every scoop is like manna from heaven. Wes was no different.

My adrenaline carried me quickly from the newspaper office, past the restaurant with the striped awnings and outdoor seating, and around the corner, where I spotted Gordon's mustang convertible. Top down, shiny. Probably hand washed to keep it in pristine condition.

Frank had resisted the temptation to spend any of the drug money he'd accumulated. That didn't seem a problem for our friendly realtor. People would expect Gordon Fike to have a new car now and then, so no suspicions would be raised.

Maybe that was his logic when he found himself unable to resist the lure of a bigger boat. A new home on the beach would likely be next.

I opened the front door. Dollyene, the receptionist, was gone. On the edge of her desk was an antique brass hotel desk bell and a printed sign: *Ring for service.*

Ding. Ding. The harsh sound reverberated through the main room and down the hallway that led to Gordon's office.

"Give me a sec, I'll be right out." It was Gordon's voice.

"No rush. It's Leslie Elliott."

"Have a seat," he yelled.

I walked over to the framed photograph I'd seen before of Frank, Janis and Gordon in happier times. On Dreamcatcher. I could see why both Frank and Gordon were captivated by Janis.

Even though she still claimed him as her territory, Frank said the love between them was long gone. Chemistry between people lasts two, maybe three years, a psychologist friend once told me. Even though I was proof of that, the statement always filled me with a sadness.

Apparently, though, it was downhill after that for the Johnsons, especially with Janis wanting more than Frank could give her. Why then would she be interested in Deputy Webster, a man who lived over a store? No time to think about that now.

"Leslie! Nice to see you." Gordon Fike came into the outer office wearing a pale green polo shirt, open to expose the King Neptune figure nestled in his dark chest hairs. From the photo I'd been staring at, I knew there were more hairs on his arms and down his back. Dark ones that some women find attractive.

He was carrying a briefcase, black with gold letters in one corner: GAF. I had a college roommate named Sharon O'Brien who insisted on sporting the initials SOB on her luggage. Sharon was not a son-of-a-bitch, but Gordon Fike was a gaffe, a man who'd made serious blunders in his life and would be paying for them someday soon I hoped.

"I've been thinking about what you said, Gordon. Maybe I am interested in a house. Something closer to the village. The north end of the island is so far away from everything. Although it's quiet and beautiful there; a great secret."

His face lit up like a Christmas tree. "I have several places you could invest in. Big enough for you and your mother. The way property values are climbing around here, you could double your money in a couple of years. Maybe less. But you have to act soon, before the boom passes."

"Let's go now. I'm free."

"Would that I could," Fike said, shrugging and extending his hands in a gesture of helplessness. "I'm meeting a prospective buyer for my boat. I've been itching to get a new one and now that business is picking up, well…."

"Your *Kadey Krogen*?"

"Why yes. How did you know about my boat?"

"I was with Peter, Peter Thompson in Key West, and we met Raul, uh, Pinelli, I think his name is. He flew back with us to take a look at your boat. Peter thought it was yours or that maybe you were selling it for someone else. He wasn't sure."

He looked a little nervous, but I pretended not to notice.

"It's mine. I'm, uh, looking to unload it."

"You know what they say. The two happiest days in a boat owner's life are the day he buys his first boat and the day he sells his last one."

Gordon Fike laughed, trying to sound casual, but I could see the wheels turning.

"I'd love to go with you and see Raul again. Such a nice man. Then maybe we could look at houses later."

"Not a good idea," he said.

"Why is that?"

He pulled a handkerchief out of his back pocket and wiped his brow. Some of the hairs from his thick mane were plastered to his forehead even though the temperature was 68 degrees, with a significant breeze coming out of the northwest. I figured he was delaying, searching for a better explanation than the truth.

"In fact, I'd love to ride in your convertible."

He let out a sigh that sounded like a tire going flat. Long and slow.

"Okay, okay. But if it looks like I'm getting close to making a deal, you'll need to exit. Go below and fix yourself a drink or something."

"Aye, aye captain."

Fike's boat, tied up at the marina on the east side of the island, was a honey of a craft. Not that I know much about boats. But it was pristine, one of my main requirements for life, and had adventure written all over it.

As we climbed on board, he described it like the salesman he was. "Mint condition, 48-feet. You could live on this boat, Leslie. I'm asking half a million for it. At that price, it's a steal."

"I was hoping for something a little more grounded," I said, and flashed a smile his way. "Why are you selling it?"

"I'm looking for something newer and, um, smaller. *Kadey Krogen* has a new model 44-footer out. I saw one the other day. Tied up a couple of boats down from me. Had to stop myself from drooling when I walked past it."

He pointed out the steps to go below and said, "Hey, why don't you go and pour yourself a drink. You can see for yourself it's as nice as your condo. Nicer. Rustle up some snacks. When the potential buyer gets here, we can join you; take the boat out for a spin."

I didn't mind being his wait staff if I could stay and watch the dynamics among these three creeps.

Gordon headed for the ladder to the topmost part of the boat, the flybridge, I thought I heard him say. When he'd disappeared, I pulled my cell phone out of my purse and sent a text to Wes Avery.

On Fike's boat in marina. No trouble yet. Alert Frank. #555-0081.

I could have bypassed Wes and gone directly to Frank. But Wes was a neutral party in whom I had total trust. Even though we were close, Frank was still a question mark; a small one. I hit *send* and then shut off the phone to save the battery.

The gallery, living quarters – I wasn't sure what to call it – was well-maintained, with gold carpeting, cherry wood paneling, several cozy seating areas, a full-sized stainless-steel refrigerator and stove in the small kitchen and a queen-sized bed to the front of the boat. Gordon was right. I could live and write on something like this if I wasn't prone to seasickness and didn't have a mother and daughter in tow.

Near the kitchen, I sat down on a bench that would give me a good view of the dock. I wasn't sure what time Raul was expected, or if he would come alone. I checked my watch. Five minutes 'til 2. There was no one around. Just me below and Gordon above, separated by little distance but a big lie that the realtor had been living.

My goal was to get Gordon to reveal the truth. But did I really expect him to confess all to me? That hadn't worked with Jamie alias Peter Thompson. Not even with Frank.

I felt a sudden uneasiness. It started in my arms and hands and worked its way down to my feet. My right heel was bouncing up and down in time with my randomly swirling thoughts. I got up, opened the refrigerator door and was relieved to see it was stocked with water, soft drinks and a couple of bottles of Chardonnay. I toyed with the idea of opening one of the wines but reached for the water instead.

Maybe being on this boat with Gordon, Raul and perhaps Jamie Thompson wasn't such a good idea, after all. Certainly, Raul didn't trust me. Even if I played the role of coy girl who was enjoying being the only female on the boat, I would be outnumbered if something went wrong.

The text I sent to Wes Avery seemed such a smart move five minutes ago. Now I realized how ridiculous it was. If I didn't show up, it was probably because I was dead. I needed to get the hell away from the boat. My flight mechanism kicked in. I grabbed my purse and headed up the steps two at a time. I couldn't see Gordon. I grabbed onto the piling and hoisted myself onto the dock.

I stopped to catch my breath. My legs were shaking from the rush that had carried me up and out. My heart was beating twice as fast as it needed for the amount of exertion I was putting out. I looked around the marina, trying to calm myself.

Steady girl. You're safe.

When events start to overtake you, it's impossible to tell how much time has passed. Was I standing there for 15 seconds or 5 minutes? When I decided my body was ready to move, I looked up and saw them walking toward me.

There was nothing menacing about their approach. I don't think they realized it was me. The two of them – Jamie, alias Peter, and Raul – were gesturing, talking over each other as they came closer.

I had a couple of options. Neither involved calling 911. Jumping off the dock might work. I was a good swimmer. But there was nothing subtle about hurling myself into the drink. One of them might be better in the water than I was. Instead, I clutched my purse, took an exaggerated look at my watch and plastered a big smile on my face as they came nearer.

"Hey, fellows. What a surprise! I was looking forward to a boat ride when I realized I'm supposed to meet Wes Avery, the new editor at the newspaper. He and I are old friends. He wants me to do some stories, mostly things that will interest women."

Jamie alias Peter grabbed my arm and leaned down to give me a kiss on the cheek.

"What a disappointment, Leslie," he said, flashing an exaggerated frown my way. "Gordon called to say you were onboard…uh…what's your boat's name, Gordon?"

I turned around to see the realtor standing behind me.

"Willing Sailor."

"I get it," I said rather loudly. "Willing seller! Willing buyer and you have a real estate deal. Very clever, Gordon." My laugh was over the top. "Gotta go. See you guys around."

I stepped forward. Pretend Peter stepped aside to let me pass. Raul stood firm, looking more like an impenetrable wall than a man. He grabbed my arm and held tight.

"No podemos dejara ir. Tengo la sensación de que ella sabe demasiado." He spoke to Jamie. It was obvious that Gordon, like me, had no idea what he was saying.

"¿Qué quieres hacer con ella?" Jamie responded. "Si se desaparece, hemos terminado aquí, amigo."

Desaparece sounded a lot like *disappear*. The adrenaline was flowing again. Maybe jumping into the water wasn't such a bad idea.

"No estoy dispuesto a dejarla ir…no todavía," Raul said.

"If you would please step aside, I'll be out of your way and you can check out Gordon's boat," I said, trying to buffalo Raul.

A cruel smile crossed his lips. Maybe a body block or a foot sweep would work on him, sending him into the drink and out of my way. I always thought big in these instances. That's what the survival guides said to do when confronted by a wild animal. Make yourself look large.

"Leslie, hey Leslie." All four of us looked toward the direction of the voice. Wes Avery, in his white leather tennis shoes and jeans, with sweat marks on his blue polo shirt and his face beet red, was walking briskly toward us. Raul dropped my arm.

"Am I that late for our meeting?" I said, checking my watch again. "I thought it was at 2:30."

"No, 2," he said. "The sheriff's right behind me. I told him I was coming out here to look for you because you were late for our meeting. Don't want to keep Harry waiting."

"Perhaps you could take a rain check on your meeting," Raul said. I swallowed hard, trying to look unconcerned. *Not on your life.*

"I don't think so," I said and moved quickly past the three men, greeting my friend with a kiss on the check and a whisper: "You just saved my life."

CHAPTER 41

"Start packing. I have an early Christmas present for you," I shouted as I entered the front door of Mother's condo.

It was nearing 6 o'clock. My hands were still clammy, my body jittery, from the events of the afternoon. I was surprised I hadn't heard from Frank, but my focus for the moment was getting Mother, Deb and Scooter off the island as soon as possible.

If Gordon, Jamie or Raul was determined to send me a message by hurting them, there wasn't much I could do. I'd have my hands full keeping myself safe. They needed to leave.

At the sound of my voice, Mother emerged from her bedroom. She had on a figure-fitting, short-sleeved pink dress, with a colorful shawl over her arms. Her blue eyes sparkled from under false eyelashes. Her lips were soft pink against the slight tan of her skin. She looked great, happier and younger than she had in years.

"You want me to pack? Oh no, dear. I have a date. He's picking me up in 10 minutes."

"You have a date?" Did I hear my mother correctly?

"Don't sound so shocked. I've been told I'm still an attractive woman."

"Don't get me wrong, but who is this person?"

"Gale Gammon. What a lovely man. I met him at the community theater. He was trying out for the lead role in the spring musical. I was wiping away the tears from his beautiful performance – such a voice – when he stopped at my seat and introduced himself."

"You hardly know this man and you're, what, going out to dinner with him?"

She gave me a wave of the hand that indicated I didn't know what I was talking about. I'd seen that gesture plenty of times. It meant she wasn't to be challenged.

"He's taking me to the hotel dining room. Such a classy person."

"At least you'll be safe there, with lots of people around you." I wanted to appear concerned but not so much that I frightened her.

"Really, dear, your imagination is beyond belief. I never knew you were so, uh, skittish. This island is the safest place in the world. Not like those communities where drugs and murder are rampant, like Chicago."

Right. No drugs or dead bodies on this island.

"So why should I be packing?"

I grabbed a bottle of red wine from the fridge, where I had to put it to keep it from going bad in a humid climate. I removed the cork and poured myself a glass.

"Can I get you some?"

"Oh no. I want to be a good girl tonight," Mother said and giggled.

Good grief, Mother! I took a long sip, trying to forget about the boat and my rescue by Wes Avery. If he hadn't shown up when he did, I might have been dead or swimming for my life in the middle of the South Pass. For all my bravado, the thought of being alone with those three men was still scaring the bejesus out of me. And they could be coming after me and my mother as we dithered here.

"I've decided to send you, Deb and Scooter to Islamorada for two weeks," I said. "To the Cheeca Lodge and Spa. On me."

"Islamorada? Why aren't you going?"

"Honestly, Mom, I need you to act as babysitter to make sure that Deb and Scooter have a good time. When they return, their house should be close to finished. I hope."

I couldn't go, I told her, because I had too much to do. Needed a break from houseguests and was eager to sleep in my own bed again. Being alone would be good for me. Allow me to sort out my feelings for Frank and give me some time to work on my novel, which was at long last taking shape in my mind. Besides, Meredith would be here before we knew it.

"Well, I suppose. If you really want me to go."

"And if you and the singer hit it off tonight, maybe he can join you. Couples massages, candlelight dinners by the ocean. And if your friend isn't interested, there are always cute cabana boys to wait on you hand and foot."

Mother's eyes brightened.

"I'd feel bad about leaving you alone. You, uh, should, uh, come with us," she said. The hesitation in her voice meant she didn't want me there. Deb and Scooter would be enough responsibility for her. If she could figure out a way to dump them and still have company, she'd be all over it.

She checked her make-up and hair in the full-length mirror in the dining room, breathed into her hand to make sure her mouth was fresh, then turned to me. "When do you want us to leave?"

"Tomorrow. You can pack in the morning and be on the road by one o'clock or so, in my car. That gets you there before dinner."

"I can do that. And I do need a vacation from all this fun." She giggled. "There's my date now." Someone had just knocked on her front door. "Come on in!" she trilled.

Gale Gammon, I assumed, came through the screen door like a Shakespearean actor making an entrance from stage right. He was pleasant looking and may have been really handsome when he was younger. In his late 70s I guessed, with thick gray hair that curled up in back, a scar across the bottom of his chin and a barrel chest. Diamond stud in one ear. *Such a with-it AARP member,* I thought.

When he reached out to greet me, I noticed he was missing the last two fingers on his right hand.

"Got on the wrong side of a circular saw when I was in my 30s," he said, recognizing the expression on my face. He exposed a set of gleaming white teeth. False I assumed, but his smile was genuine.

"Why I never even noticed," Mother said. She seemed almost giddy, smiling and laughing as we made small talk. After a few minutes, she slipped her arm through his, and they sauntered out the door like two people who'd known each other for years.

Deb and Scooter protested my generosity at first and then declared themselves more than willing to go on a two-week, all expenses paid vacation as a courtesy to me.

"With us gone, you and Frank can have the place to yourselves," Deb had said, winking at me and giving Scooter a nudge with her elbow.

The concrete sea wall had absorbed the evening's chill and was passing it back to me. I could feel it through the jeans I'd slipped on: cold on my rear end and an uncomfortable coolness traveling up to my mid-section. I needed a jacket but wasn't inclined to move away from the large glass of wine I'd poured and taken with me to the water's edge. I wondered if I was becoming an alcoholic.

It was close to 7:30. The moon was half full and rising from the other side of the island. In its glow, I could see the gentle waves before they met the wall, where they delivered a rhythmic slap. The cadence was almost hypnotizing.

I shivered at the reality of my situation. Is this what death by freezing feels like? I asked myself to keep a distance from the idea of death by some bad guy's hand. First cold, followed by detachment, then disorientation and the finality of it. Had I become numb to the dangers I was pursuing?

Foolhardy and stupid. No one had called me that to my face, but I was sure Frank and probably Wes were thinking that. For sure Deb and Scooter thought it.

The boat's running lights, tiny pinpricks, were visible seconds before the sound of the diesel engines. I stood up, brushed off the back of my jeans and backed across the patch of sand that led to the steps.

If it was someone I didn't want to see, I could make it up the steps and into Mother's lanai in a few seconds. The pepper spray gun was in my nightstand drawer. This time I wouldn't hesitate to use it.

"Leslie. It's Frank. I need you to come with me."

How did he see me? He was a shadowy figure against the backdrop of the North Pass. A hooded presence beckoning to me, his voice reaching out over the still water.

"I'm freezing out here. I'll get my jacket and be back in a sec."

I dashed up the stairs and sent a text to Wes. *If you don't hear from me soon, call Sheriff.*

He responded immediately. *Christ. What now?*

Explain later. With Frank. Not sure what's happening.

I wrote a note to Mother. *Gone with Frank on his boat. You and Rankins are registered at hotel. Leave as early as you can tomorrow. Love, Leslie*

CHAPTER 42

He pushed the hood back from his face, wrapped his arms around me and enveloped my mouth with his. The new beard growth was still prickly compared to the softness of his lips. It did not interfere with the electricity between us.

"Are we sailing away to some warmer climate?" I said when we broke apart. His body was like a furnace. I wanted to stay as close to him as skin.

"Um," he said, as he grabbed my hand and led me onto the boat and into the cuddy cabin. He took the wheel, turned it around and headed for the open water.

"No, seriously, where are we going?" I said as I snuggled close to him.

"Trust me," he said.

Oh, lord, I thought. *Here we go again.*

Dreamcatcher veered to the right and passed under the causeway. We were out into open water again. It felt like Frank was pushing the engine to its maximum as we flew toward our destination. I had no sea sickness. *Weird*, I thought. *But true.* I had to smile to myself.

After about 10 minutes, he took another right and slowed down. When we were on top of the long dock that jutted out into the water by Frank's storage building, he jumped off Dreamcatcher, threw the thick rope around the piling and pulled it tight.

As I stepped off the boat, he took me in his arms once more. "Whatever happens next," he whispered in my ear, "I need you to go along. It will be a big help. Bruce knows. You'll be okay. I would never let anything bad happen to you. Never."

I searched his face for understanding. *Whatever happens next?* I didn't like the sound of that. *And you weren't there when I was on Gordon's boat and Raul could have had me dead had it not been for Wes. Wes, not you, Frank.*

He leaned in and kissed me again, lingering. *And Leslie melted*, I thought in my writerly way.

My heart was engaged but my senses were telling me something wasn't right. I opened my eyes. Off Frank's left shoulder, I could see a figure walking toward us on the dock, his chest heaving as though he was in a hurry. It wasn't the deputy, it was Gordon Fike.

"Took you long enough," he said. "We've got work to do. If you wanted one last piece of ass from this meddlesome bitch, you should have gotten it sooner."

Anger raged through me, fueling my arm to deliver a slap across Frank's face. Behind that physical act were years of frustration and anger directed this night at the fisherman but delivered to all men who'd hurt and betrayed me.

"Bastard!" I whispered.

Gordon's laughter bounced off the water. Frank made no move to rub the spot on his cheek.

"You might need to tie her up," he said, switching his eyes from me to Gordon. "She's too much woman for you."

The realtor grabbed my arm and pulled me toward his boat, which was also moored at the end of the dock. "I've got a gun. I'll use it if she gives me any trouble."

"I told you I'd take care of her in my own way, Gordon." His voice was like ice. "Me, not you. After tonight she'll be out of your hair for good."

"Yeah, yeah. You took care of the dog and gave me the mutt's head in a paint can. This time you can keep her body parts for your own use."

Frank turned his back to us, released the ropes and climbed aboard the Dreamcatcher. I watched him leave, my body trembling, my heart breaking even as my mind reeled with hatred toward him.

Gordon manhandled me onto his boat, leading me down the steps to the room I'd been in before, the kitchen, or whatever. He was mumbling something about my mother sitting on the front row of the church and judging him. I wasn't sure what he was talking about.

He pulled the gun from his pocket and put it on the edge of the table. It was black, worn. I wondered if Gordon had ever fired it. It certainly looked used. Would he have the nerve to shoot me?

"Sit over there." It was the same bench I'd been on earlier that day waiting for Jamie and Raul to show up. "And don't do anything stupid for a change. "

He took his seat, inches from the gun and a bottle of beer that was almost gone. I noticed several other empties in the nearby trashcan.

"You had to stick your nose in our business," he said. "Too bad 'cuz you're a nice-lookin' lady. But you were about to ruin everything."

"How so?" If Frank was going to "take care of me" later, I was determined to have all of my questions answered before this was over – as my favorite poet Dylan Thomas wrote.

"We could have gone on forever, bringing drugs in, shipping them to Canada, and no one would have been the wiser."

"I must say, Gordon, if you are the man behind the drug idea, it was a stroke of brilliance."

A prideful smile crept across the fat man's face. He reached up and stroked the gold dolphin around his neck. "I thought so, too."

"Yeah. Who would suspect that you, a sniveling pig of a man, would have the brains to put together something like this?"

He raised his arm as if to give me the back of his hand but then let it drop. "You are a bitch, just like your mother. She saw me the day I left the church to pay off Frank for killing the dog. When I returned, she sat there, her nose in the air, scowling at me, judging me. Maybe I should tell Frank to do her in, too."

Frank killed the dog? A dog. Not Whalen. My mind whirled again, off kilter for the 90th time in this nightmare of my own curiosity.

Gordon chugged the remains of his beer and belched, tossing the bottle into the trash where it crashed onto the others.

"I finally realized what was going on this afternoon and was going to confront you. But when I saw you, Raul and Jamie…."

"How in the hell do you know about Jamie?"

"I figured it out after I learned that Peter Thompson had a look-alike cousin who was part owner of the yellow house. How did you convince him to get involved – to take his cousin's place – after the murder?"

Gordon didn't even react to that word. He was cocky, in fact, and this made me even more nervous. I might know a lot, but it didn't matter; I was pretty sure I was going to be shark bait before the day was out.

"Thompson wanted a bigger share or he was out. I never counted on his reaction to the mutt's death. He took out after our Spanish-speaking friends on Frank's boat. They killed him, dumping his body overboard. Frank was plenty pissed, but what could he do. There were two of them, one of him."

He scowled at me. "That damn body kept washing up after the storm. Luckily, Frank saw it the second time and retrieved it before that stupid deputy could find it."

"So, you contacted Jamie to keep up the pretense?" I asked, already knowing the answer.

"Jamie was involved from the first. Peter would take the drugs up north and deliver them to his cousin who'd set up one hell of a distribution network. I'm not sure how much he cared about Peter. When he learned he was dead, he was more than happy to take his cousin's place. Said he loved it down here. Was lookin' to find a plaything."

"It's Jamie I know, Jamie I had dinner with that night at the Tarpon Bar?"

"Yep. He was scared you were on to him when you found the pinky ring on the beach. You just had to keep askin' all those questions."

The wrist twist that Jamie had given me. God, I was slow on the uptake.

Gordon's face turned an even deeper red. He picked up the gun, waved it at me and then turned his back to me as he reached into the refrigerator for another beer. "Goddam women. Always spoiling everything," he said under his breath.

"Can I have some water?"

"Sure. Why not." He handed me a bottle, still holding the gun in his hand. I had no illusions about overpowering him. My only hope was Wes Avery. It had been almost two hours. My plan was to get more information out of Gordon and be rescued before anything happened to me. I didn't know if it would work. How would Wes know where I was? I plunged in again.

"Who set fire to Deb and Scooter's place?"

"It was one of Raul's men. If he'd done a better job, Deb and Scooter would be out of their misery and out of my hair."

"But you were the one that raised money to have their place fixed up."

"Frank made me do it. Said he was out of the deal if I didn't take care of them. He felt sorry for them, I'm guessing. People like them – the rats and mice of the island – they need to go. This is a rich man's playground now."

I was shaken by what he'd said. He gulped a big swig and went on talking.

"They'll be gone soon. Medical bills, insurance and taxes will eat them alive. Good riddance to bad rubbish. Before this deal is done, I'll be living on this island like the rest of them. Big house, nice boat, fancy cars. Still selling real estate to keep up the pretense. You wanna see my ticket to the good life?"

Gun in hand, he directed me to the back of the room where the sleeping quarters were located. Stacked on and around the queen-sized bed I'd seen earlier were brown packages filled with what I assumed was cocaine.

He told me then that when Frank and another man named Cruz finished transporting the drugs to Jamie's plane, they were coming for Gordon's stash – and me. That made him grin. I didn't say anything, just looked at him, trying to contain the trembling that was shaking up my insides.

He continued talking about this being their last shipment for a while, thanks to my interference. A second delivery had been made earlier in the day, offshore of one of the neighboring small islands.

As I tried to think of some way to get off the boat before Frank and the other man showed up, he talked on. It was a risky transfer for them but worth it, he said. "After tonight, we'll be set for several years. Once the heat is off, we can start up again: the heat that is going to be generated when you turn up dead." He grinned at me again. I wanted to slap his ugly face.

"Not sure what Frank has in mind for you," he went on. "But his neck's on the line. And knowing the bastard as well as I do, I don't see a future for you."

That particular line filled me with dread. Maybe he did know Frank better than I did.

247

CHAPTER 43

Frank said I should trust him. Then he handed me over to a man who had a gun and no moral compass that I could discern.

I checked my watch. It was after 11. Mother was home from her date and probably in bed. She'd read my note, assumed Frank and I were on a trip. By tomorrow at noon, she and the Rankins would be heading to Islamorada, giving no thought to me.

They might call during their two weeks away but wouldn't realize I was missing until they returned. If something did happen to me – if Frank's words had been a lie – then Mother would be all right financially. She'd have her condo. My daughter, Meredith, would inherit the other residence. Both would have monthly allowances and would console each other, I hoped. I wanted to weep for us all.

I sat there, looking out the boat's window at the darkness, trying to calculate a miracle and realizing that I needed to do more than pray.

"Bet you didn't suspect your boyfriend was involved in this," Gordon said. He reached under the table and pulled out a bottle of Dewar's, pouring himself a generous glass.

I sparked up a little at this: he might become so drunk he'd pass out.

"You thought Frankie was in love with you, didn't you, honey? He's so fuckin' good lookin', you women can't help yourselves when he's around. Spread your legs for him just like Janis did all those years ago."

God, he was crude.

He set the glass down on the table with a clunk, reached over for the scotch and poured himself another glass. He was already slurring his words.

"I'll have one of those," I said, hoping to encourage him to drink more.

"You will? Thas nice. Could be 'nother couple hours. Might as well make the most of it. You so willing to fuck Frank, maybe you'll give me a try. I'm pretty good in bed." He belched loudly. "Scuse me."

"I bet you are, Gordie." *You disgusting piece of garbage. No woman in her right mind would want to get between the sheets with you.*

He leaned back in his chair, almost falling off and then righting himself.

"And what did he tell you about Janis?" he asked me. "That she was the one who wanted the divorce? Naaaaaah, he kicked her out 'cuz he was screwin' Jewel, Gator's mom."

Oh, wonderful. If true, one more strike against a man I thought was too irresistible for words.

"Thass what Janis told me, and she wouldn't lie. Started up with her couple of years ago. He's waitin' to get cussstody of Stevie, then he's takin' Jewel, Gator and Stevie and gettin' outta town. Leaving you behind, baby. Dead mose likely. Along with that mother of his. She's a beeitccch jus' like yours."

Maybe he'll pass out. Oh, please pass out.

"When that SOB Frank's long gone outta here, he'll get the blame for all this sssshit. No one 'cept you suspecks me. And you'll have vanished. Piff-poof."

His round face reddened even more – it was almost mesmerizing – as he moved from laughing to a coughing spell. "Geez, I gotta take a piss."

He stood up, swaying, and staggered off toward the toilet. I watched in disbelief as the buffoon took the gun with him and left me all alone. My head was reeling from everything Gordon told me, but I needed to focus. I had three minutes at the most.

I ran to the cabin door. It was unlocked. I sprinted up the steps and stepped up on the edge of the boat, jumping onto the dock. In the dark, I'd misjudged the distance. I lost my balance, landed on one knee, and got up, limping at first as I moved down the wooden planks.

Shouts came from Gordon's boat, but I didn't dare look back. When I reached the shell path near Frank's shack, I headed down the asphalt road toward the lights of the village running like the wind, ignoring any pain from my knee, or soon, my lungs. This was my life here. I ran.

I could feel the dark liquid oozing down my leg. I hoped whatever scar my fall produced would serve as a future reminder to keep my curiosity in line.

The sheriff's office was about a mile from me. Was it manned at night? I couldn't be sure. Didn't Frank mention Bruce? He did. If he wasn't there, maybe there would be someone at the fire department.

Down the road I saw a pair of headlights, close together in a box shape, coming my way. Golf cart. I stepped off the road, seeking refuge behind a large royal palm. I couldn't make out the cart's occupants when it sped by me and turned left. When it got to the dock, two figures hopped out and started in the direction of Gordon's boat.

"Leslie!" I heard my name and recognized the voice.

"Wes. Wes." I screamed as I turned around and, then, hope in sight, started limping to where I'd escaped from sure death.

Wes doubled back and was now running toward me. Close behind him was a man I didn't recognize at first. When he passed under a small light on a nearby house, I saw Deputy Bruce Webster. I was glad it was him.

"You okay? Look at your knee," Wes said when he met up with me. He pulled a handkerchief from his back pocket and began dabbing at the wound. I put my arm on his shoulder to steady myself.

"I'm fine now. Not fine. I'm alive. That's all I want to be right now, alive."

The deputy was wearing civilian clothes, a pair of jeans and a jacket, and didn't have his gun where I could see it. I hoped it was someplace in his possession.

"It's Gordon Fike," I said to him. "He's out there on his boat, drunk. And the sleeping quarters are filled with drugs. He's got a gun." I couldn't seem to catch my breath.

"A gun?" By the deputy's reaction, I could tell he'd left his behind. I wanted to yell at him. *If Frank did contact you, why don't you have a gun with you?*

There was a scream from the direction of the dock and a loud splash. Wes and the deputy took off running; I limped along behind.

In the light at the end of the dock, we could see Gordon thrashing around in the water, his arms flailing. The deputy looked at Wes. "Man, I can't swim."

"Neither can Gordon," I said.

"I'll save the dirt bag," Wes said. He dove in, approaching Gordon from behind and slipping his arm around his chest. "Take it easy, asshole. I got you."

"Wheresss my gun! Wheresss that bitch! Goddammit!"

"A room full of drugs? Guess ya were right all along," the deputy said as he emerged from below deck and watched Wes sidestroke with his heavy drowning man along the edge of the dock and then onto the beach area. Wes was nicer than me. I'd have let him sink.

"Well, Wes," I said to my dripping friend as Bruce Webster, deputy, stood watch over the weeping realtor. "I got the connections I needed today. Not the ones I wanted."

I hoped he couldn't see the tears in my eyes.

‿◯‿

We dropped Gordon off at the sheriff's office, locking him up in the old-fashioned jail. It had one cell that was only used on holidays, when visitors had too much to drink. The deputy notified Sheriff Fleck, giving him a brief rundown of the evening's events, knowing the sheriff would show up soon. Webster also grabbed a shotgun and a heavy-duty flashlight.

Better late than never, I thought.

He was on the phone again with the sheriff as soon as we arrived on Oceanview Drive in a county-owned SUV. Except for the cleanup that occurred when Jamie Thompson arrived to take the place of his late cousin, the yellow house had remained unchanged, guarding its secrets well.

"We're here at the house. Looks like no one's around," the deputy whispered on his phone. "Got the newspaperman and Ms. Elliott with me. They refused to be left behind. She'll be fine. She's tougher than you think."

It was past midnight. If the plan was to pick up drugs and transfer them to Jamie's plane, they must have come and gone by now. We slipped through the fence and entered the house through the perpetually unlocked door on the lower level. Our destination was the closet on the third floor. As we headed up the stairway, I noticed the drywall dust had been replaced by sandy footprints.

When we arrived at the mystery door, the deputy shined his flashlight on the handle and gave it a turn. It opened. Inside were individual packages, each about 8 inches by 4 inches, stacked in rows approximately 6 feet wide and 4 feet high. By the pile were six satchels. Bruce opened them all, exposing neat piles of hundred-dollar bills. And in the last one, a white envelope.

"Jesus. There's a lot of money in there." Wes reached in his pocket and pulled out his Marlboros, offering one to the deputy.

"What's in the envelope?" I asked.

Deputy Webster, who seemed mesmerized by the sight of the contraband, handed the envelope to me. I opened it and read aloud:

Report to police that twin-engine plane registered to Peter Thompson, scheduled to arrive in Toronto approximately 3 a.m. from Florida, is carrying drugs. Pilot is Jamie Thompson of Toronto Canada. Passenger could be Raul Pinelli of Miami.

More drugs are on boat, Willing Sailor, owned by Gordon Fike and on the boat, Vida Buena, registered to Pinelli. Both are docked south of the marina. Drugs also in house at 450 Live Oak, rented by Thompson.

For more info on the contents of this closet, contact Don McKechnie of the DEA in Miami.

Remains of Peter Thompson, murdered by Pinelli associate, Ben Cruz, on my boat, the Dreamcatcher, on October 21, are located behind the shack on the island located at 27.7N/82.3W. I witnessed the murder and the dumping of Thompson's body into the Gulf. I later retrieved the body from the shore and buried it.

I swear the above statements are true.

Frank Johnson.

The paper was notarized earlier in the day by Grace Land, whose name I recognized as the elderly mother and secretary of Frank's attorney.

"Son of a bitch," Deputy Webster said, running his hands through his slicked back hair. "This is some story." He looked at me but said nothing.

"I'll testify that Jamie Thompson and Raul Pinelli were together in Key West and here on the island this afternoon," I said. "They also know Gordon Fike, who held me at gunpoint for at least two hours while even more drugs were being transferred from this house to the plane at the airport off island."

"So, where's Frank?" Wes asked. No one had an answer.

CHAPTER 44

Two days after the discovery, a press conference was scheduled on the island for 2 p.m. Sheriff Fleck had spent the better part of the morning preparing. Even did his own ironing, putting creases down the sleeves and pants of his tan uniform. His black shoes shined like patent leather.

All of those details came from Deputy Webster, who'd visited the local barber the day before. The deputy's hair was no more than an inch all over; the back of his neck clipped and shaven. He was clutching a law officer's hat under his right arm as he waited for the press conference to begin. I'd never seen him look so official or so ill at ease.

There were at least three television cameras in front of the buff brick structure that served as the city services headquarters for the sheriff and fire departments.

A handful of reporters, including Wes Avery from the island newspaper, stood in the area cordoned off for the news media. Television reporters had come from as far away as Naples and Sarasota. Wes had gotten his scoop, tweeting out teasers that morning of what was to happen at the press conference.

Curious and shocked residents had also gathered after the news from Wes's tweets spread throughout the community. While the realtor liked to say that his status among locals was no better than a used car salesman, Gordon was being characterized by many as a pillar of the community and the church.

As word of my involvement spread among the crowd, some locals gave me the eye, as though I was somehow responsible for Gordon's moral decline. Mother and Deb Rankin had delayed their trip to Islamorada to stand next to me in the crowd, with Mother giving anyone who looked in my direction her most menacing scowl.

Promptly at 2 p.m., the sheriff cleared his throat and introduced himself, his deputy and DEA agent Don McKechnie, a stereotypical fed in a tan suit and aviator sunglasses. While the others remained silent, their arms folded in front of them, Sheriff Fleck detailed the story.

About a year ago, Gordon had set up the operation that brought drugs up from Miami. Although there was no way of telling how many drugs had been run through the island network, this latest haul was valued by the DEA at more than $10 million.

The drugs, delivered by boat, were stored in a house on Oceanview Drive and then transported by van to the small airport off island. There, a Piper Chieftain was waiting to take them over the U.S. border for distribution in Canada.

The house and plane were owned by Peter Thompson of Toronto, believed dead. Further details would be available once a coroner's report was issued on bones discovered on a nearby island.

Thompson's cousin, James J. Thompson, also of Toronto, was wanted by law enforcement for his alleged role in the operation. James Thompson and a passenger identified as Raul Pinelli from Miami left the area in a small plane around 9 p.m. the night before last. A search was under way for the plane, which had not arrived at its stated destination.

Wes asked the first question. "Sheriff, it's my understanding that a local fisherman, Frank Johnson, was also implicated in this operation." He shot me a sympathetic glance. A buzzing noise moved through the crowd.

"Uh, yes. I believe Agent McKechnie can answer your questions about that individual," said the sheriff.

The agent who had once been Frank's partner was tall and lean, with a crew cut. I'd seen him on Fort Myers television whenever there were stories about big drug busts. He stepped to the microphone with confidence, speaking out in a baritone voice that resounded with authority.

"In answer to your question, I can say that Mr. Johnson's role in these events has not been determined but is under investigation. There is no arrest warrant out for him, and no plans to issue one at this time."

There was another murmur through the crowd. I heard a little whimper from Mother. "Oh, I hope he isn't one of them."

"Where is Fike now?" a female TV reporter asked.

"He's being held in Miami where drug trafficking charges will be filed against him and the others when they are apprehended."

The press conference continued for another 15 minutes, with the sheriff giving Deputy Webster a pat on the back for his good work. No mention of me, thank God. I preferred not to be acknowledged for my dubious involvement.

When the press conference ended, Deb and Mother offered their goodbyes and headed for my car where Scooter was waiting. Deb promised not to have too much of a lead foot, but she wanted to arrive in Islamorada before midnight.

"Be safe. By the time you get back, all of this will be a distant memory," I said. I hoped that would be the case.

I waited until the crowd cleared and the reporters had packed up their microphones before I approached Deputy Webster. He was standing off to one side, shifting from one foot to the other.

"That seemed to go okay," I said.

"Yep. I should have listened to ya from the beginnin'," he said, grinning at me.

"How were any of us to know that my theories had some truth to them?"

"I gotta be honest. I thought ya was a crazy woman. Didn't care for ya much at first, but ya've grown on me." He produced a soft laugh and then blushed. "The next time ya come to me with some half-baked idea, I might listen to what ya have to say."

I reached up, giving him a kiss on the cheek. "I think the days of my snooping are over. I'm sticking to my fiction from now on. Bruce, do you know where Frank is, um, and how he was involved?"

"Don't know exactly. Doesn't seem like Agent McKechnie's in any hurry to find him. I'm thinking he was on our side. On my own, I checked both houses this morning and it sure looked like Georgia and the kid, Jewel and Gator, had cleared out in a hurry. The dog, too."

"I guess he was in love with Jewel." The words came out easily but hearing them hit me hard.

"Can't say. If he was, he never talked about her. But he sure did love that kid Gator like he was his own."

"What about Janis? I, um, thought she might be here today."

"I told her not to come. She was pretty mad about the whole thing. Frank takin' Stevie and all. Them not even divorced yet. I didn't tell her this, but I know Frank won't abandon her. He's always good to his women. He'll work out somethin' once he and the others get settled. Somewhere."

"Somewhere." I repeated the word, feeling empty inside.

ееꓳСее

It had been three weeks since the press conference. Life had returned to something that resembled normalcy. I hadn't heard from Frank.

I took my morning walk past the yellow house, which still had crime scene tape strung along the fence. I wondered if the house would ever be finished. Perhaps it would be seized by the feds, as often occurred in drug-related cases. That would not make the neighbors happy. It could sit half-completed – an eyesore – for years and a threat to nearby property values.

Mother and the Rankins, Deb and Scooter, had enjoyed their vacation on my dime. When she returned, Mother had plenty of news.

"There IS sex after 70," she had said when she walked in the front door of my condo. She was wearing a big straw hat and a white lace sundress. I can't say that it suited her, but she certainly looked happy. Thrilled might be the better word.

"Welcome home, Mom." I gave her a hug. "I hope you're not talking about the cabana boys."

"Don't be ridiculous. I'm talking about a real man. Gale came to visit for three days. He's amazing for his age. He must take pills, but who cares as long as it works."

"Good for you, Mom." Even though I was destined to be alone like the spinster ghost in the Tarpon Bar, I was glad Mother had found someone.

Deb and Scooter stayed two days at my place and then moved into their repaired house, complete with new furniture, landscaping and a year's worth of lawn service paid for, in advance, by Gordon Fike.

"That man was a saint," Deb said. "Maybe he'll get off with a light sentence. Scooter and I are thinking about testifying on his behalf."

I groaned, stifling the urge to share everything I knew about Gordon, including his role in the fire and his observation that Deb and Scooter and their kind – the folks he called vermin – needed to be gone from the island. They were happy, for now, and that was all that mattered to me.

The price for their stay in my condo was a new mattress for my bed and a thorough house cleaning before my darling Meredith arrived to spend her Christmas break with me. I vowed that as soon as she left, I'd return to my writing and not be sidelined by any other strange happenings on the island.

Although there was no update from the sheriff or his deputy on the drug case, Wes had called to report that the wreckage of Peter and Jamie Thompson's plane had been found in a remote area about 20 miles from the Canadian border.

Strange that he'd made all those trips and this was his first – and deadly – accident.

Most of the plane and its contents were burned beyond recognition, although investigators had found body parts and traces of cocaine.

Wrapped up in a nice little package, I thought as I took a load of laundry out of the washer and plopped it into the dryer in advance of Meredith's arrival.

The only missing part of the puzzle for me was the whereabouts of Frank and his family and the $3 million in drug money from his safety deposit boxes.

The question of the dead dog had been answered when the vet's office called to tell me that Frank was the man who brought Whalen in to check on his shots. I already knew that. But, apparently, while he was there, he charmed the 18-year-old receptionist into giving him the carcass of a stray dog found in the road and brought to the vet for disposal. She'd been afraid to tell anyone what she'd done but finally confessed.

At least that was something in Frank's favor. He figured out how to substitute an already dead look alike so he didn't have to kill and decapitate the lovable Whalen.

I didn't care whether he was a drug dealer or an undercover agent, I told myself. Frank had used me. It had happened to me before, and it never felt good afterward.

If he was working with his former partner, Agent McKechnie, his work was serious and secret and maybe saved lives. But for a while – I couldn't predict how long – he'd ruined a part of me. The part that was just starting to trust and was open for love had closed down again.

"Hellloooo!" A small voice called from the direction of the screen door.

"Be right there," I yelled. I slammed shut the dryer door, turned the timer to 45 minutes and pushed the *start* button.

When I rounded the corner, I saw a large bouquet of flowers and a pair of short legs in jeans and tennis shoes.

"It's you again," I said, when the tiny gray-haired lady walked through the door and set the red roses on the counter.

"Yes. You're my last delivery of the day, thank heavens. I must say that you have some boyfriend. Last time it was white roses and hydrangeas. This time two dozen roses, all blood red."

"I'm so sorry you had to carry those up the steps," I said, reaching into my pocket for another $20 bill.

"It's all part of my job," the woman said. "Oh, I almost forgot. Be right back."

I watched her walk down the steps, open the back of the van and produce a white box wrapped in a red ribbon. She trudged up the stairs and handed me the package.

"Darn. You should sign for this, but I left the sheet in the van."

"Don't worry. You've delivered it, and I have it. I don't want you walking up the steps again. I give you permission to put my initials on the receipt."

"Thanks again for the generous tip," she said, grinning.

The card on the envelope had my name on it but no indication of who'd sent the flowers. Maybe they were from my friend Tim Fletcher. He'd listened to my tale one evening and commiserated with me. He was planning on visiting me after the first of the year and advised me to "stay out of trouble or I'll be coming down to bring you back north." Why did men always want to take charge of me?

I opened the envelope and pulled out the white card that had tiny roses in one corner. Printed in thin, block letters: *It's not over.* No signature.

"It's not over," I said aloud. "What's not over?" I studied the card for a minute, looking for a signature, anything, and then laid it carefully on the table.

My body was suddenly chilled. *Roses the color of blood…my blood? It's not over… not over…not over. Something's wrong, terribly wrong,* that little voice inside me said.

The red ribbon on the white box came off with a pull of the bow's two ends. I lifted the top. Inside was another box, wrapped in brown paper and addressed to the flower shop. With it was a folded piece of paper that instructed the florist to put the box in a gift package and deliver it and two dozen red roses to Leslie Elliott. The box was mailed from some town in Florida I'd never heard of.

From the utility drawer, I took out a knife and split the pieces of heavy tape. The brown paper fell away, revealing another, smaller box. Becoming exasperated at the elaborate packaging, I opened it and lifted off a rectangular piece of cotton.

There were no other words. There didn't need to be. The contents said it all: A pinky ring, gold with a silver face and an eagle on top.

I stood there, trying to make myself numb to the message from Jamie Thompson. The plane was down, Wes had said. The wreckage had DNA samples, which turned out to be from Raul. No mention of Jamie. I figured they would determine his remains some time.

I picked up my cell to call Deputy Webster. Or maybe Wes Avery. The deputy was probably with Janis. And Wes? I'd already put him in harm's way once. I couldn't do that to my friend again.

"Siri…" I paused.

"What would you like to me to do?" the female voice said.

"…call Frank Johnson."

"Calling Frank Johnson," Siri responded.

The phone rang twice. When the familiar voice answered, *Leslie*, I tried to speak but the words wouldn't come.

"Don't say anything. I know he's alive." The phone went dead.

He? Did Frank mean Jamie was alive?

A feeling of numbness came over me. I poured a glass of wine and went out to the lanai. The sun was beginning to set. These days, so close to the winter solstice, the light faded fast after 5 p.m.

I sat down on one of the Adirondacks and pulled a throw over my legs. I watched the waters of the North Pass slow, then turn to glass. Overhead, the skies that had been bright pink, striated with shades of purple and yellow, faded to black.

The buzzards that had haunted the island for so long had departed. A cold snap did in the red tide, or so Mary Sanders said. With their food source gone, the big carrion birds had left in search of other graveyards. Now it seemed the human scavengers – those that feed off the plight of others – were returning, hoping to feast on my carcass.

I searched the strip of sand, tracing it from underneath my condo until it widened into the public beach farther down. Faint lights from waterfront residences reflected in the stilled surf, save for the space where the yellow mystery house stood. As always, it was dark.

As my eyes adjusted to the diminishing light, I could see the solitary figure walking my way. Head down, hood overshadowing face, hands in his pockets. I leaped up to get a better look.

I'd been naïve and foolhardy these last several months, but I'd only been scared, really scared, a couple of times. As I watched the man come closer, I felt a tingling unlike any other climb up the back of my spine to my neck and converge into a body-wrecking shudder. Is this what real fear is?

Should I call 911? Get the pepper spray? Accept my fate? I stood there frozen.

The stranger stopped and looked in my direction. The light from a neighboring condo exposed the dark goatee on the lower half of his face, but the hood kept his features and eyes hidden.

Suddenly, a low whistle escaped his lips, summoning. Another figure emerged from behind the bushes and ran to the stranger's side.

"Here, boy. Good dog," the familiar voice said.

I sat down and waited, the tension draining away.

He was keeping his word. He was on his way.

(end)

ABOUT THE AUTHOR

Susan Hanafee is an award-winning former journalist whose career as a reporter for *The Indianapolis Star* spanned three decades. She formerly headed corporate communications for IPALCO Enterprises and Cummins Inc. She resides in Boca Grande, Florida.

Hanafee's blogs can be found on www.susanhanafee.com. Her previously published books include *Red, Black and Global: The Transformation of Cummins* (a corporate history); *Rachael's Island Adventures* (a collection of children's stories); *Never Name an Iguana* and *Rutabagas for Ten* (essays and observations on life); *Leslie's Voice* (a novel).